The Kingdoms of Laos

The Land of a Million Elephants

The Kingdoms of Laos

Six Hundred Years of History

Peter and Sanda Simms

CURZON

To TIAO INKHAM RANGSI

First Published in 1999
by Curzon Press
15 The Quadrant, Richmond
Surrey, TW9 1BP

© 1999 Peter and Sanda Simms

Typeset in Baskerville by LaserScript Ltd, Mitcham, Surrey
Printed and bound in Great Britain by
Biddles Ltd, Guildford and King's Lynn

British Library Cataloguing in Publication Data
A catalogue record of this book is available from the British Library

Library of Congress Cataloguing in Publication Data
A catalogue record for this book has been requested

ISBN 0–7007–1125–2

Contents

Foreword

FEW COUNTRIES CAN compete in remoteness and romance with the faraway land of Laos, once one of the three kingdoms of Indochina, with Vietnam and Cambodia. French administrators who served long in Laos were said to have succumbed to a certain dreamy, live-and-let-live attitude that made them suspect in the colonial service. Impoverished, and fervently Buddhist, Laos suddenly found itself in the Cold War cockpit in the late 1950s and early 1960s when East and West vied to fill the vacuum left by the departing French.

The outgoing President Eisenhower told the incoming John Kennedy that Laos was the hot-spot that was going to cause him the most trouble in the new administration. Kennedy, who never learned to pronounce Laos properly (he rhymed it with *chaos* instead of *house*), went on national television with maps and charts to describe the West's alleged vital interests there and the all but incomprehensible politics that pitted princes and their various political factions against each other. Kennedy tried to piece together a coalition of Lao forces and a withdrawal of foreign advisers – an agreement which nobody kept. There followed a tragic clandestine war as the United States tried to organize resistance to the Vietnamese and Lao Communists who needed eastern Laos for the 'Ho Chi Minh Trail' to transport men and material down into the maelstrom of the Vietnam War.

Both the Americans and the North Vietnamese used their proxies in Laos to fight a shadow war, while the number of bombs dropped on the tiny country rivalled all the bombs dropped in World War II. Seven months after the fall of Saigon, Laos was taken over by the Communists, who abolished the monarchy and sent the former, pro-Western elite, including the King, into re-education camps from which many never returned.

There have been many books about the tragedy of modern Laos, but little has been written about the ancient origins of the people who infiltrated south from China into the mountains and valleys of what are now Laos, Thailand, Northern Burma and Assam half a millennium ago. Theirs is a fascinating story of conquests and defeats as kingdoms came and went, of a time when white elephants could be a *casus belli* – as rich and colourful a canvas as historians have ever painted upon.

Peter and Sanda Simms have filled this gap with verve in this detailed history of Laos from the beginning of the 14th century until the coming of the French a hundred years ago. They have woven memoirs and travellers' tales with scholarly translations from ancient texts.

Peter Simms, an Englishman who began his east-of-Suez life in World War II India with the Bombay Sappers and Miners, was studying Sanskrit at Cambridge when he met his future wife, who was reading anthropology there. Sanda is a princess from the Shan States in Northern Burma. Her father was the first President of the independent Union of Burma after the British left, but was overthrown in a coup which led to decades of ever-more repressive army rule, which exists to this day.

Sanda went on to an academic year at the School of Oriental and African Studies in the University of London, and then joined Peter in Bangkok where they were married. In the mid-fifties they spent six months walking over north Laos in that last period before war overcame the region. After a stint in Rangoon, which became impossible for them after the coup, the Simmses ended up at the University in British Guyana where Peter wrote his well-received political analysis, *Trouble in Guyana*.

The lure of the East was too strong, however, and the Simmses ended up back in Laos in the mid 1960s, when they took up newspapering. Peter was hired by Time Magazine in Laos and was later sent to Singapore and then Bangkok as the Vietnam War escalated. It was in Bangkok, where I was sent by Time in 1969, that I got to know the Simmses. Sanda was beautiful, soft-spoken and aristocratic. Peter, in those days, was a Conradian expatriate – an old Far East hand who already knew more about the Orient than I would ever know. It was no surprise to me that Peter later served as the model for John le Carré's *The Honourable Schoolboy.*

Peter gave up journalism to join the intelligence branch of the Hong Kong police, and later served the Sultan of Oman. But with this important, well-researched and fascinating book, the Simmses have returned to that magic place which they were fortunate enough to have known in that twilight time when the old Laos was about to disappear forever.

H.D.S. Greenway, Needham, Massachusetts

Preface

WE HAVE WRITTEN this history as a tribute to a great nation. One that at the moment is severely divided, but hardly more severely than on a number of other occasions in the past. It was while we were writing an account of the events between 1945 and 1975, many of which we experienced at first-hand, we came to realise that, however terrible they were, many of the events we were recording had happened before, and yet Laos and the Lao people have survived. We hope this book will be a tribute to the greatness of the Lao and that one day we shall all see the emergence once again of the kingdom of Laos as an independent and united nation.

Another reason for writing this book has been the remark, so often made to us by our Lao friends in exile, that there was no general history book on Laos they could give to their children to help them understand the country that was their birthright.

This is in no way to under-estimate the great achievements of Maha Sila Viravong and ML Manich Jumsai who have done so much to bring to light the Annals and many other historic writings to be found in the libraries around the world, especially in Bangkok. Their work is highly notable. We also wish to refer the reader to some of the great works of Charles Archaimbault, of Henri Deydier, Pierre Bernard Lafont, Paul Le Boulanger and other French scholars. Among the modern Lao scholars we must mention Saveng Phinith, whose translation of the Annals of Luang Prabang we relied on so heavily. He is one of the many Lao historians who are currently working in the field of Lao studies. There is also a modern school of western historians in Australia with Stuart Fox who have made original contributions towards the unlocking of the past. We are particularly indebted to Stuart Fox's thoughts on the times of the Mahadevi.

We hope this history of Laos from the triumphant conquests of Fa Ngum to the French takeover at the beginning of the twentieth century, will also provide the historically all-important links to events and relationships in its neighbouring states. We believe that it is only with such a panoramic view that many of the occurrences can be understood.

We trust that we have written as reasonably an accurate account as is possible with the present studies of Lao history. Where there have been a number of differing accounts we have included the more important, either in detail or with a reference. We also hope that beyond all else this history may afford a mirror to the past into which young and old may look and see why it is still worth doing all in their power to re-create a just and democratic country, presided over, if the people wish, in the proud tradition of the past, by a Royal Family, who have, with their subjects, suffered so much since 1975.

We were present at most of the major events in Laos between 1955 and 1975. At times, we had the privilege of being allowed to cross the lines when Prince Souvanna Phouma's Neutralist government was functioning on the Plaine des Jarres. We used to fly from Vientiane to Khang Khay in the little opium planes, a traffic that as usual managed to transcend frontiers, to meet Prince Souvanna, as well as the Pathet Lao and Communist leaders, who were officially headed by Souvanna Phouma's half-brother, Prince Souphanouvong. With them were many civil servants and students whom we had known before the country had become divided into two parts.

We have so many people to thank and, of those many, we would especially wish to mention the following: Charles Archaimbault, Koupranom Abhay, Bandith and Sophie Phraxamai, Chao Sanhprasith na Champasak, Jean Deuve, Diane Baude, Max Duvaux, Helen Cordell, Phagna Houmphanh Saignasith, Tiao Inkhamrangsi, Phagna Inpeng Suryadhay, Dr. Tiao Jaisvasd Visouthiphongs, Tiao Mangkra Souvanna Phouma, Tiao Mantharangsi, Jany Morgan, Tiao Savivanh Manivong, John Steed, Dr. Manas Chitakasem, Chao Sopsaisana Southakakoumar, and Tiao Suchindarangsi.

We would especially like to mention Diane Baude who spent many hours searching the museums and archives in France tracing our requests for photographs. Chao Sopsaisana Southakakoumar very kindly read the chapter on Xieng Khouang and pointed out the ambiguities in the accounts of Chao Noi's alleged betrayal of Chao Anou.

Phagna Inpeng Suryadhay has been concerned with so many parts of the history and, with Koupranom Abhay, commented especially on the Champasak chapter and the importance of the Chaomuongs of that kingdom.

Finally, Phagna Houmphanh Saignasith and Jean Deuve were constantly helping us with the 1945 to 1975 book, until we decided to put it on one side while we completed this history. They both read the final chapter of this book and made highly pertinent comments and threw a great deal of illumination on some of the events.

In the production of this book our thanks must go to David and JB Greenway, who shared many experiences with us in Southeast Asia. They read and commented on the beginning of the book and David earned our gratitude by very kindly agreeing to write the Foreword. Our thanks are also due to Malcolm Campbell, the Publisher of the Curzon Press, and Marie Lenstrup, the Administrator. Especially notable was the contribution of Jonathan Price, the Chief Editor. LaserScript under David McCarthy ensured that the final product met their highest standards.

To the many other people who helped us and we have not recorded their names may we say thank you very much indeed. We owe a very great deal to all the suggestions, criticisms and help, but there will still be some errors and they must remain our responsibility.

Peter and Sanda Simms
London

Illustrations

Genealogical Tables

Maps

CHAPTER ONE

Where the Lao World Began

IN THE EARLY morning the Mekong River is covered by a dark, heavy mist. Gradually, it begins to lighten, a silvery luminescence shines through it, soon one can begin to distinguish the shapes of trees, of a pirogue and the small waves beating against the bank. As the moments pass, the mist becomes diaphanous, then, suddenly, it clears and one can see the trees, houses and people on the opposite bank. For a while there are still some dark patches of mist on the rising hills beyond. Then they are gone and everything is clear, fresh, and sparkling in the sunlight. It is a moment of ethereal calm and freshness.

The beginnings of Tai history are the same: first darkness, then increasing transparency, then clarity. However, as one traces the course of historical events, unlike the mists along the Mekong, there are many dark patches that we shall never see through.

Today the Tai race comprises the Lao, the Thai of Thailand, the Shans of Burma, the Ahom of eastern Bengal and several million descendants in China and Vietnam. The first historical accounts of the Tai are to be found in the Chinese chronicles and these go back well over a thousand years. Before those times, we have some knowledge of how the Tai lived, their rulers, the way they fought, and even their sexual relationships. It was during those earlier years of prehistory that small Tai settlements gradually spread across the southern half of what is today China.

Where did it all begin? Thirty thousand years ago, the lands from the Yangtze River to the South China Sea and the Bay of Bengal were inhabited by a people who were remarkably homogeneous: they spoke the same language, although doubtless divided by innumerable dialects, they used the same tools, and, throughout the vast area, they lived and behaved in much the same way. About ten thousand years ago, new peoples entered the region with different languages and customs and, through intercourse with them, new ideas and technologies were created and the earlier homogeneity was lost.

1

The Tai Discover their Individuality

IT WAS DURING this period of change that the Tai began to develop their own very individual way of life. When we come to the earliest accounts of the Tai, which are to be found in the Chinese chronicles in the sixth century BC, around the time of the Buddha, the Tai had already created a distinctive way of life. It was to be the foundation of their culture and beliefs until the middle of this present century. It was about this time that they started to call themselves, Tai, meaning, to be free. Their communities were spread over a great area from the Yangtze River southwards, as far as the southern boundaries of Yunnan and eastwards to the China Sea.

Their staple diet was 'wet' rice, so they built their villages in river valleys where there was plenty of water and level ground that could be flooded in the growing season. While the Chinese and Vietnamese built their houses on the ground, the Tai houses were always raised above the ground on stilts, just as they are in the villages today. These and other differences placed them apart from their neighbours, and helped to preserve their sense of identity and their individual customs and traditions.

Although the Tai were spread widely across the different provinces, they were not the rulers of the lands they inhabited. Instead, the Tai communities developed as small groups, each group being a part of a Muong. In physical terms a muong was, and still is today, anything from a hamlet, or a village, to a large town and all the land between it and the next town. Each Muong had a chief, a *Chaomuong*, who was the ruler and, more than that, represented the spiritual essence that bound the whole Muong together.

The Tai Way of Life

THIS SOCIAL STRUCTURE, the muong, tied all the individual families together. It proved to be immensely strong. Muongs might be shattered by war, or by a natural disaster, but, like the cells of a body that has been damaged, the survivors came together again and recreated themselves, so far as they could, in their original form.

In the country to the north of Yangtze River occupied by the Chinese people there was overpopulation and land was at a premium. In the south, however, the soil was rich and plentiful. When a Tai village outgrew the land that was suitable for paddy fields, the younger generations moved further down, always *down* the valleys, or, if that was not possible, over the hill-line into the next valley. There was no shortage of land to the south and east.

As land was plentiful, manpower became the most valued asset. With more people one could grow more, one could work less and enjoy an easier, richer life. Without the pressures that existed in the north, Tai society was much more open, and women, unlike those in Chinese society, were regarded as equal partners.

It is no wonder that, in comparison with others, the Tai thought of themselves as being free. Their life created an easy-going attitude to life, 'Mai pen rai' is the Thai expression, or 'Bor bin nyang' in Lao, meaning simply, 'Relax, don't worry!'

The year was divided into two natural periods: the months of hard work, planting and harvesting, and the rest of the year that could be given up to more pleasant things. In the relatively free months, visits could be made to distant relatives. If some members of a family felt like a change they would pack up a few presents and be away from their village for days, even weeks, at a time. In this way, even though relatives lived in muongs that were quite far apart, they could still keep in touch. Out of these relatively frequent contacts, a cohesion pervaded the system of muongs and of the Tai people as a whole. This was to be an inheritance that was preserved until recent times.

In those days, there were no hard and fast frontier lines. One state merged into another, often with a neutral area between, where sometimes the villages, or even quite large towns, paid tribute to two rulers. There was, therefore no difficulty in crossing from one kingdom to another. All rulers encouraged trade and with it the free movement of people.

The Future Lands of the Tai

No ONE HAS yet thought of a satisfactory name for the region of which Laos is the heartland. Today it comprises Burma, Cambodia, Laos, Thailand and Vietnam and the northern states of Malaysia. Within the limited choice available, 'Indochina' is probably the most appropriate. So long that is, that the term is understood to mean only that India and China played a part in the formation of the social structures of these countries. The term 'Indochina' should not be taken to mean that, in historical times, either the Indian or the Chinese races populated these countries.

From India, the contributions were commercial, religious, and the provision of a clearly defined social framework. Their religious and philosophical ideas began to enter Indochina from about 200 BC, or even earlier. Indian concepts were to become the foundation of all thought. Equally important, through the Brahminical teaching, India gave the countries of Indochina the concepts of kingship and a social hierarchy.

From China, the contribution was diplomatic and political. Whenever possible, China sought to dominate any Indochinese state it could control. It tried to make them into Chinese provinces, or, if that was not possible, into vassal kingdoms. Since this was only possible in areas where they could send their armies, the main Chinese influence in Indochina was felt only on the coastal regions: that is the lands that now form part of today's Vietnam.

It was in Neolithic times that a new wave of people, who were later to be called the Mon–Khmer, reached Indochina. Again it is difficult to find a satisfactory name for them but today's Malays and Indonesians are also their direct descendants, and they are often referred to as the Malay–Indonesians. They spoke a pre-Khmer, Austro–Asiatic language. They gradually spread through Indochina, just as the Tai were to do later. Traces of their settlements have been found as far north as Luang Prabang in Laos. Even more important, these peoples were dedicated sailors and it is probably they, rather than the Indians, who dominated the trade routes from India to the Indonesian archipelago and the ports of Indochina.

The Indian Legacy

UNTIL RECENTLY IT was thought that the beliefs in Hinduism and Buddhism were spread by the Indian traders. It is now considered unlikely that ordinary, uncultivated merchants would have had the ability, or the power, to make such dramatic changes. It seems more likely that the rulers of the Indochinese states invited Brahmins and Buddhist monks to come and teach and from them was developed a new social structure.

One of the reasons that the rulers invited them was the need for a ceremonial form of enthronement that set the ruler apart from everyone else and gave him divine, or magical, powers.

A new king needs to display a guarantee of his divine right to rule that only an older civilisation can give, since it is backed by an accepted religious hierarchy that possesses ceremonies hallowed by age and tradition. These conditions were amply met by the Brahmins. So well did the Brahmins fulfill this role that even now, centuries after Buddhism has been recognised as the acknowledged religion, they still perform important national ceremonies such as the consecration of the Kings of Thailand and Laos. As well, in everyday life in weddings and other family ceremonies, the Brahmins play their part in most of Asia today.

The Brahmins brought with them strong deistic beliefs, as well as a social structure that was based on the four ranks of society: the religious men, the warriors, the merchants and the outcastes. While this social order was accepted as the theoretical basis, it was never applied in any Indochinese society with the rigour that is found in India. This is a clear indication that the rulers and peoples were not Indian themselves.

At the same time, the Brahmins brought Indian legends, the Vedas, the Puranas, the great epics, as the Mahabharata and the Ramayana, and other religious texts. With them came the pantheon of Hindu deities and their powerful influences.

Siva, Creator and Destroyer

OF THESE, THE deity that was to dominate all the others was Siva. Originally he was the third deity in the trinity of gods. However, for many he became the supreme deity, representing the two most important aspects of life: creation and destruction. His symbol was the Linga, a representation of the human phallus, portrayed by a single column of stone with a rounded

ILLUSTRATION 1 Hindu figures from Wat Phu

© Peter & Sanda Simms

5

top. From the great Siva sprang the prosperity of the harvests, the ever multiplying family, and the increasing riches of a great country.

His other symbol was a cone to represent Mount Meru, the centre of the world that was, like Olympus, the home of the Gods and the source of all power. Representations of Mount Meru are to be found throughout Indochina. In Laos there is Wat Phu and in Cambodia the greatest representation of all, Angkor. The mountain and the Linga became the two most powerful symbols of the pre-Khmer and Khmer world.

As the god of destruction Siva was known as Rudra, or Maha Kala, and it was possibly this duality of being both the creator and destroyer that made him so attractive to the people of Indochina. According to their ancient religion, human sacrifice was essential to propitiate the Spirits, *Phi*, to ensure a good harvest, and the welfare of the community. Siva fitted perfectly into this traditional pattern.

Although the main Brahminical beliefs were centred around Siva, the second most popular deity, Vishnu, also had many followers at all levels of society in the Indochinese kingdoms. However, on balance there is no doubt that the Sivaite practices were dominant. It is impossible to be more explicit as the whole question is complicated by one of the contemporary beliefs that combined Siva and Vishnu into a single Godhead.

Also important in the mythology of the earliest Indochinese empires were the beliefs in the Divine Spring, the fountain that brought youth and goodness, and the mythical, but extremely powerful, Nagas. *Naga* is the Sanskrit word for a snake. The legendary Naga had the head of a human being, the thickening neck of a cobra, and the tail of a snake. This may not sound very attractive, but they could assume human form, or even the appearance of a particular person. A female Naga, if she chose, could be irresistibly beautiful in human eyes. Any human children born by a Naga would usually possess superhuman powers and could look forward to a life of greatness.

All these early beliefs have continued into the Tai world in various ways and have formed the basis of many Lao legends. It was, for example, a Naga that chose the site for both Luang Prabang and Vientiane. Such legends, enriched and refined by Buddhism, have given a beauty and deep symbolism to the legends of the creation of the Tai world and of Laos in particular.

The great empire of Funan

DURING THE FIRST century two great empires were founded in the Indochinese peninsular. The greater of these was Funan. At the height of its power it stretched from the South China Sea to the northern parts of modern Siam and, probably, covered most of the present Malaysian peninsular.

Funan is not the name its people called their country. This has been lost. The name Funan is the modern pronunciation of the two Chinese characters, *b'iu nam* found in the Chinese chronicles. These the Chinese adapted from the second word of the title of the king, *Kurung Bnam, King of the Mountain. Bnam* is *Phnom* in modern Cambodian, as in the name of the present capital, Phnom Penh, and has the same meaning as the older word, *mountain*.

The influence of Funan on the formation of the Indochinese kingdoms, including the future Tai nations, was as crucial as Rome had been in the social and cultural development of Europe.

Funan first grew up to the north of the swampy, mosquito-infested delta of the Mekong river. Its capital was Vyadhapura, the *City of Hunters*, standing south of the confluence of the Tonle Sap, probably near present day Bnam, or else Chau Phu, then known as Chau Doc.

Its initial wealth came from its position on the trade routes, especially from India to China, and its ports were soon crowded with Indian traders, first as visitors, later as residents.

All that we know about Funan is through Chinese sources and they are remarkably sparse. Between 245 and 250 CE, a member of a Chinese mission wrote an account of a visit to Funan, an account that is spoilt in part by some of its extreme statements. He was called K'ang Tai and he says that the people lived in walled towns with palaces and dwellings. They practised a simple form of agriculture, but they were far more than a simple peasant society. They made and wore engraved ornaments and paid their taxes in gold, silver, jewels and perfumes. They had books and libraries and used an Indian script. The Chinese chronicler could not, however, resist describing them as ugly, black, fuzzy and, very improbably, that they went naked. Perhaps, by this he meant that the upper parts of their body were uncovered. Despite their ornate sarongs, embroidered with gold and silver, they must have seemed 'naked' when compared with the elaborate robes of a Chinese mandarin.

The first known king of Funan was Kaundinya who reigned in the latter part of the first century and the last recorded king was Rudravarman, who acceded to the throne in 514 and is not heard of after the year 539. But before going into the mysterious end of the Funan empire, we need to look at its powerful neighbours, Champa and Chenla.

The Empires of Champa and Chenla

THE CHAM PEOPLE were among the very first of the colonisers of Indochina, possibly predating the Mon–Khmer. There was probably a Cham kingdom based on Wat Phu in the centuries before the Christian era, but the first recorded Kingdom of Champa dates from 192 CE. It came into existence when an official in the Chinese prefecture around Hué realised that the Chinese control over the territory was so weak that he could take over the prefecture and declare it an independent country.

This he did and the Chinese Court was forced to accept the situation. They continued to refer to it as Lin Yi and this is the only name we have for the country until the seventh century, when the name Champa is found on an inscription.

By the seventh century Champa was already in decline. Its territory in the Mekong valley had been overrun by Funan. Champa withdrew to its original homeland along the coast of Vietnam. Although never so powerful as Funan, it had been proved to be an extremely powerful and civilised nation. In the Mekong Valley its centre had been around the great temple complex Wat Phu, near present day Champasak town.

Even though diminished, Champa managed to survive and was to be a considerable nuisance to both of its immediate neighbours the Vietnamese and the Chinese. Then in 1287, the Vietnamese defeated a Mongol army of 300,000 troops near Hanoi and from that time onwards, they were able to resist any encroachment by Champa and could launch retaliatory attacks against her. The end came in 1471 when the Vietnamese captured the Champa capital at Indrapura and according to their claims slaughtered its 40,000 inhabitants. From that time on, Champa ceased to exist.

It is in 550 CE that we first learn of Chenla. Its boundaries were approximately those of the Champa territories in the Mekong valley. It was at that time a vassal state of Funan. The kings of Chenla were also believers in the Sivaite cult and Wat Phu was to be one of the greatest centres of their nation.

The New Year Sacrifice at Wat Phu

IN 1950 THE life of Chenla as it was nearly a thousand years before still lived on in the oral history of Champasak. Chao Siromé of the royal family of Champasak described to us the annual ceremony that used to be performed at Wat Phu. He placed it in the times of the Chenla kings.

ILLUSTRATION 2 The Grand Stairway leading up to Wat Phu

© Peter & Sanda Simms

It was in the times before Buddhism had exerted its full influence, and, he said, once a year in the sixth month, when the blossoms of the frangipani were falling, the King of Chenla used to mount the great causeway, flanked by thousands of brilliantly dressed soldiers, up the steep side of the mountain and entered the temple of Wat Phu.

Two virgins were awaiting him clothed in the finest silks and cloth of gold, perfumed with precious unguents, powdered, and immaculate. Solemnly he prayed and then turning to them consecrated them to eternal marriage with the guardian spirit of the mountain. For all their fine costumes they still lacked one thing, a blazing red flower with its stalk twisted into their hair behind their ear: the final happy symbol of a maid going to her marriage. These two symbolic flowers the king of Chenla handed to them as their final ornament.

Then to these two shy and radiantly beautiful girls, he would offer some rice spirit. Hardly had their lips touched it, than swords fell upon them and they were hacked to pieces at the feet of their god: their gorgeous costumes of gold, silver and brilliant colours, the red flowers of marriage, their bathed and perfumed bodies, were all soaked and spoiled in their own blood. The sacrifice of the two maidens was the price the people paid for one more year of prosperity and for the glory and continuation of their king's reign. From this destruction, Chao Siromé said, people believed there would be creation.

In 514 Jayavarman, one of the greatest of the kings of Funan, died. King Jayavarman had a son by a concubine named Rudravarman. On his death, Rudravarman murdered the rightful heir, whose mother had been a queen, and assumed the throne. By doing this he divided the ruling family into two factions, each with different beliefs in who had the legendary rights to the throne. Rudravarman managed to preserve his hold on the throne until 539. This is the last date that any mention is made of him. What exactly happened then may never be known, but sixteen years later, in 550, King Bhavavarman I of Chenla, his grandson, annexed Funan and founded the kingdom of the Khmer that was to become Angkor.

Chenla's annexation of Funan did not extend to the network of states that had been its vassals and stretched across the whole of Indochina. However the new Chenla–Funan state was immensely large and powerful, covering modern southern Cambodia, Cochin China, northwards along the Mekong from Stung Treng up the Wat Phu and Champasak to the area around the Mun river and, possibly, even beyond the present boundaries of Laos as far north as Nanchao in China.

In the eighth century dynastic quarrels caused Chenla to be divided into Upper Chenla with its capital near Wat Phu. It became known as *Wen Tan* to the Chinese and, since its frontiers were contiguous with China's in places, the two countries maintained frequent contact. Upper Chenla's last mission to China was in 799 CE and after that, it passed into obscurity to be inherited by the growing empire of Angkor.

The southern territory now referred to as Lower Chenla was popularly known as *Water Chenla*. It was a maritime power that had its capital in the Mekong delta. Compared to Upper Chenla, it was to have a turbulent history for its first hundred years, suffering especially from the attacks of pirates. To escape their raids it gradually moved its capital further and further inland, until about 889 CE, the construction of Angkor was started and a new empire was born.

Dvaravati: The City of Gates

POSSIBLY AS A result of Chenla's annexation of Funan, a new state was created. It was called Dvaravati, *The City of Gates*, named after a legendary city in the Mahabharata. The people were Mon, the oldest inhabitants of present day Thailand and Burma. The Mon were to be found among the neolithic colonisers of Indochina.

Their capital was at Nakhon Pathom, thirty-five miles west of modern Bangkok. Nakhon Pathom lay on a neolithic trade route, forming an important meeting place for merchants from Tibet, China and those from the Chinese and Indian Oceans. As well as being a trading emporium, it soon became the centre of Indian studies in Indochina. Phya Anuman, the Thai scholar, was to claim to the British historian D.G.E Hall that it was from Nakhon Pathom that Buddhism reached Burma.

Nakhon Pathom stands at the confluence of the Mae Khlong and Khwae Noi rivers. The Khwae Noi descends from the Three Pagodas Pass, which was to be the gateway for so many invasions from Burma.

Dvaravati is thought to have coexisted with Funan and remained independent until the eleventh century when it was annexed by Angkor. Its Mon people had long before spread up the river valleys and formed an important part of the population of both future Thailand and Burma.

The Tai and the Chinese Administrations

IT WAS AMONG these civilisations that the Tai people would come to settle. But in the centuries before this happened, the Tai in China with each new generation found themselves forced to expand. New muongs were created and these remained linked by blood ties with the old ones. The first Chinese records of the Tai show that they mostly inhabited the territory to the south of the Yangtze river.

In the five centuries between the ninth and fourth century BC, the Chinese tried to impose their culture, and whenever possible, their administration on the peoples in these southern regions. It was a switchback ride: when their northern provinces gave the central government trouble, the southerners were left to look after themselves. Whenever the north was quiet, the south could expect the Chinese to try and impose their domination.

Between 246 BC and 209 BC the Chinese annexed the two provinces of Kwangtung, adjoining present day Hong Kong, and its southern neighbour, Kwangsi, bordering on Vietnam. The inhabitants of the lowlands of these two provinces were composed of Tai, or Vietnamese, while on the higher reaches were the Meo, or as they call themselves today, the Hmong, the Yao and other hill peoples.

From these records, it can be seen that the main body of the Tai people was already spread from the banks of the Yangtze River southwards to Yunnan in the west, and to the Red and Black Rivers above Hanoi in the east. The Tai in China can best be imagined as the palm of a hand. From this palm stretched 'fingers' of small muongs running southwards down the Salween, which rises to the west of Nanchao through the Shan States to the Gulf of Martaban; the Menam Chaophraya, near the mouth of which lies modern Bangkok; the Mekong, which runs from Tibet through Laos and Cambodia to Saigon; and the Red and Black rivers, which as a single river pass through Hanoi.

In the first centuries of the Christian era, the Chinese decided to take direct control of the rich coastal regions running from the north to as far south as today's Vietnam. At that time the Vietnamese were then a relatively small group of people inhabiting the area around Tongking and some of the coastal strip south of it. They were a very distinct race and for a thousand years, from 111 BC to 939 CE, the Chinese were to try, but fail, to sinicize them.

As a result of this drive southwards by the Chinese, the Tai to the north of the Red River came under direct Chinese rule. They have come to be known as the *Chuang*, while those in the Vietnamese areas are known as the *Tho* and the *Nung*. Once separated geographically, none of these Tai was to rejoin the main Tai body who migrated south into Indochina.

By 69 CE the Chinese directly administered what is now Yunnan. From there they extended the territory to create the prefecture of Yung Ch'ang between the Mekong and the Salween rivers. Their objective was to control the trade route that passed across northern India to Bactria, now northern Afghanistan, and from there to the Roman Empire.

Although the trade route brought in revenue, the Chinese found that maintaining the prefecture of Yung Ch'ang was, in times of trouble, too much of a drain on their resources. In 342, they closed the prefecture, leaving the merchants without any official protection. It was to be another two hundred years before the route opened to regular traffic again. When it did, it was under the protection of Nanchao.

The Creation of Nanchao

THE CHINESE WITHDRAWAL from the direct control of their western frontiers continued. In 713, the central government decided to place the responsibility for the Yunnan region in the hands of Chinese officials in Szechwan Province, who were to maintain control through the local rulers in Yunnan.

Although the Tai, or Ai–Lao as they were called by the Chinese, formed the majority of the population of Yunnan, they were not its rulers. In the early part of the eighth century, one of the Yunnanese chiefs was Chao (Prince) Pi-lo-ko, the ruler of the principality, Mengshe. With Chinese encouragement he conquered the five other major principalities around Lake Tali to become the chief ruler. The Chinese officials in Szechuan referred to him as *Nan Chao*, the *Southern Prince*. It was not long before the name was used to refer to the region, as well as to the Prince.

The decision to place the power in local hands was to prove a costly decision for the Chinese. In 748, Ko-lo-Feng, the adopted son of Chao Pi-lo-ko, inherited Nanchao and made his capital near Lake Tali, probably at Taho. He continued his father's extension of the kingdom and decided to reopen the lucrative trade route to the West. His campaign was so successful that he not only opened the trade route but quickly subjugated the Pyu in Upper Burma and eventually extended his conquests as far south as the Irrawaddy delta.

Ko-lo-Feng's increasing power caused concern among the Chinese officials. When a Chinese military governor insulted him, Ko-lo-Feng killed him and declared Nanchao independent. The Chinese sent an army against him which he defeated. In 753, as a proof of his independence he formed a military alliance with Tibet.

In the same year the ruler of Upper Chenla visited China and accompanied the Chinese army in one of its attacks on Nanchao where he witnessed the complete destruction of the Chinese army! Ko-lo-Feng beat

13

off three more Chinese campaigns against him before the Chinese found themselves involved with other problems in the north and were forced to leave him to pursue his conquests without their intervention.

Ko-lo-Feng and his son pushed further eastwards and by the end of the century had conquered most of southern China and raided Tongking and even Annam. By 791, China was stronger and Ko-lo-Feng's grandson, I-mou-hsun, wisely accepted Chinese suzerainty and Nanchao became a vassal state.

The Tai of Nanchao

THERE SEEMS TO be no doubt that neither Pi-lo-ko nor his adopted son, Ko-lo-Feng, was Tai. The language of Ko-lo-Feng is known and is closely related to that spoken by the Lolo people, now to be found largely in Burma. No words of Lolo language have ever been shown to have any relationship with the Tai language. Also, the kings of Nanchao followed the custom of taking the last syllable of their father's name as the first syllable of their name. Thus, Pi-lo-*ko*'s recognised son was *Ko*-lo-feng. Again no such custom has been found in Tai ruling families. All the evidence is, therefore, against the Tai being rulers of Nanchao, or of the rulers of Nanchao being those named in the greatest of Tai legends, that of Khun Boulom.

However, much more important, since the Tai formed the majority of the population of Nanchao, it must have been the Tai, who made up the bulk of the Nanchao armies. It was, we may assume, largely Tai soldiers who conquered Burma from the hills in the north to the Irrawaddy in the south. It was Tai soldiers whose glorious conquests covered southern China and northern Vietnam. Such experiences burn deeply into the racial consciousness.

The Tai were already living in Indochina under the rule of the Khmer and Mon. The time was coming when they would decide to unite their scattered muongs and become the princes of the lands where, until then, they were only settlers.

The Tai Movement South

ABOUT THE SIXTH century the Khmer in the Lopburi area spoke of the local Tai as inhabiting *Syam*. This is an indication of how they had already spread throughout Indochina. In this same period they already formed a very important group within the city of Muong Swa, today's Luang Prabang, the royal capital of Laos until 1975.

Tradition has it that this was the first Tai capital in Indochina, possibly in the Tai world, in which case it would have pre-dated Sukhothai, 1238.

The arrival of the main body of the Tai in Lan Xang, modern Laos, is recounted in a number of versions of the Khun Boulom legend. All the versions clearly place the descent of Khun Boulom on his mission to repopulate the earth as being in the Black River valley. His kingdom was around today's Dien Bien Phu, the *Valley of the Angels*.

It was at Dien Bien Phu in 1954 that the French army tried for an overwhelming victory against the Communist Vietnamese – and was defeated. The battle of Dien Bien Phu was their last throw, it was followed by the loss of the whole of Indochina.

Dien Bien Phu: The Valley of Angels

THE LEGEND OF Khun Boulom takes place in the valley lands of Muong Thene, which was the richest and largest muong and is now known as Dien Bien Phu. The Tai living in the valley of Muong Thene were on the edge of the demarcation laid down by the Chinese and Vietnamese. From linguistic evidence they appear to be the forebears of the present Black, Red, White and other upland Tai peoples, and are now referred to as the Sipsong Chau Tai.

Just to their south along the valley of the Nam Ou and the parts of the Mekong close to Luang Prabang, then called Muong Swa, are those who were to form the northern Lao and the Tai of the Sukhothai kingdom. While those to their east around Xieng Khouang were to populate central Siam (Thailand) and southern Laos.

The Legend of Khun Boulom is of great antiquity. In some versions of the legend one finds the story of the Flood and the almost total destruction of mankind. In these versions the Khun Boulom legend is integrated with some of the oldest memories of man. With such a venerable past, it is therefore probable that the lists of fourteen kings that preceded Khun Boulom are clan memories passed down from generation to generation: each new king being added to the list as he succeeded to the throne.

Before examining the legend any further, the following is a very freely translated version based largely on that in Le Boulanger's history of Laos.

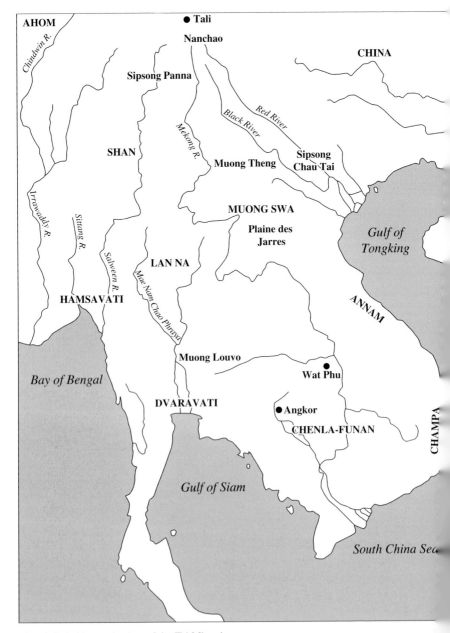

MAP 1 Indochina at the time of the Tai Migrations

The Legend of Khun Boulom

THE KING OF Heaven, Phya Thene, looked down on the world in sorrow. All was without order or purpose and he concluded that the only solution was to send down a race of great men who would do good.

He looked around his counsellors, and decided on the wise Khun Boulom as the one best able to reign over the earth. With him he sent two divine wives, who were called Nang Et Keng, the first wife, and Nang Yomakara, the second wife.

Khun Boulom appeared on earth riding on a white elephant whose ears were completely black, while its tusks were curved, shimmering and crossed over each other.

Khun Boulom and his great cortège of attendants crossed the vast plain of Muong Thene, which is today known as the valley of Dien Bien Phu to a place called Na Noï, the *Small Rice Field*.

There he and his attendants found a giant gourd plant that grew in the centre of the Lake Kouva. The gourd was entwined with a vast fig tree that reached unbelievably high up into the sky.

ILLUSTRATION 3 The Phou Gneu Gna Gneu: the Magical Great Ancestors, Lao New Year, 1956, Luang Prabang

© Peter & Sanda Simms

17

In some versions, the liana continued to grow and it soon covered the whole sky and the sun could no longer be seen. With the darkness came bitter cold and Khun Boulom gave orders for the liana to be cut down. However when the people approached it with their axes it was quite obvious that whoever cut it down would have no chance of escaping. When it fell, its great trunk and branches would crush them to death. Nobody dared to attack it and it continued to grow larger and larger. It would not be long before everyone died of cold and shortage of food.

Then two old people, who had come down from heaven with Khun Boulom, decided that they must sacrifice themselves. So Phou Thao Gneu, and his wife, Mae Ngam, volunteered to cut it down. In return, they asked that for ever after their death they would receive offerings, and their spirits would be invoked at the beginning of every meal. The people immediately promised them their wishes would be honoured.

Everything happened just as expected. After three months and three days, Phou Thao Gneu and his wife hacked away the last of the supporting roots and the liana fell. As they had known, they were killed, but sunlight and warmth came back to the earth once again.

Ever since then, the two old people have been revered under the names Phou Gneu and Gna Gneu. In Luang Prabang they are also known as the *Ho Tevada Luang*, the *Magical Great Ancestors*, and their masks and costumes are kept in Wat Aram, a pagoda that is kept closed all the year round except when it is opened for the ceremonies and celebrations of the Laotian New Year.

In other versions there is no mention of the Phou Gneu Gna Gneu and the account tells how the giant liana, or fig tree, helped support two immense gourds that had sprung from the plant. Khun Boulom pierced the gourds and from them immediately poured out, far beyond the powers of anyone's imagination, gold, silver, fabrics, perfumes, seeds, men and women, cattle, buffaloes, pigs, dogs, chickens, ducks, and other living creatures who spread across the earth.

His two wives had given him seven sons, Khun Boulom separated the people and divided them among the seven kings who were his sons and so formed the great Tai world.

To Khun Lo, the eldest son, he gave the beautiful Muong Swa, or Lan Xang Hom Khao, the *Land of the Million Elephants and White Parasols*. Khun Lo was to change the name of the capital to Muong Xieng Thong, *The City of the Flame Trees*.

To his second son, Chet Chuong, he gave the Kingdom of Muong Phoueune, today's Xieng Khouang, which comprised what was later to be called the Tran Ninh Plateau and the Valley of the Nam Nhiep running south to Borikane.

To his third son, Ni Fa Lane, he gave Muong Ho, the Sipsong Panna, the *12,000 Rice Fields*.

To his fourth son, Chu Song, he gave Prakan, which to this day is the Tai country of the Upper Tongking and the Black River Valley, the Sipsong Chau Tai.

To his fifth son, Saya Phong, he gave Muong Niuon, that was to be the kingdom of Lan Na, the *Land of the Million Rice Fields*, which was later to be ruled over by the Chiang Mai dynasty.

To his sixth son, Kham In, he gave Muong Louvo, (sometimes known as Lan Piyeau, the *Million Granaries)* that was to become Siam, today's Thailand.

To his last and seventh son, Louk Poun, he gave Hamsavati whose capital was Pegu on the plain formed by the deltas of the great Salween River that flowed from the Tai homeland and, to the west, the Irrawaddy River.

Before sending them to found their kingdoms, Khun Boulom exhorted them to live as good neighbours, the older not quarrelling with the younger, 'Go and remember that you all have the same father.' Unfortunately, they did not listen to their father's advice

Another version of the legend provides an explanation for the presence of another race the Kha or Lao Theung, the earlier Khmer peoples. In this version there are three gourds, instead of two. The first was opened using a red-hot iron and the people who came out were blackened by the soot. The other gourds were opened with chisels and the people were, therefore, fairer in colour.

Another version of the legend includes the story that is to be found in legends throughout the world, including the indigenous tribes of the Americas. In these versions the King of Heaven was disgusted by the human race and decided to destroy it except for three chiefs who, under his instructions, built an ark and survived the deluge. In this version there are three gourds and the first is opened with a red-hot iron and the people, as in other versions, came out blackened by the soot.

There is no evidence that about the time of the expansion of Nanchao, at the end of the eighth century, that the Tai conquered all of the seven areas that were given to Khun Boulom's sons. But from linguistic evidence it is clear that from about 800 CE large groups of Tai moved into Laos, Thailand and Upper Burma and continued to do so for the next two hundred years. Tai mercenaries are to be seen on the friezes in Angkor.

It was a mere trickle southwards compared to what would come later, but it prepared the ground for the subsequent mass migrations. In 1096, the small Tai state of Phayao was created to the east of modern Chiang Mai. Very recent excavations have shown that about 1200 CE there was a Tai town named Souvannakhongkham, some 235 miles to the northwest of today's Vientiane.

The Mongol Invasion

THEN CAME A dramatic change. In 1211 Genghis Khan led his Mongol army into northern China and conquered the ancient Chinese empire. The subjugation of the Chinese territory was not completed until 1223, but the repercussions were immediately felt throughout the kingdom, even as far south as Nanchao.

The trickle of Tai emigration started to be a mass movement. In 1215 the Tai state of Mogaung in northern Burma was founded, to be followed in 1223 by Mong Nai in what are now the Shan States. It was about this time that the mass migration down the Nam Ou to Luang Prabang took place. There were already Tai, whom we may now call Lao, living there. It was at that time that the vestiges of Khmer rule were extinguished and it became a Tai state ruled by Tai.

In this mass movement, there were so many Tai that they could no longer settle in with the original inhabitants. Those who were not Tai were driven out of the valley land and up into the hills. These were the Khmer, Mon, Cham and other indigenous peoples who had to settle on what land they could work on the slopes and uplands. They became the Lao Theung, or as they were called then the *Kha, the slaves*.

One wave of Tai followed another. In 1229 the Tai founded the Ahom kingdom in today's Assam. In 1238, two Tai chiefs defeated the Khmer governor of Sukhothai and the foundations of present day Thailand were laid.

In 1253, Kublai Khan, the grandson of Genghis Khan, attacked and captured the kingdom of Nanchao, causing what Coedès calls the great 'effervescence' of the Tai, who like swarms of infuriated bees spread down the Indochinese peninsular. It was at this time that the Tai country of Lan Na, *The Thousand Rice Fields* was created. Their first historical ruler was Phaya Mangrai, who founded Chiang Rai, the *City of King Rai*, on 12 April, 1296.

From Nanchao, Kublai Khan reconquered the whole of southern China and the region around Hanoi. In 1271 he sent envoys to King Narathihapate, the king of Pagan, who refused to receive them. Two years later Kublai Khan sent a second mission and King Narathihapate was foolish enough to execute them. In 1277, Kublai Khan ordered a Tartar force from Yunnan to attack Pagan. It defeated the Burmese. Unfortunately a second Mongol army, which arrived a little later, was defeated and this emboldened King Narathihapate to challenge Kublai Khan once again. When the Mongols returned to answer the challenge, Narathihapate's army was annihilated and he fled to Bassein.

The Mongols made approaches to the Khmer, offering them protection in return for acknowledging Mongol supremacy. The Khmer were foolish enough to reject the proposal out of hand. The Mongol policy from then on was designed to weaken the Khmer rule in the Indochinese states. Taking advantage of the situation, the Tai king, Rama Khamheng, reached agreement with the Mongols and began a series of attacks against the nearby countries that were vassals of the Khmer.

He was able to take over the whole of the Mon country along the Menam Chaophraya valley and in the surrounding Mon populated towns around Chiang Rai. In Rama Khamheng's life time Sukhothai embraced Luang Prabang and Vientiane, so ending Khmer rule in the north for ever.

When Rama Khamheng died in 1298, his son, Lo Thai, was unable to hold his father's kingdom together. Luang Prabang and Vientiane were able to return to independence, becoming Lao towns under Lao rulers.

By 1299, the Mongols were finding themselves over-stretched. They decided to hand over Pagan to their Tartar allies. King Narathihapate had been murdered by his son. The traditional royal bloodbath had followed as one contender for the throne after another tried to massacre his way to power. The eventual winner was a Prince Kyawswa. The Tartars offered him the throne as a vassal. It was to be only a temporary respite for the Burmese.

In Burma the Tai have always been known as the Shan. The Shan have kept their identity and maintained their own language. While the Burmese civilisation in the rich Irrawaddy Valley has influenced the Shan, especially those along the western borders, the Shan have always felt an affinity with their Lao and Thai neighbours and have shared a common cultural background throughout the centuries.

In 1299 three Shan chiefs murdered Prince Kyawswa, bringing an end to Burmese rule for the next two hundred years. The Shans gradually took over the whole country. Setting up kingdoms under their Saophas, *The Lords of the Sky,* such as Yawnghwe, Hsenwi, Hsipaw, and Kengtung, to name only a few.

From then on, the way was clear for the Tai to take over most of Indochina. The greatest of their warrior kings that came into being was to be a Lao, Prince Fa Ngum.

The Tai Brotherhood

THE DESCENDANTS OF Khun Boulom's seven sons have survived in Laos, the Shans States, Thailand, Assam, in the Tai in parts of Cambodia and in Vietnam and, finally, in their original homeland south of the Yangtze, where they are still to be found across the whole of the south of China.

Today there are at least seventy million Tai peoples in Southeast Asia. Of these, the Lao account for probably three and a half million in Laos, with an estimated twenty million Lao living in Thailand. Surprisingly, they are almost equal to the number of Thai in Thailand, who number about twenty-seven to thirty million.

There are about three and a half million Shans in Burma. The Nung and Tho in Vietnam are about 400,000 and the Chuang in Kwangsi and Kwangtung are around eighteen million. To these are to be added several million more in China who cannot be identified, including those on the island of Hainan. In addition, there are the Ahom in Bengal.

And, finally, there are the unnumbered thousands in exile in France, Britain, Australia and the United States. It is to them that this book is dedicated.

CHAPTER TWO

Laos: The Paradise of Riches

THE MASS MIGRATIONS of the Tai in the thirteenth century were both arduous and dangerous. Most of the migrating families followed routes that had already been travelled, and they probably had guides. Even so, whether they were entering today's Burma, Thailand, or Laos, they would have had to face the freezing hardships of crossing at least one mountain divide and each must have taken its toll of the old and the weak. The mountains towered some 3,000 to over 6,000 feet above the struggling groups of migrants as they pushed their way up into the passes. At night, the temperature probably fell below freezing, something that would have been unusual in the villages they had just left, where year-round it was more likely to be about a pleasant 20°C.

On each side of the paths was a thick, often impenetrable, jungle: vast trees, giant lianas, and a lush undergrowth hid everything in a moving green sea of leaves and rustling branches. Tigers, wild boars, snakes, even swarms of hornets, were a threat to their lives. Hundreds must have died of exhaustion, through accidents as they navigated the rivers, or stumbled through tiredness and tumbled down the steep ravines.

They had to try to lead their buffalo, pigs, and dogs, while carrying in their baskets chickens, cooking utensils, blankets, agricultural tools, weapons, and any other personal possessions that they wanted to salvage from their past life.

It was a completely different journey to those taken by the Tai in the earlier centuries. Then the migrants had always known that they could go back to their homes and to safety. In this mass migration there was no going back. They had to find land in time to plant and to harvest or they would die. If they should have to fight to obtain land, then, even though exhausted by the journey, that is what they would have to do if they were to survive.

Although the journey over the mountains and beside the fast flowing streams was difficult, these migrating groups were not entering a wilderness, nor a country of savages. For over six thousand years, just as in China, root crops, bananas, gourds or cucumbers, rice and yams had been grown by the indigenous peoples. They used water buffalo for hauling their carts and ploughs, for meat and for hides. They raised and ate chickens, pigs and other domesticated animals. From far back, there had been prosperous Stone, Iron and Bronze Age settlements in the region, some of them close to modern Luang Prabang, which the future Lao people were approaching

On the Plaine des Jarres there had been a well organised society of a people who loved jewellery, and treasured their own personal possessions. It had had a clearly defined hierarchy that used iron and bronze. The hundreds of great jars, some over five or six-foot tall that still lie scattered across the plain, were probably part of an elaborate burial practice. The life on the Plaine des Jarres had not been a culture unique to the Plaine, but had formed part of a wider culture that had spread at least as far south as Savannakhet and Keng Kok.

The Tai were moving into lands that were already inhabited land, but fortunately for them they were entering a land where the ruling power, the Khmer empire, was in decline. It had been the greatest empire to that Indochina had ever known. But now it had overstretched itself and was weak; the outermost territories were only waiting for an opportunity to break free from the Khmer.

The bulk of the migrants, once they were out of the high ridges and climbing down into the lower valleys found themselves entering first a temperate, then a semitropical, and finally, the fertile valleys with a tropical climate. Now that the forest lay above them, it no longer seemed the fearful place they had known on the march. Instead it was to become an inexhaustible source for the hunter, as were the fertile lands beside the rivers for the farmer, and the rivers themselves for the fisherman. They had entered the paradise envisaged in the Khun Boulom legend.

The City of Flame Trees

JUST AS THE legend of Khun Boulom says, the Tai people formed themselves into seven principalities that were soon to become kingdoms. Those who descended the Nam Ou came to Muong Swa, or as it is known today, Luang Prabang. The city was many centuries old, and was said to have been founded by two hermits who came from the high plateau lands of Tibet near the source of the Mekong River. As the hermits descended the river, they were looking for a place to found a new city. Just to the south of the confluence of the Nam Ou and the Mekong, they were struck by the beauty of the flame trees and decided that it would be there that they would found the city-state to be called, *Muong Swa*. Although the town came to be known as Xieng Dong Xieng Thong, *The City of the Flame Trees beside the River Dong*, It was also often referred to as Muong Swa.

Xieng Thong was most probably its name when the Tai came to take possession of it somewhere about 1250. It too had been a part of the Khmer empire. As the Khmer influence diminished, then vanished, so did its monuments and temples. In Luang Prabang today, the former Xieng Thong, only a stele of Vishnu remains as a memory of the once all-powerful race of Khmer warriors.

Buddhism was also known to the thirteenth century inhabitants of Xieng Thong. Before the Christian era, Buddhism had divided into two different followings, the Mahayana from North India and Tibet, and the Theravada, or Hinayana, from the south and Ceylon. Although Buddhism certainly had its following in Xieng Thong, the strongest influences were exerted through the much older worship of Spirits and the Deities of the Earth. These beliefs would not have been significantly different to the beliefs of the Tai migrants.

While living in China, the Tai had also certainly come into contact with the far newer philosophy of Buddhism. It is in 65 CE that the Chinese first mention the arrival of Buddhism. It had come by sea from southern India, or possibly Ceylon, and was Theravada in form. However it was so alien to any previous Chinese philosophy that they found it completely unacceptable until they had given it strong Taoist overtones.

As the legend of the founding of Muong Swa shows, Buddhist monks from Tibet were already proselytising along the Mekong and the other rivers flowing to the south. As well as the Theravada Buddhism with its Taoist overtones, the Tai in Nanchao must certainly have become aware of Mahayana Buddhism from at least the times of Ko-lo-Feng, if not far earlier. However, judging from the outlook and beliefs in the times of Fa Ngum in the fourteenth century, spirit worship, with the propitiation of the gods by human and animal sacrifices, was still their dominant belief.

There is no record of the date when the Tai came to settle in Xieng Thong, nor is there any account of how they came to be its rulers. The lists of 35 legendary kings that were originally handed down orally are without any indication of the dates when the kings of Muong Swa ruled.

Khun Lo, the eldest son of Khun Boulom, is the thirteenth king on some of the lists. The first, Phaya Nan Tha, was said to have come from Ceylon. The eighth, Thao Tiantha Phanit, was said to be a betelnut-seller from Vientiane, who so fascinated the people of Muong Swa that they made him king. He was followed by Khun Swa, who was a 'Kha'. If these legends are to be believed there were twelve kings of other races who ruled Muong Swa before the Tai were strong enough to become the rulers.

The Birth of Lan Xang

NONE OF THIS, however, is history. It is only proper that the history of Laos should begin in the Year of the Naga, 1316, the year that saw the birth of Chao Fa Ngum, Prince Fa Ngum, who was to be the founder and creator of Lan Xang.

In that year, 1316, King Phaya Souvanna Khampong was the king of Xieng Tong. His eldest son, the Crown Prince, was Chao Fa Ngiao. One does no know why, but he had a bad reputation and people referred to him as Chao Phi Fa, *Prince Evil Spirit.*

According to legend, it was in the same year that King Souvanna Khampong was crowned, that Chao Phi Fa's wife gave birth to a son, Chao Fa Ngum. Chao Phi Fa was to have two sons and two daughters. It is still early in the history of Lan Xang and the mists of time still cover these first years. Some records say that Chao Fa Ngum was the elder, others that he was the younger. Whichever he was, his birth was not auspicious. He was born with thirty-three teeth already formed. The mandarins told his grandfather, the King, that this was a sign that Chao Fa Ngum would do great harm to the kingdom.

Again, it is not so surprising that there are two very different accounts of what happened next. In one account, Chao Fa Ngum was allowed to live but, when he was about six years old, his father, Chao Phi Fa, was accused of committing adultery with one of the Khmer concubines of the King, his father. So Chao Phi Fa, his ill-omened son, Fa Ngum, and their attendants were placed on a raft and, under escort, were cast off to float down the Mekong.

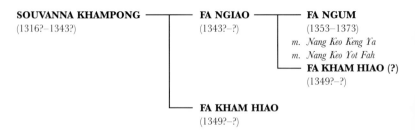

GENEALOGICAL TABLE 1 The First Historic Kings of Lan Xang

More probable is the second account that says King Souvanna Khampong thought the omen accompanying Chao Fa Ngum's birth too important to ignore. Since the young prince was of royal blood, it was not advisable to kill him, so he was set adrift on a raft with thirty-three people in attendance, including two wet nurses and six others who were to become his fighting companions in later life. Three of these were Ba Chi Kae, Ba Lim and Ba Lu.

In this account, Fa Ngum is not accompanied by his father, who remaining at Court could have succeeded to the throne when his father died in 1343.

After about a year, they reached the island of Khong and from there they made their way to the court of Angkor, the Khmer capital. They were received by the king, Jayavarman Paramesvara (1327–1353?). The Khmer empire, as we have seen, was the direct descendant of the empires of Funan and Chenla. It had been founded around 802, but it was not until 889 that its fourth king, Yasovarman (889–900), began the construction of a resplendent capital with the vast representations in stone of the Sacred Mountain, Mount Meru, the portrayals of the legends of the Mahabharata, of the Ramayana, and of the Hindu and Buddhist stories. Angkor was of a splendour and magnificence that mankind has probably never again equalled in any other construction in the world.

In earlier days, the Khmer kings had been so powerful that they employed hundreds of thousands of people on building temples, monuments, processional ways, creating statues, paintings, complex dances, and music, while still having sufficient manpower to keep their armies in the field and maintain their rule over even the most distant parts of their empire.

By the time that Jayavarman came to the throne, Angkor was severely weakened. It had seemingly squandered its resources not only in building its spectacularly magnificent capital, but, as well, by trying to defend what had by then become an over extended empire.

In 1282, there had been nothing that Angkor could do to stop the Tai king of Sukhothai, Rama Khamheng (c.1275–c.1317), declaring the independence of Sukhothai and with it claiming the suzerainty over the former Khmer vassals, Xieng Thong and Vientiane. Before he died, Rama Khamheng had been able to extend Sukhothai's rule over the greater part of the former Khmer territories in the west of the Chaophraya Valley. It was, however, to be only a brief flowering for Sukhothai as, on Rama Khamheng's death, his descendants proved unable to hold his kingdom together, and it was gradually taken over by new and more vigorous Tai states.

ILLUSTRATION 4 Buddha Rupas within the entrance

Illus. 4, 5 and 6 © Nicholas & Suchinda Thompson

ILLUSTRATION 5 Entrance to the Caves

ILLUSTRATION 6 Inside the Pak Ou Caves

At the Court of Angkor

THE ARRIVAL OF this Tai prince, Chao Fa Ngum, seemed to King Jayavarman to offer an opportunity to regain the former Khmer influence in the north. He made him part of his family and gave him Phra Pasman, a Buddhist monk, as his tutor. When Chao Fa Ngum was old enough, he further cemented their friendship by giving him his daughter, Princess Keo Keng Ya, as his wife. She was to be Chao Fa Ngum's only true love. When she died, as we shall see, he was left so desolate that even his warrior companions could do nothing to fill the sense of emptiness that followed.

King Jayavarman had only recently become converted to the southern school of Buddhism, the Theravada, and he maintained close contact with Ceylon, which had become the authoritative source of all matters of Theravada doctrine.

In 1343, the King of Xieng Thong died and it is not clear who succeeded him. The most probable is Chao Fa Ngum's father, Chao Fa Ngiao, known as Chao Phi Fa. Whoever did become king, it was not until six years later, in 1349, that Chao Fa Ngum requested his father-in-law, King Jayavarman, to give him an army to recover his throne. He was by then thirty-three years old.

Why was there a six year gap between the death of King Souvanna Khampong and the request to march against Xieng Thong? One possible answer is that his father, Chao Phi Fa, had quite legitimately succeeded to the throne in 1343 and had died in 1349. The throne was once again vacant. Fa Ngum had accepted that his father should succeed his grandfather, but on his father's death, he believed that the crown should have passed to him. However, instead it had passed to another claimant, who was called Chao Fa Kham Hiao. Probably he was Chao Fa Ngum's uncle, but he may have been his brother. If this is so, and Chao Fa Ngum was the elder, he would certainly have had good reason to try to take back the throne through the use of force.

With the Princess Keo Keng Ya, Ba Chi Kae and the others who had been exiled with him, Chao Fa Ngum set off at the head of a Khmer army that was to be known as *The Ten Thousand*. The Prince of Champasak tried to stop them, but they brushed his army aside and fought their way up to modern Thakhek, where they rested for a while.

From there, Chao Fa Ngum sent out his generals on marauding trips to bring back the submissions of the local rulers and with them the spoils of victory. In Khammouan he was given 100 elephants with 200 mahouts accompanied by 200 men and women, as well as gold and silver, silk curtains, and carpets. His generals returned with ever more wealth and, most importantly, men and women captives, to be used as troops, servants and porters for the army.

Chao Fa Ngum moved north. He crossed the Nam Kading, which, in 1960, was the last defence line for Captain Kong Lae against General Phoumi Nosavan's army. From there he marched on Paksane and sought the help of the Tai kingdom of Vientiane, to give it its modern spelling.

Vientiane was as old as Xieng Thong and was one of the most powerful of the Tai kingdoms. It had earlier probably been a Mon city and was then called Chandapuri, from the Pali meaning, *City of the Moon*. Vieng is literally a wall, or palisade, and possibly for this reason some Lao scholars do not accept that it was called Vieng Chan, *Wall (?City) of the Moon*, but instead say that it was Vieng Chanh, *Palisade of Sandalwood*. Whichever it was, we have chosen to refer to it as Vientiane from here onwards.

Vientiane, however, refused to give Fa Ngum any assistance. While Fa Ngum was deciding what to do, he was approached by Chao Thiem Kham Nho, the son of the king of Muong Phoueune, now modern Xieng Khouang, who had been sent into exile for what seems to have been a common fault: that of seducing one of the concubines of the king, his father. Chao Thiem Kham Nho (1350–1374) offered to be Chao Fa Ngum's vassal, on condition that Chao Fa Ngum would help him fight his father and win back the throne.

Chao Fa Ngum readily agreed as he was afraid that the king of Muong Phoueune might make an alliance with Xieng Thong and he would then have had to fight their united armies. With his new ally, he advanced up the Nam Nhiep and routed the Phoueune army. After that, Chao Fa Ngum appears to have spent nearly a year in Xieng Khouang.

Annam Accepts Fa Ngum

THEN, INSTEAD OF marching against Luang Prabang, Chao Fa Ngum led his armies across the Tran Ninh plateau to today's Sam Neua. As he approached the border with Annam, the King of Annam sent a high ranking mission with valuable presents and a proposal that was very favourable to the warrior prince.

The Annamite mission told Chao Fa Ngum that their king wished to have a permanent border agreement. He proposed that if the houses in a village were built on stilts, then it would be Lao territory, if built directly on the ground, then it would be Vietnamese. This was a system that was to be used again in the nineteenth and twentieth century when the French decided on the frontiers between Laos and Vietnam.

In addition, the natural divide of the Annamite range of mountains running north to south would form the border. Where the rivers ran to the sea it would be Vietnamese, where they ran into the Mekong valley, Lao.

As a result, Chao Fa Ngum was able to annex several towns and there was peace with Annam that was to last for a century. This agreement recognised both Chao Thiem as ruler in his new kingdom of Xieng Khouang and Chao Fa Ngum as the future king of Xieng Thong.

From the borders of Annam Chao Fa Ngum took his army up the Red River Valley and along the Black River to Dien Bien Phu, where Khun Boulom had arrived from heaven. He subdued all the Tai muongs and following the southward course of the rivers reached the Nam Ou and sailed his army down to its confluence with the Mekong. He then made camp only a few hours to the north of Xieng Tong.

The king of Xieng Thong, who was either Fa Ngum's uncle, or possibly his younger brother, sent out his armies on three occasions and three times they were beaten. Finally, as Chao Fa Ngum's army approached his capital, overwhelmed with shame, the king hanged himself in his palace. The mandarins who had earlier voted against Chao Fa Ngum hastened to offer him the crown.

Chao Fa Ngum Crowned King of Lan Xang

In 1353, Chao Fa Ngum (1353–1371) was crowned. One of his earliest acts was to call his new country Lan Xang, the *Million Elephants*. He spent some time organising his administration, but to him it was far more important to fulfill his dream of a great and united Lao nation. Impatient to add to his victories he appointed Queen Keo Keng Ya as his regent and left Xieng Thong in her hands, while he sought the homage of the northwest.

He made a series of campaigns obtaining the submission of Chiang Saen and Chiang Hung in the Sipsong Panna. He extended the boundaries of Lan Xang as far as Kengtung, now in the Shan States, and advanced on the frontiers of Lan Na whose capital was Chiang Mai.

King Pha Yu (1337–1355) of Lan Na immediately raised an army, but Chao Fa Ngum overwhelmed it and the king of Lan Na sent sufficiently valuable gifts that they were able to reach an agreement on their borders. Having secured his northern and eastern frontiers, King Fa Ngum then returned to Xieng Thong.

On the way back, he ordered that 100,000 Khmer living around Namtha should be removed to the region around Xieng Thong. He warned those that remained against fighting each other, or of creating any other form of disturbance. He left with them a large stone that was to be the weight of the fine that they would have to pay in gold, or silver, if they disobeyed.

He returned to Xieng Thong in 1356 and his wife, who was pregnant when he had left her two years earlier, had given birth to a son, named Chao Oun Huean. Evidently, Queen Keo Keng Ya had administered the country effectively as Chao Fa Ngum was soon able to turn his attention southwards towards Vientiane and the other states that had earlier, in 1349, refused to help him during his advance northwards from Angkor.

The Conquest of Vientiane

It was in 1356 that King Fa Ngum decided to invade Vientiane. This was not to be a war against small and disorganised muongs, but against a fully organised state that had not been frightened by the apparent invincibility of the victorious *Ten Thousand* when they had approached its frontiers seven years before.

At that time the kingdom of Vientiane was ruled by King Xieng Mung, while his son, Phagna Phao, ruled the twin city of Phai Nam, which lay opposite to modern Nong Khai.

The battle took place on the plain before Vientiane. Even allowing for the exaggeration of the chroniclers, the preparations for the battle must have been awe-inspiring. On the Vientiane side there were 500 elephants, brilliantly caparisoned, their howdahs with a fighting platform in front of them, were covered in silver and gold. Behind the elephants were 20,000 soldiers. The bodyguards of the king and the princes were brightly dressed to make them appear more frightening.

King Xieng Mung was riding on his elephant *Vangburi*, who, at its shoulders, was over twice the height of a man. His son, Phagna Phao was on his elephant called *Nang Khoi*, who was even taller, being thirteen feet high with the fighting platform above his neck.

King Fa Ngum was riding his elephant named *The Four Kingdoms of Xieng Thong*. Surrounding him were his trusted companions from the days when they had been placed on a raft and left to the mercy of the gods. Now toughened by the years of warfare they were experienced generals, princes, and noblemen, ready to take on anyone: cold blooded, death-dealing men who had never known peace.

To the sounds of conch shells, drums and shouting, the armies closed in on each other. Their trained elephants surrounded by foot troops, moving in to give their masters the most advantageous position as they stood on their platforms and fought their opponents standing fourteen or fifteen feet above the ground.

General Ba Chi Kae, one of Chao Fa Ngum's companions in exile, found his elephant next to *Vangburi* on which rode King Xieng Mung. Hand to hand they fought until Ba Chi Kae had killed King Xieng Mung. As soon as his son, Phagna Phao, saw this he decided he could not defend the twin cities. He left Vientiane to King Fa Ngum and ordered his own army to retreat within the walls of Phai Nam.

Phai Nam means *Sharpened Bamboo* and was known by this name as the inhabitants had ringed their town with barricades of sharpened bamboos so thick that they were impenetrable. Chao Fa Ngum immediately sent part of his army to surround Phai Nam, while he took the remaining troops into Vientiane to celebrate their victory.

However hard they tried. Lan Xang's generals found it impossible to break through Phai Nam's bamboo thicket. After some days they went to Chao Fa Ngum and asked him for his suggestions. His solution was simple. He ordered his Treasury to make available gold and silver and these he had turned into spears and arrows. His army advanced once more on Phai Nam and carefully aimed the gold and silver weapons so that they fell within the bamboo defences. Then the Lan Xang army pretended to retreat.

In some accounts Chao Fa Ngum left Phai Nam and went off on his southern campaign, but it seems more likely that, having feigned a retreat, the Lan Xang troops marched away and then after a day or two returned to lie in hiding watching the city.

When the people saw the riches lying among the bamboo, they immediately started to cut their way through, making paths into the barricade from both sides. Chao Fa Ngum's troops watched and when they saw that the barricade no longer provided any defence they advanced on the town, setting fire to the fallen bamboo. In moments the distraught townspeople found their homes threatened by fire, and their lives by the enemy troops. They could only surrender. From then on, in ironic memory, the town became known as Vieng Kham, the *City of Gold*.

For Tai chroniclers, Chao Fa Ngum's idea, if indeed it was his, became a favourite ruse that they told and retold, attributing it to attacks on many other cities. We can never know whether he did employ this ruse, or whether it was even at that time a chronicler's embellishment. Whether it was or not, the kingdom of Vientiane was defeated and was to be part of the kingdom of Lan Xang for the next 300 years.

It has been said that Chao Fa Ngum's ruse could not have taken place as the name Vieng Kham was already known in 1279 as it is to be found inscribed on a stele in Sukhothai that had been made on the orders of King Rama Khamheng. If this were so, it would predate by at least seventy years King Fa Ngum's capture of Phai Nam. However, it is now a possibility that the Rama Khamheng's stele was actually carved during the nineteenth century in Bangkok. If so, it was done with King Mongkut's approval by Siamese historians. It is argued that the intention was not to create a forgery, but, by imitating what King Rama Khamheng *might have created*, would be a proper way to celebrate his great achievements.

There are two different accounts of the fate of Phagna Phao, the king of Phai Nam. In one, Chao Fa Ngum was so impressed by his bravery that he made him the vassal king of Vientiane. In the other, Phagna Phao was placed in a cage and sent to Xieng Thong, where he died.

Fa Ngum takes a Census

After defeating the kingdom of Vientiane, King Fa Ngum held a census of his possessions. It was recorded that in the north of the country his army and people numbered 600,000, with 2,000 elephants and 1,000 horses. To the south, there were 400,000 men and women, 1,000 elephants and 500 horses.

His people and army therefore totalled one million, of which 700,000 were Lao and 300,000 other races. It is impossible to make an assessment of the accuracy of these figures, but they do not seem to be improbably large.

Chao Fa Ngum appears to have always thought strategically. With any victory, he looked ahead to where the next threat might be. With Vientiane now his, he turned his attention southwards and saw there a new threat to the security of Lan Xang.

With the gradual weakening of the Angkorian power, the Tai people had been able to become rulers of the lands they inhabited, even though they were often a minority. At this time, the kingdoms of Lan Na, Sukhothai, and a number of small principalities were created with the Tai replacing the rulers who had earlier been installed and supported by the Khmer.

These breakaway states were mostly on the northern borders of the Khmer empire, but a far closer threat to Angkor's sovereignty was about to take place. In 1350, a Chinese businessman named U Thong founded the city of Ayudhya, just 76 kilometres from present day Bangkok. In 1351, he married the daughter of the King of Suphanburi, a vassal of Angkor, and took the name King Rama Thibodi (1351–1369).

For the Khmer kings, Lopburi and the valley of the Chaophraya were becoming identified with the Tai people and the region called *Syam*. The people of Ayudhya were to adopt this name, which has survived to today as *Siam*. For simplicity, and to differentiate them from the other Tai in the Chaophraya valley, one may refer to them from the time of the foundation of Ayudhya as *Siamese*.

In 1352, Rama Thibodi sent an army to attack Angkor. The attack failed but he was able to extend his dominance over a large part of the western provinces of the Khmer empire, possibly as far north and east as today's Roy Et on the Korat plateau.

This was the situation in 1357 when Chao Fa Ngum had completed the capture of Vientiane. He, as the son-in-law of Jayavarman, the king of Angkor, felt he had a stronger claim to the former Khmer territory than the Siamese. Fa Ngum was determined to take this opportunity to appropriate what he guessed Ayudhya would not yet be strong enough to hold as its own.

He prepared to take his army across the Mekong and southwards into the Korat Plateau, but before doing so, he ordered 10,000 Tai families to move into the present-day Kalasin region, which had formerly been colonised by the Khmer. A further 10,000 he ordered resettled along the banks of the Mekong. This was the beginning of the Lao Isarn in northeast Thailand today.

King Fa Ngum advanced rapidly southwards, capturing the towns and taking their rulers prisoner. When he reached Roy Et he turned it into his base and sent a challenge to the King of Ayudhya asking whether he wished to fight or not.

King Rama Thibodi sent a conciliatory message reminding Chao Fa Ngum that they were both descended from Khun Boulom. He offered to give him his daughter, Nang Keo Lot Fa, when she was of marriageable age. He also promised annual gifts. At the same time he sent fifty male elephants, fifty female elephants and great quantities of gold and silver and over 1,000 pieces of rare horns.

King Fa Ngum accepted King Rama Thibodi's homage and prepared to return to Vientiane. Before doing so however, contemporary accounts provide one of the first opportunities to see how the Tai viewed warfare and the treatment of prisoners. This behaviour must have been based on centuries of Tai customs before the full influence of Buddhism was felt.

Chao Fa Ngum had captured the rulers of the Korat plateau and they were safely imprisoned in Roy Et. He was not under any threat since he had succeeded in his war against both Vientiane and Ayudhya. Yet to celebrate these victories, he prepared to order the sacrificial death of his prisoners. The account Chao Siromé of Champasak gave us of the human sacrifices at Wat Phu were not, it might seem, distant horrors of the past, but represented the reality of King Fa Ngum's time when the gods of the earth still had to be propitiated with blood.

On this occasion, it was only Phra Pasman, Chao Fa Ngum's own Buddhist tutor, who was able to persuade him that for once he should let the prisoners go. There were to be many occasions in the future history of Indochina when there was no Phra Pasman to save the lives of those who had been captured. Tradition has it that the Fa Ngum listened to his teacher and ordered the prisoners to be allowed to live. Fa Ngum returned to Vientiane where he again held celebrations and from there, in 1357, made his way back to Xieng Thong.

Sadly, although he was a magnificent general and the true founder of the immense new kingdom of Lan Xang, his successes had turned Chao Fa Ngum into a despot and tyrant. He could not bear any opposition. Even his closest advisers found that it was dangerous to make suggestions, even the smallest difference of opinion was taken as a challenge to his authority.

In these unhappy circumstances the people and the mandarins of his Court appealed to Queen Keo Keng Ya for her help. As fervent a Buddhist as her father, she decided that only through Buddhism could her royal husband become more temperate and more caring towards his subjects.

The Prabang comes to Lan Xang

THE QUEEN BEGGED Chao Fa Ngum to let her send to her father, King Jayavarman of Angkor, for monks and the *Tripitaka* so that Lan Xang might become a truly Buddhist country. Phra Maha Pasman probably was the person who took the request to Angkor as it was he who was chosen to head the delegation that returned from Angkor to Xieng Thong.

As well as the Buddhist scriptures, the *Tripitaka*, King Jayavarman Paramesvara sent one of his most sacred Buddha figures, called the Prabang, that had been given to his father by the King of Ceylon. It was solid gold and weighed 40 kilograms. According to legend it had been made in Ceylon 1,400 years earlier by some of the greatest craftsman of the times. It was a standing Buddha just over one and a half feet high, with its elbows at its sides, the forearms horizontal and the palms of the hands vertical and facing outwards: a classical posture signifying that one should have no fear. The Prabang was believed to contain four relics of the Buddha within it.

There is some doubt about whether King Jayavarman was still alive at that time, as by one account he may have died in 1357, and his successor may have acceded to the throne in 1362. However, whether Jayavarman was alive

ILLUSTRATION 7 The Prabang at the Royal Palace, Luang Prabang

© Collection Prince Mangkra Souvanna Phouma

or not, the mission is an historical fact. It became a vast cortège. Accompanying the Prabang were engineers and craftsmen, musicians and dancers, and many others to ensure that in future the Queen could enjoy some of the amenities that she had been accustomed to at the court of Angkor.

38

Also, Phra Pasman had been given twenty Buddhist monks with 1,000 lay helpers; 3,000 helpers for the craftsmen and engineers; 1,000 attendants for Queen Keo Keng Ya and some 5,000 other people. One can imagine the stir they must have caused as this immense procession slowly made its way through the countryside, building a city at night only to break it down and rebuild it at the end of the next day. Eventually they arrived at the Mekong and crossed to Vien Kham.

King Fa Ngum, who was in Xieng Thong, had been warned of its approach and had ordered all the people from the surrounding areas to be there to welcome the Prabang and the Tripitaka.

For three days they celebrated the safe arrival of the Prabang and mission. However, when they were going to continue the journey, the eight men who had been carrying the Prabang could not lift it, not even twenty-four men could move it. This was taken as a sign that the Prabang wished to remain there.

In another account, Phaya Phao, the son of the former king of Vientiane, had requested that the Prabang be allowed to remain in Vien Kham for three years and King Fa Ngum had agreed to this.

As it turned out, its stay was to be far longer. The first attempt some years later to send the Prabang to Xieng Thong almost ended in disaster. It was loaded onto a boat, but the boat struck some rocks and sank. The Prabang was miraculously rescued and returned to Wat Manorom in Vientiane. The second occasion, in 1502, nearly a century and a half after its arrival, was successful and it was brought safely by land to Xieng Thong by King Visoun.

For whatever reason, the Prabang was allowed to remain in Vientiane and Phra Maha Pasman with the Tripitaka, his monks and all the cortège went on to Xieng Thong. Wats and monasteries were built for Phra Maha Pasman and Buddhism became the recognised religion of Lan Xang. Chao Fa Ngum followed the Buddhist practice and for a short time became a monk under the Theravada rites. For the first time since its creation the kingdom was allowed to settle down to a peaceful life.

All continued well for the eight or nine years left to Queen Keo Keng Ya. But in 1368, she died, and King Fa Ngum was inconsolable. He did not care sufficiently for any of his other queens, or wives, to allow them neither to moderate his sorrow at his loss, nor to prevent his sudden indifference to both his throne and country.

At the time of Queen Keo Keng Ya's death, Chao Fa Ngum's son, Chao Oun Heuan, was only twelve or thirteen years old, too young to be a regent. King Fa Ngum handed over the affairs of the kingdom to his mandarins placing all the power in their hands. So began a period of

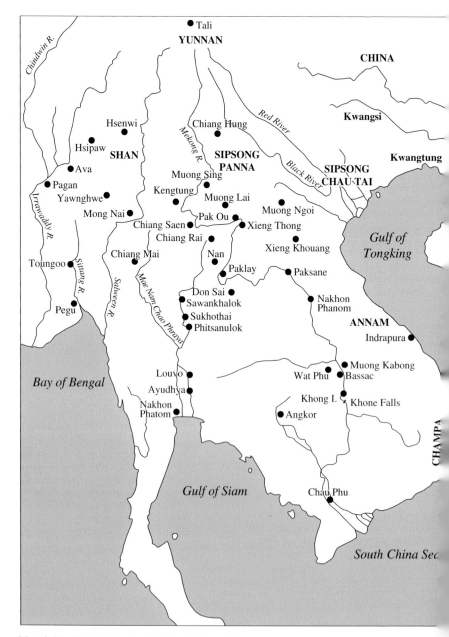

MAP 2 The Tai World in the 13th to 15th Centuries

misrule. His companions in war, and the mandarins of the Court, began to rob the Treasury and the people. Worse still, law and order disappeared and only power and position counted, so that a man could not even protect his wife from the demands of those who were more powerful than he.

While this was happening, King Fa Ngum levied new armies and started on new wars of expansion. It was more than the people would bear. There is once again doubt about the dates but it seems probable that about 1373 he was forced to abdicate in favour of his son, Chao Oun Hueun, and was exiled to Muong Nan in today's northeast Thailand.

Looking back, whatever may have been his faults, Chao Fa Ngum turned the ancient Muong Swa from a group of feuding Tai principalities into a nation. He forged a nation that through all her vicissitudes has survived to this day.

His vision was to create the greatest of the Tai nations. This he did. One must set against the horrors of war that he brought to tens of thousands of people, the stability of the nation he created and his greatest of all gifts, even if given reluctantly through his love for his Queen, that of Buddhism. Buddhism was to prove his most precious legacy as it gradually took root and became the very essence of Lao life from the days of Lan Xang to present times.

CHAPTER THREE

Through Chaos to a New Order

Mystery: One

T WO MYSTERIES SURROUND the abdication of Chao Fa Ngum c.1371 and what was, probably, a twenty-two year's delay before the coronation of his eldest son, Chao Oun Hueun, who then took the regnal name of Sam Sen Thai (1373–1417).

The first mystery is when did Chao Fa Ngum die? By some accounts it was in 1373, two years after his abdication. In others, it was twenty years later in 1393. Did his death take place at this later date and was it only then that the coronation could be held?

The kings of Laos have always attached a particular importance to their coronation. The late revered King Savang Vatthana, when he acceded to the throne in 1959 on the death of his father, did not hold a coronation immediately. His reason was that he did not wish the ceremony to be performed until Laos, divided by the Geneva Conference of 1954, was once again united. In fact, it was never reunited and King Savang Vatthana was never crowned.

Did Chao Sam Sen Thai have the same regard for principle, believing that he would consider himself a usurper were he crowned while his father lived? Or was it impossible for him to get the nobles of his Court to agree to his coronation?

Mystery: Two

THE SECOND MYSTERY is who was Chao Sam Sen Thai's Queen from Ayudhya? In 1356 when Chao Fa Ngum received tribute from the Ayudhyan king, Rama Thibodi (1351–1369), he was promised the king's daughter as soon as she was of marriageable age. Her name was Nang Keo

Lot Fa. Although more than fifteen years were to elapse between the Ayudhyan submission and Chao Fa Ngum's abdication, there does not appear to be any record of her arrival at the Court of Lan Xang. Whatever her age when she was promised to Chao Fa Ngum, there was certainly sufficient time for her to be sent to Xieng Thong and to be received as one of Chao Fa Ngum's queens.

The all important question is whether King Rama Thibodi kept his word or not. The doubt arises because Chao Sam Sen Thai is recorded as having a queen from Ayudhya and her name was Nang Keo *Yot* Fa, not so very different from Nang Keo *Lot* Fa, who was promised to Chao Fa Ngum.

Whether or not she was the same person will be of paramount importance when we come to study the decade when the Maha Devi, the *Great Goddess*, or more descriptively the *Lady Macbeth* of the Laotian Court, dominated the kingdom. She crowned first one king, let him rule for a few months, or a year or so, then had him assassinated, before choosing another of her relatives. If we knew who she was, we might be able to understand why she found it necessary to order so many murders. One result was that the consolidation achieved by Chao Sam Sen Thai was swept away in the decade of misrule under the domination of the Maha Devi.

The Reign of Sam Sen Thai

BY THE LAST quarter of the fourteenth century the great Mongol Empire found it increasingly difficult to exert any control over the Tai regions in southern China and modern Vietnam. Even their tenuous hold in northern China was soon to be ended by the anarchy that followed a calamitous series of floods and widespread famines. These terrible conditions provoked the Chinese into rebellion and led to the founding of the Ming Dynasty.

In 1389, during the subsequent reorganisation, the Ming emperor ordered a census in all the provinces that had previously been administered by the Mongols. Chao Sam Sen Thai also ordered a census, and some historians assume that it was the same time as the Chinese census.

Chao Sam Sen Thai's census was solely of the Lan Xang army. It showed there were 700,000 soldiers, of which 400,00 were Lao Theung, the former Khmer and Mon peoples, and 300,000 were Lao Soum, those who were of Tai stock.

The census provided the inspiration for Chao Oun Hueun's choice of his regnal name: *Sam Sen Thai*, the *Three Hundred Thousand Tai*. He was half-

Khmer through his mother and his taking this unusual name could have been interpreted as a token gesture to his nobles that he would not favour the Khmer in any matters affecting the two groups at Court.

Deadly Feuds

THE ABDICATION OF Chao Fa Ngum was the result of a palace revolution that must have been carried out in great secrecy and with considerable danger to the participants. However, Chao Oun Hueun, who by then was only seventeen, was not crowned immediately. It is evident that the Court was split between two factions, each of whom feared for their lives if the other were to gain dominance.

On one side were those who owed their positions to Chao Fa Ngum, to his one-time companions-in-exile, and to his Khmer Queen.

The other faction comprised the noble families of Xieng Thong, those who predated Chao Fa Ngum's accession and had fought against him when he returned to claim the throne. If the king of Ayudhya did send his daughter, Nang Keo Lot Fa, to be one of the other queens of Chao Fa Ngum, her Siamese, that is *Tai* background, and her personal interests would have made her a natural ally of this faction.

The differences between the two groups were very marked both by race and by customs. The Khmer dynasty could look back over more than one thousand years of sovereignty, the Xieng Thong Court a little over one hundred. They were separated by their religious beliefs which were significantly different, the Buddhism of Angkor and those of the Tai Menam Valley against the northern forms of Buddhism from Nanchao. Added to these were the differences of language, of dress, of their favourite foods ... a thousand times a day the differences must have jarred, creating ever-present causes for annoyance, if not hatred.

Was the Court so evenly divided that they could not agree on Chao Oun Hueun's coronation? It must be remembered that even to this day the eldest son, or next in line, has no legal right to the crown. The selection of who is to be king is decided by members of the royal family, often in consultation with the most influential mandarins. Did the Ayudhyan faction have another candidate for the crown?

While the Khmer Queen, Keo Keng Ya, lived there can have been no question which faction was dominant. By the time Chao Fa Ngum died, the scene was set for a showdown between the Khmer faction and the old Tai and Ayudhyan group.

The Coronation of Sam Sen Thai

THE TWO FACTIONS at Court finally accepted Chao Sam Sen Thai's right to be king. By one account this was only achieved, against accepted law, by his marrying his own stepmother, Chao Fa Ngum's widow, Queen Keo Lot Fa, the Ayudhyan queen. If this was in 1393, it would support the idea that it was only then that Chao Fa Ngum died.

The reign of Chao Sam Sen Thai was a quiet and prosperous one. The only trouble came at the beginning when the ruler of Chiang Saen, one of his vassals, disputed his right to the crown. Chao Sam Sen Thai was forced to send an army against him and, winning the battle, reclaimed his allegiance.

He was accepted by all his neighbours. The kings of Lan Na, and Chiang Hung each sent him one of their daughters to marry, so creating an alliance with their respective countries. As we have mentioned, the king of Ayudhya also sent one of his daughters, possibly Nang Keo Yot Fa.

The New Order

WHEN THE CENSUS had been completed, Chao Sam Sen Thai set about the task of consolidating the vast empire Chao Fa Ngum had created. He decreed that society should be divided into two social classes: nobles, possibly 'executives' might be a better term, and commoners. The nobles were those who were concerned with the administration of the country and ranged from princes of the blood to simple officials, such as tax collectors. All the others, merchants, artisans, peasants, were the commoners. Perhaps the four tiers of the Hindu caste system influenced the king's ideas, with the nobles representing the ruling warrior class, the *kshatriya*, and the commoners the *vaisya*.

Although the appointment to many posts was theoretically by popular vote, it appears that most posts, such as Chaomuong and Headman, usually remained in the same family and were passed down from father to son. Looking at it from this point of view, one can see that the 'executive' class as a whole had some right to the term noble, since they possessed a birthright.

Lan Xang society at the time also had a class of slaves. There were a number of ways for people to become slaves. The most common was probably through capture after battle, and the second, by falling into debt where failure to repay entailed compulsory service to the creditor. Apparently, there were also slave traders who abducted people, and

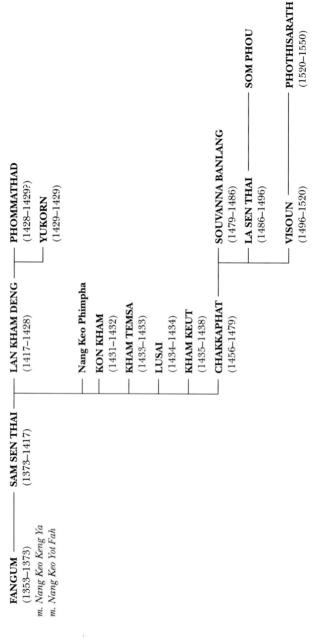

GENEALOGICAL TABLE 2 The Kings of Lan Xang – Fa Ngum to Phothisarath, 1353 to 1550

brought them to sell quite legally in the markets of Xieng Thong and the other towns of Lan Xang. A practice that was to be found in many countries at that time, such as the *sudras* in India, and the serfs in Europe.

Chao Sam Sen Thai also turned his attention to his army. He decided that an army of 150,000 men would be sufficient. He divided this into five groups of 30,000 soldiers, supported by 20,000 porters. He also divided his army into three groups: the first for internal policing, the second for protecting the borders or for fighting abroad, and the last as a reserve.

The soldiers fought on horseback, or on foot and were generally armed with lances and swords. They did, however, have some rifles that fired stones. At the beginning of Chao Sam Sen Thai's reign the rifles were imported, but towards the end of the reign the Lao began to make them for themselves.

When Chao Sam Sen Thai died in 1417, aged sixty, he left a rich and prosperous nation that was efficiently organised and defended by a well-trained army that had helped to ensure the peacefulness of his reign and had deterred attacks by his neighbours.

Chao Lan Kham Deng: the last years of peace

THE ELDEST SON of Chao Sam Sen Thai, whom we know only by his title *Mun Bun*, was, for some reason that is not known, passed over and a younger brother, Chao Lan Kham Deng, then aged 30, was elected in his place. Chao Lan Kham Deng (1417–1428) was to reign for eleven years and they were to be the last years of undisturbed peace that Lan Xang would know for nearly two decades.

However, four years after he ascended the throne, a very serious incident occurred that was to cause a devastating war some fifty years later. Ever since the treaty between Chao Fa Ngum and the Annamite king, relations between the two countries had been extremely warm. It was natural that when the Chinese attacked Annam in 1421, Chao Lan Kham Deng should offer to send an army to help the Annamites and this was gratefully accepted. At that time the ruler of Annam was Le Nga, who had usurped the throne. That he was a usurper may have had something to do with the inexplicable action on the part of the Lan Xang army which, on arrival at the battle ground, immediately passed over to the Chinese side.

Fortunately for Le Nga, his troops were able to beat the Chinese and to send the Lan Xang army ignominiously back beyond its borders. Le Nga did not appear to show any resentment and the relationship between the two countries, at least on the surface, continued to be harmonious. Le

Nga's successors were not so forgiving, and a legacy of hatred was to bring disaster to both countries.

Seven years later Chao Lan Kham Deng died and with him the stability and peace that both he and his father had created. It had been an unremarkable reign and he is remembered chiefly for the two monasteries, Wat Bothe and Wat Suanthen, he had built. In Wat Suanthen he is believed to have placed the ashes of his father, King Sam Sen Thai.

His own ashes were placed in a new monastery called Wat Manorom, which was still to be seen in 1975.

Maha Devi: the Years of Blood

THE SECOND MYSTERY will remain unsolved until more evidence is found. As mentioned earlier for over a decade, from 1428 until about 1442, the country was completely dominated by a woman known only by the title Maha Devi, *Great Goddess*. There have been many attempts to find out who she was, but no one has yet been able to find irrefutable proof of her identity. However, her title is a vital clue. Only the senior queen has a right to the title *Maha Devi*, so she must have been the senior queen of Chao Lan Kham Deng, or of his father, King Sam Sen Thai. Or even, and this is not improbable, since she was 95 when she died, she could well have been the queen of King Fa Ngum.

Maha Sila Viravong believes she was Nang Keo Ketkesy, the sister of King Sam Sen Thai, whose mother was the Khmer princess given by Jayavarman Paramesvara to Chao Fa Ngum as his Queen. If, as appears extremely probable, the Court was divided into two fiercely antagonistic Khmer and Ayudhyan factions, Nang Keo Ketkesy would have been the natural leader of the Khmer faction.

Le Boulanger and M.L.Manich Jumsai see her as Nang Keo Phimpa, who was the daughter of Noy Nong Hiao from Xieng Thong. Her father was said to be Chao Fa Kham Hiao, who may have become the king of Xieng Thong when Chao Fa Ngum was in Angkor. If so, it was his accession that had made Chao Fa Ngum decide to fight for the throne. If Nang Keo Phimpa was the Maha Devi, she would have favoured the old regime, the Xieng Thong and Ayudhyan faction, over the Khmer faction.

In the Chronicles the name of Chao Sam Sen Thai's queen from Ayudhya is Nang Keo *Yot* Fa. This is so close to the name of Chao Fa Ngum's widow, Nang Keo *Lot* Fa, that it could be a mistake, or even an intentional red herring to disguise, as we shall see, what may have been an unnatural marriage.

The most recent dramatic suggestion, partly based on a doctorate thesis by Amphay Doré, is by Stuart-Fox of Queensland University. He argues that the Maha Devi may have been Nang Keo Lot Fa, the wife promised to Chao Fa Ngum by King Rama Thibodi of Ayudhya.

If so, she either arrived at the Court of Xieng Thong too late to marry Chao Fa Ngum, or she was Chao Fa Ngum's widow. If Chao Sam Sen Thai married her, he was marrying his legal stepmother. Such an unusual, if not unnatural, marriage could only have been agreed to by Chao Sam Sen Thai for political reasons. This would suggest that conscious of his being half-Khmer, he may have felt he had to accept this marriage to prove his neutrality. This also suggests that the Ayudhyan faction may have been the more powerful, although not strong enough to be the dominant faction.

Chao Lan Kham Deng's death opened the gates to a bloodbath that was to last twelve years or more. The Maha Devi seems to have become a ruthless, autocratic figure driven by her own lust for power for herself, for her lovers, or for a young man whom she raised to the rank of the Chief Minister, and may have made her husband.

From the string of murders that followed the death of Chao Lan Kham Deng, it is obvious that she did not have her own way entirely. But she was prepared to assassinate anyone who seemed to be a threat to her, or would not do exactly as she wished.

In the years of anarchy that followed, it would have been more than any chronicler's life was worth to record the true course of events as one assassination followed another. Historians have managed to find a rough path through the maze of happenings, but the actual dates, and sometimes even the sequence of the events, are frequently impossible to untangle.

The Ill-fated Kings (1428–1440)

THE FIRST KING was Lam Kham Deng's son, Thao Phommathad (1428). His reign was short-lived. He survived only ten months before he was assassinated. He was followed by his younger brother, Chao Yukorn (1429–1430), who after eight months learnt that he too was to be murdered and fled. However, there was to be no escape. The assassins caught up with him, and he too died. There is no agreement on how many kings reigned in this decade. Some believe six, some seven.

The third king was probably Chao Kon Kham, the only son of Chao Sam Sen Thai and Nang Noy On So, the princess who had come from

Lan Na. He survived for eighteen months before being killed (1431–1432).

He was followed by Chao Kham Temsa (1433), the second son of Chao Sam Sen Thai and Nang Keo Sida, the daughter of the ruler of the Sipsong Panna. The next was Chao Lusai (c.1434), another son of Chao Sam Sen Thai, but the name of his mother is not known. The sixth king was slightly more fortunate. He was Chao Khai Bua Ban (1435–1438), who was either a son of Chao Lan Kham Deng, or a nephew of Chao Sam Sen Thai. His reign lasted for three years.

The last of the kings was Chao Kham Keut (c.1438–1440), who was also a son of Chao Sam Sen Thai by a palace maid. He claimed to be a reincarnation of his father and is believed to have ruled for two years.

It is possible that the Maha Devi, about 1440, became the first and only Queen of Laos. If so, she reigned for two years and then the nobles, revolted by so much bloodshed, took her, then reportedly ninety-five years old, and her young husband, tied their feet together and left them on a rock to die of thirst, or starvation, or whatever might bring about their death.

Her death did not solve the problem. The sixteen years from 1440 to 1456 were years of strife and unhappiness. The people wanted quiet and stability, but there seemed to be no way of achieving this. In 1440 Vientiane rebelled in an attempt to find its own peace in independence, but the revolt was put down and it remained under Xieng Thong.

By 1453 the different factions had fought themselves to a standstill and an interregnum was agreed upon with the administration of the country being vested in the two chief monks.

No modern historian, nor even the Chronicles, is in complete agreement over the events of these turbulent years.

The period of the interregnum, under the Council headed by the two chief monks, lasted about three years. They then offered the throne to Chao Vang Buri, a son of Chao Sam Sen Thai and his Ayudhyan queen. Chao Vang Buri was then aged about forty-three. If Nang Keo Lot Fa was the Maha Devi, she would have been more than fifty when Chao Vang Buri was born. This would seem to exclude her from being his mother. We must, therefore, conclude that either Nang Keo Lot Fa was not the 'Ayudhyan' queen, or, quite possibly, Chao Sam Sen Thai also had a second queen from Ayudhya.

Earlier, while the bloodbath was taking place at the Court, Chao Vang Buri had been Governor of Vientiane and had been invited to become king, but had wisely refused. This time he accepted. If, as is believed, his mother was an Ayudhyan princess, then we must assume that the

Ayudhyan faction had finally triumphed. It was probably in the year 1456 that he was enthroned and took the regnal name of Chakkaphat Phaen Phaeo (1456–1479).

The kingdom at last seemed to be able to look forward to a time of peace. And for twenty-three years, the country prospered. King Chakkaphat had six sons and, as they came of age, he sent each of them to administer a province.

The White Elephant and War with Annam

To THE EAST of Lan Xang, the Annamite kingdom under King Le Thanh Ton (1460–1497) had begun to pursue a policy of aggression towards its neighbours. So far as Lan Xang was concerned, the Annamites had never forgotten the incident when the Lan Xang army had changed sides and joined their enemies, the Chinese. They had not been able to punish Lan Xang before as threats of invasions from the Chinese to their north, and from the kingdom of Champa to their south, had kept them fully occupied.

Then in 1471, King Le Thanh Ton attacked Indrapura, the capital of Champa, bringing to an end over one thousand two-hundred years of its independent existence. His army overwhelmed the defenders and razed Indrapura, near modern Hué, to the ground, killing at the same time its forty thousand inhabitants. Champa never recovered and ceased to exist as a kingdom from that time on.

By 1478, King Le Thanh Ton felt it was the time to take his revenge on King Chakkaphat and his people. He began to collect his armies along the Annamite border in preparation for an invasion.

At the same time the ruler of one of Xieng Thong's vassal states, Muong Kon Thao, captured a White Elephant and sent it to King Chakkaphat as an expression of his loyalty. When the king of Annam heard of this, he immediately sent an ambassador requesting that the elephant be taken to Annam so that his people might see it.

King Chakkaphat did not wish to send the White Elephant. Instead he ordered a gold casket to be made so that he could send King Le Thanh Ton clippings from the elephant's nails and hair. However, his Chief Minister, his eldest son, Chao Kon Keo, decided that the Annamite king's request was an affront, as it had been couched in terms that would be used by a sovereign lord to his vassal. He therefore filled the gold casket with the elephant's dung. This he gave to the ambassador for delivery to the king of Annam.

Another story is that King Chakkaphat and his chief minister sent the casket to Muong Phoueune for the ruler to forward to Annam. He,

51

however, in order to cause trouble, removed the clippings and substituted the dung. If so, he was later to receive his desserts as King Le Thanh Ton decided he was a liar and cut off his head.

When the King of Annam opened the casket, he was so enraged that he ordered his armies, who were already in a state of readiness, to cross into Muong Phoueune and from there to attack Xieng Thong.

King Chakkaphat placed his son, the Chief Minister, at the head of an army of 200,000 men and 2,000 elephants to march against the Vietnamese. At first, on the *Plaine des Jarres* in Muong Phoueune, they ambushed the Vietnamese army. For three whole days the armies struggled for supremacy with thousands being killed on each side.

Finally the Lao had to fall back and in the next battle all the commanders were either killed in the fighting, or captured, and executed. The Chief Minister, Chao Kon Keo, fled on his elephant to the nearest river and tried to escape in a pirogue, but it overturned and he was drowned.

When news of the disaster reached King Chakkaphat in Xieng Thong, he collected his family together and fled down the Mekong to Vientiane.

The battered Annamite army continued its advance and occupied Xieng Thong. However, Chao Then Kham, one of the king's sons, who was governor of Muong Dan Sai brought up his army and attacked the Vietnamese. The Vietnamese were still disorganised and exhausted after the campaign that they were unable to resist the fresh troops. By the end of the battle only 600 out of the original 4,000 Vietnamese soldiers survived. These were driven back to Annam.

Peace Returns

Chao Then Kham returned to Xieng Thong where he sent a delegation to his father inviting him to return to the throne, but his father, humiliated by his flight, declined, saying that Chao Then Kham should accept the crown, which he did, taking the regnal name of Souvanna Banlang (1479–1486). He had taught the Annamites such a lesson that they and Lan Xang had good relations for the next two centuries. His father lived on for a few more months and died in the same year, 1479.

King Souvanna Banlang did not have any children and was succeeded by his brother who took the regnal name La Sen Thai (1486–1496). He maintained the closest relations with Ayudhya and encouraged commerce between the two countries. His other great interest was in the furthering of Buddhism and his ten years' rule left a stable and increasingly prosperous

ILLUSTRATION 8 King Visoun built the magnificent Wat Visoun Maha Viharn for the Prabang at the beginning of the sixteenth century. It was destroyed in 1887 when Luang Prabang was sacked by the Ho pirates. The above is a nineteenth century French drawing.

country. He was only thirty-three when he died and his son, Chao Som Phou, was either seven or nine years old. Chao Som Phou's uncle, Chao Visoun, the brother of King La Sen Thai and the third son of Chakkaphat, acted as his regent (1496–98) for nearly two years until Chao Som Phou (1499–1500) was crowned. The young king, however, was only to reign for another year before he died for reasons that are not known.

The crown then passed to his uncle, the Regent, Chao Visoun (1501–1520), whose name means *Lightning*. His was to be a long and prosperous reign. He, too, was deeply religious and one of his first acts was to send to Vientiane for the Prabang that had been there since the arrival of the mission of Maha Pasman in 1359. The Prabang was to become the palladium of Lan Xang.

King Visoun had a magnificent Wat built for it that was named Wat Visoun Maha Viharn. It was built of teak, highly ornamented and rectangular in shape with the sides sloping outwards from the ground level to meet the roof. It was designed in the shape of a traditional coffin as a reminder of how ephemeral life is.

Sadly, when Luang Prabang was sacked in 1887, this most beautiful Wat was burned to the ground and the only memory of it is an engraving by the French artist Delaporte. Fortunately the Prabang was no longer housed there. Wat Visoun was rebuilt in 1898 in brick and stone, but cannot be compared to the original that King Visoun built in the sixteenth century.

King Visoun encouraged the arts and had the Tripitaka translated from Sanskrit to Lao. As well, the Sangharaja, the head of the Buddhist Sangha of Laos, made the first compilation of the Khun Boulom legends and had them engraved on palm leaves.

King Visoun moved down to Vientiane and ruled from there for many years, but Xieng Thong remained the official capital. When Chao Visoun died in 1520, his son and heir, Chao Phothisarath was to continue his father's defence of Buddhism. He was the first king to develop an active interest in foreign diplomacy. He was also the first king, for over half a century, to have to face an armed invasion of his country: this time from the western borders.

King Phothisarath's reign (1520–1550) was to see the beginning of two hundred years of warfare that led to the destruction of the mediaeval kingdoms of Burma, Ayudhya and, indeed, of Lan Xang itself.

CHAPTER FOUR

Pride brings Disaster

By the beginning of the sixteenth century, the Lan Xang of Fa Ngum had changed beyond all recognition. Chao Fa Ngum had created a nation out of a large number of small muongs, who voluntarily, or by force, acknowledged the sovereignty of Lan Xang. When King Visoun died, these small groups had become a network of principalities and chiefdoms who were allowed their local independence in return for the payment of an annual tribute and the provision of soldiers and supplies in times of need.

Their independence depended on their distance from Xieng Thong, the greater the distance, the greater their independence. Their independence also depended on the power of their immediate neighbours. Muong Phoueune, for example, was, at different times, claimed as a vassal by both Lan Xang, Vientiane, after 1707, and Vietnam and in some years had to pay tribute to all three.

As King Visoun's reign drew to an end, Lan Xang was for the last time for many years at peace with its neighbours. Their mutual treaties were cemented by intermarriages and common interests. But these untroubled times were not to last. In the next two reigns, Lan Xang, then the largest of the Tai nations, became involved in a series of wars. Its history became irrevocably bound up with those of Lan Na, Ayudhya, and Burma.

To discover what happened, it is no longer sufficient to look only at the Annals of Lan Xang. The Lao chroniclers had often to be circumspect in what they wrote and it was sometimes healthier to omit, or distort, some facts. It is often possible to get a clearer view by looking at the histories of their neighbours. However, although these other accounts can sometimes be illuminating, they are frequently almost impossible to correlate as any one incident is rarely given the same date by the different chroniclers. These differences can be so great that it is impossible even to decide on the order, never mind the precise dates, of the different events.

Chao Phothisarath ascends the throne

In 1520, on the death of King Visoun, Chao Phothisarath (1520–1550), his son, came to the throne. His reign began with one of those incidents that no chronicler has dared to explain fully. King Muang Kaeo (1495–1526), the king of Lan Na discovered that one of the most sacred of his country's Buddha figures, the Phra Saekkham, was missing. He immediately instituted a nationwide search, sending groups of twenty men throughout the region looking for it. One of these groups came secretly to Xieng Thong and found the Phra Saekkham standing next to the Prabang statue.

One night, they broke through the bars of the eastern window of the wat. As they took hold of it, the Phra Saekkham fell to the ground, either because it was heavier than they expected, or because it did not wish to be taken back to Chiang Mai.

The noise woke the guardians of the wat, who arrested the twenty men and took them before King Phothisarath. With great magnanimity, he refused to punish them and had them sent back to King Muang Kaeo with a letter. The Chiang Mai king was so impressed by the behaviour of Chao Phothisarath that he had one of his daughters, Nang Yot Kham Tip sent to Xieng Thong to be Chao Phothisarath's Chief Queen. This was the beginning of a close relationship between the two countries. As lesser Queens, Chao Phothisarath was to marry princesses from the royal families of Ayudhya, Muong Phoueune and of the Khmer kingdom.

Three years later, in 1523, he sent a mission to his father-in-law, King Muang Kaeo asking whether he might have copies of the Buddhist scriptures, the Tripitaka. King Kaeo was obviously pleased by the request and sent him sixty volumes and also a number of monks to help his Sangha. Two years later, Chao Phothisarath decided to return to the monkhood for a short period, and was once again ordained, some of his teachers being monks from Chiang Mai.

Following his ordination, Chao Phothisarath embarked on a major venture that was to bring him fame among his neighbouring rulers, but was not to bring good fortune to him, nor to his country. Until then, Buddhism had flourished side by side with the worship of the ancestral Spirits, who were to be found everywhere. They lived in sacred places in the mountains, streams, and trees, as well as protecting each person's family and household.

The Proscription of Spirit Worship

IN 1527 THE King issued an edict proscribing Spirit worship and any other beliefs that were associated with the traditional religion. He ordered the destruction of all shrines throughout the kingdom. Even the shrine of the guardian spirit of Xieng Thong itself did not escape destruction. It was completely demolished and on its site, King Phothisarath had a new Wat, Wat Sisouvanna Devalok, constructed to cover the once holy place for ever.

Contemporary and later historians have recorded this edict as a highly meritorious act. His fellow rulers were reported to have greatly respected his actions and to have shown their approbation by sending him valuable presents. But looking back, one can only wonder what harm was also done.

Many of the traditional beliefs were based on centuries of knowledge that were the basis of all Lao medicine and was of vital importance in everyday skills such as those of the midwives. Admittedly much of this knowledge was to live on. This can be seen in the medicine still practised by the *Boun Mo* today, in the celebrations of *Pi Mai*, the giving of a *bassi*, and a host of other customs that have continued to form a very important part in Lao life.

Making Buddhism the state religion would eventually contribute a large part to the charm and individuality of Lao life, but, at the time, it was not strong enough to bring an end to many of the cruelties of contemporary warfare, such as the killing of prisoners and their families, when the king, or general, felt the occasion warranted it. However, it did give to the Buddhist clergy, the Sangha, far greater power to influence events. We saw how Phra Pasman had obtained the life of the ruler of Roy Et and his other prisoners from Fa Ngum. From the time of King Phothisarath, the Sangha became increasingly involved in such humanitarian acts, concerning itself with trying to save the lives of captives, or of the people in villages and towns that had resisted an attack.

At the time, the proscription must have been traumatic and created many enemies within Lan Xang. It is impossible to judge how deeply it struck, nor how many people paid lip-service to it while continuing to respect the *phi* more or less as they always had. However the Edict may have been less draconian than it seems, and may well have been mitigated by the traditional wisdom and good nature of the Lao people.

About 1532, King Phothisarath became involved in a dispute with Muong Phoueune. The Xieng Khouang Annals do not agree about how this dispute turned into a war between the two countries. The most probable account of the events says that the king of Muong Phoueune, the Annals do not agree on who the king was at the time, decided not to send the triennial tribute to Lan Xang. King Phothisarath therefore sent a

ILLUSTRATION 9 The Great Buddha in Wat Mai, Luang Prabang

© Collection Prince Mangkra Souvanna Phouma

58

mission of three of his mandarins to inquire why it had not arrived. When after two years he had not heard from the mission, he made further inquiries and discovered that the king of Phoueune had had the three Lan Xang mandarins killed.

Although it seems unlikely that two years would pass without the news of such an important event getting back to Xieng Thong, it does give an indication of how long such discussions could take. When Chao Phothisarath learnt of the fate of his mandarins, he immediately sent an army into Muong Phoueune to force them into submission.

In another account, the new king of Muong Phoueune, fell out with his uncle, who was his Sen Muong, or Viceroy. Their disagreement was so severe that the Viceroy thought it wiser to leave. He came to Xieng Thong and Chao Phothisarath offered him refuge. He immediately began to turn the king's feelings against his nephew, the king of Xieng Khouang, and, as a result, Phothisarath decided to send a Lan Xang army to bring Muong Phoueune to heel. The King of Muong Phoueune put up a vigorous resistance and the campaign lasted more than two years before Muong Phoueune was finally conquered. It was Chao Phothisarath's first intervention abroad and signalled the end of a period of peace that had, for more than 100 years, favoured Lan Xang.

The Move to Vientiane

INNOVATIVE AS EVER, in 1533, Chao Phothisarath was the first of the Lan Xang kings to move his court to Vientiane. Xieng Thong still remained the official capital, but he built a great palace in Vientiane and preferred to work from there. There was much to be said for the choice. Vientiane lay in a rich and fertile plain and could provide all the food necessary for a rapidly growing administrative centre. It was also the crossroads for much of the overland commerce between the Tai kingdoms of the Menam Chaophraya valley, as well as the trade that entered the Mekong Valley from the Annam, Champasak and the Khmer kingdom.

Another and very good reason was that to the south the Tai kingdom of Ayudhya under its new king, Chairacha (1534–1547), was becoming increasingly aggressive. His aim was to extend Siam's frontiers on every side, including the Lan Xang territory that Fa Ngum had taken from the Khmer empire. With Vientiane as his administrative base, Chao Phothisarath was better able to defend the Korat plateau, the vassal states around Khammouan and Champasak, as well as the hill states along the Annamite Chain.

It was a time of change for the entire region. In what is now Burma, the Tai people were then, as today, called Shan. In 1299, the Shan taking advantage of the weakened state of Pagan had attacked and destroyed it utterly. Emboldened by their new found power, they started on the piecemeal conquest of the whole of modern Burma.

Sadly, they were not to produce any single king with the strength and vision of Fa Ngum. They were, therefore, never able to achieve the unity that made Lan Xang a nation. Instead, they founded a number of independent principalities and kingdoms, some of which exist to this day. Lacking any unity other than that of their Tai race, their splintered power did not pose any threat beyond their borders. Because of this, Lan Xang was able to thrive and grow rich, concerned only with maintaining good relations with its neighbouring states of Lan Na, Ayudhya and the Vietnamese kingdoms.

The nearly 250 years of Shan supremacy in Burma was rapidly coming to an end. One year after King Phothisarath came to the throne, a Burmese, Tabinshwehti (1531–1550), made himself king of the city state of Toungoo. Toungoo was originally a Mon town, but its population had been considerably enlarged by the great influx of Burmese refugees created by the Shan capture of Ava in 1525 and 1527. They were only too willingly to join any army that would fight against the Shan.

Tabinshwehti unites Burma and attacks Tai world

TABINSHWEHTI, GRASPING THE opportunity, decided to conquer the surrounding states and to build a Burmese empire. He first attacked Kyaukse, a state to his immediate north that was considerably richer and more fertile than Toungoo. Having conquered that, he turned his attention southwards. He captured Prome and, on the death of the king of Pegu, took and held that town. With this capture he gained an even larger Mon population who gave him their support. As well, he found there a contingent of Portuguese mercenaries. They were to make a valuable addition to his army and, at times, he was to employ as many as 700 of them as fighting soldiers.

From there he continued his campaigns southwards into modern Tenasserim. His continuing successes led him to make a quick march on a Tai muong near Krai, then went on to attack the villages of the Arakan on the west coast. This was too much for Ayudhya. In 1538, King Chairacha sent an army to raid Tavoy and recapture Muong Krai. At the time, Tabinshwehti was too occupied with other campaigns to retake it, but

Siam's action decided him that he should launch a major battle against Ayudhya as soon as he was strong enough.

The next year in 1539, Chao Phothisarath accepted a Siamese noble who had fled from Ayudhya to Vientiane and had asked for asylum. Until that time, Lan Xang and Ayudhya, united by generations of marriages, had been on the friendliest terms. We have found no explanation for Chao Phothisarath's subsequent actions. Perhaps he had become alarmed by the expansionist policy being pursued by King Chairacha. Whatever the real reason, he decided to make the Siamese prince's complaints a *casus belli* and launched the first Lan Xang attack against Ayudhya. As an illuminating side note on the warfare of those times, King Chairacha refused the challenge and after a while Chao Phothisarath's army accepted his decision not to fight and returned to Vientiane!

First break in Lan Xang and Ayudhyan relations

IT WAS, HOWEVER the end of the peaceful relationship between Lan Xang and Ayudhya. From then on, Ayudhya would always be grateful for any support Lan Xang might give her, but she viewed Vientiane as an untrustworthy ally that would place her own immediate interests before any treaties, or other obligations.

In the next year, 1540, King Chairacha felt strong enough to take his revenge. He despatched an army which captured Vieng Kouk and from there crossed the Mekong and camped a few kilometres away from Vientiane at Sala Kham.

Five days later, Phothisarath attacked. The Siamese army fought tenaciously and it was only after a fierce battle that the Vientiane troops were victorious. The Siamese army fled, leaving behind them thousands of casualties. For the moment Lan Xang was safe, but the Siamese did not forget the reason for their attack and nor, indeed, the bitterness of their defeat.

Palace Revolt in Lan Na

WHILE THESE ATTACKS and counter attacks were being carried out against each other, the world of the Tai was beginning to crumble. In Lan Na, King Ket Chettharat (1526–1538) was forced into exile by his nobles and generals. His son, Thao Chai (1538–1543) was placed on the throne. However, he proved to be unbalanced and by 1543 the nobles of his court decided that his unpredictable cruelties had become unbearable and he was assassinated.

King Ket Chettharat was invited back (1543–1545), but he only lived another two years before he too was assassinated by some of his nobles. On his death there was no direct male heir and the Court was divided over whom they should choose. Their first choices were between the Shan Saopha of Mong Nai and the Shan ruler of Kengtung. There was some delay over Mong Nai's acceptance. The nobles of Chiang Mai then decided that as Chao Phothisarath's First Queen was the daughter of a former King of Chiang Mai, he should be offered the throne.

A message was sent to Xieng Thong and Chao Phothisarath happily accepted the crown on behalf of his son, who was then either twelve or fourteen years old. By other accounts, the decision to invite Chao Phothisarath had not been based so much on his First Queen being from Lan Na, as the fact that during the deliberations of the Lan Na Court, a Lan Xang army had begun to advance on Chiang Mai.

Before these arrangements between Lan Na and Lan Xang could be concluded, the ruler of Hsenwi, a Shan, arrived with an army saying he wished to punish the persons responsible for the death of King Ket. There was a terrible battle outside Chiang Mai lasting three days and three nights before the Hsenwi Saopha accepted defeat and fled to Muong Lamphun. From there, on 25 June 1545, he sent a message to King Chairacha in Ayudhya asking him to send an army to take Chiang Mai.

Princess Chiraprapha becomes Regent

IN THE MEANTIME, Princess Chiraprapha, a daughter of King Ket, was made Regent (1545–1546) by the nobles of the Court. She was to prove to be a brilliant diplomat and a wise ruler. She had an immediate opportunity to display these qualities. Even before the Hsenwi ruler had invited the Siamese intervention, King Chairacha had decided that the vacant throne of Chiang Mai was the means towards making Lan Na a part of Ayudhya.

When the Siamese army approached, Queen Chiraprapha pretended that King Chairacha had come to pay his respects to her father. She had her mandarins take gifts to Chairacha, thanking him for coming and inviting him to share in the merit of the ceremonies.

Chairacha decided that as he had been invited to participate in the funeral ceremonies, it would be ill-omened to continue in his earlier intention of attacking Chiang Mai. The Princess's diplomacy had triumphed and Chairacha gave up the idea of taking Chiang Mai by force. Instead he donated 5,000 pieces of silver to build a monument for King Ket. He was later to attack Chiang Mai, but Queen Chiraprapha had managed to win an important breathing space.

Later, the Shan ruler of Mong Nai, who had originally been offered the crown, belatedly decided that he had a right to the throne. He mustered an army and launched a serious attack on Chiang Mai. The Shan managed to throw a bamboo bridge across the moat and plundered the northern part of the town. But the townspeople were able to beat off the attacks in hand to hand fighting and removed the earth as the Shan tried to fill in the moat. Eventually the attackers gave up and returned to Mong Nai.

Chao Setthathirath crowned King of Lan Na

KING PHOTHISARATH, WITH his son Chao Setthathirath, and the nine highest ranking mandarins and 300,000 attendants with 2,000 elephants and an army of 200,000 soldiers left Xieng Thong to celebrate the coronation in Chiang Mai. The chronicles frequently increase any numbers by the degree of importance of the person concerned. It is, therefore, usual in order to arrive at a more accurate figure to divide any number by ten. In this instance, 300,000 seems improbable and perhaps should be reduced to about 3,000. The logistical problem of feeding so many people on a march from Xieng Thong to Chiang Mai defies the imagination.

Even so, it was certainly a vast procession for so important an occasion. It passed through Chiang Saen, then Chiang Rai where the Court spent nine days in ceremonies and celebrations before going on to Chiang Mai.

Here the coronation took place. Wyatt's translation of the Chiang Mai chronicles describes how the mandarins and officials of Lan Na with all the royal paraphernalia, elephants, horses and all the panoply of power came out to welcome Chao Setthathirath (1547–1550) who then put on white garments and, just as today, held in his hands a bowl with flowers, rice, gold, silver and candles while making his obeisance before the Buddha.

He then entered the city, took his place on the jewelled throne and later reverenced the Emerald Buddha. He was given as Queens, two very young royal princesses, Nang Thip and Nang Tonkham, who were the daughters of King Ket.

While Phothisarath was still in Chiang Mai, Tabinshwehti, the Burmese king, sent a delegation proposing an alliance against Siam. Tabinshwehti suggested that once the alliance had been agreed they should launch a joint attack on Ayudhya. Phothisarath procrastinated. He decided to send three of his mandarins to Toungoo to make a more detailed assessment and to report to him later.

Tabinshwehti in proposing the alliance with Lan Xang was hoping to use King Phothisarath as a catspaw. His real aim was to destroy the Shan in Burma and, as soon as he had achieved that, to annihilate all of the neighbouring Tai, whom he hated no less than the Shan.

Burmese march on Ayudhya

In 1548, while Phothisarath was still in Chiang Mai, Tabinshwehti mounted his attack against Ayudhya. He had turned the original rabble he had taken from the streets of Toungoo into an army made confident by its successes against the petty states and kingdoms in Burma.

His army was the equal of any that the Tai could mount. It must have looked extremely powerful with its richly caparisoned elephants, its cavalry, the thousands of foot soldiers, and, around Tabinshwehti, his own personal guard of some 400 Portuguese in their strange European helmets, with their quilted cotton armour and tortoise shell shields.

The Portuguese mercenaries were armed with short swords, bows, wooden, or rush, lances and some rifles. They also mounted a detachment of canon. The canon were not very powerful and their rifles not very fast firing. For all that, the Portuguese must have looked highly impressive and their appearance on the battlefield must have been unnerving, especially to the elephants, who, until then, had been the main armoured force surrounding the kings.

This great Burmese force climbed over the Three Pagodas Pass and made its cumbersome way down to Ayudhya. Here the Burmese prepared to bring all the fearsome power of their combined Asian and European arms to bear against the citizens of this Tai state. Instead of panic and flight, they were met with jeers and derision from the citizens of Ayudhya. The people quickly realised that their canons were too small to make any effect on the walls and, with ample supplies of food and unlimited water, the besieged dared them to stay as long as they wished.

The Burmese found themselves powerless to break through the fortifications and their eventual retreat would have been a rout had they not by chance captured the Siamese King Chakraphat's (1548–1569) eldest son, Ramesuen, and the Governor of Phitsanulok, Maha Thammaracha. Using them as hostages, they were able to negotiate their safe return to Burma. The victory for Ayudhya was not unalloyed. The

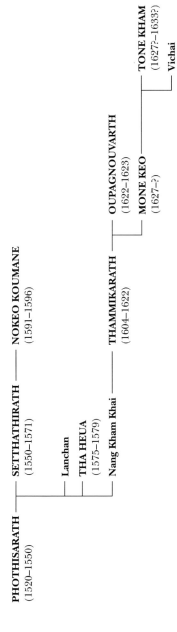

GENEALOGICAL TABLE 3 The Kings of Lan Xang – Phothisarath to Tone Kham, 1520 to 1633

ILLUSTRATION 10 Morning market in Luang Prabang

Burmese took back with them a burning desire to revenge themselves on the hated Tai for this their first and most ignominious defeat.

Chao Phothisarath is difficult to understand. While he had not agreed to join the Burmese, neither had he made any move to help Ayudhya, who for over 200 years had been Lan Xang's ally, resist the Burmese attack.

Perhaps, one day we may find out whether his policy was founded on personal pique, or based on what he felt was strategic necessity to reduce the growing power of Ayudhya.

Leaving his young son, Chao Setthathirath, as king of Lan Na, he started his march back to Xieng Thong. It was a leisurely journey. On the way back the king and his ministers camped at various places in the jungle and hunters were sent out to capture wild elephants. According to contemporary accounts, these totalled 2,000, but again, one must allow for some exaggeration.

The Story of the Emerald Buddha

ONE OF THE most revered of the Buddha rupa in Chiang Mai was the Emerald Buddha. It was in front of this most sacred Buddha figure that Chao Setthathirath's coronation had taken place. The Buddha was carved from green jasper and was believed to have been first discovered in Chiang Rai about 1434 or 1436. But its history went back far earlier to 43 BC when the Lord Abbot Nasena in modern Patna in India had had it made. It was believed to have remained in Patna for about 300 years, until in troubled times it was taken to Ceylon for safety.

Then some time after 1044, King Anawrahta (1044–1077) of Burma sent a mission asking whether it might be given to him. His request was granted but the ship carrying the Emerald Buddha was blown off course and the Buddha was next found in modern Cambodia. From there, Buddhist monks took it to Ayudhya, and other cities, before it arrived in Chiang Rai. Here the people were afraid that it might be stolen, so they covered it in gypsum and a coat of lacquer. Its true eminence was forgotten and it was only at the beginning of the fifteenth century that it was rediscovered.

When the king of Chiang Mai was told of the discovery, he came in procession to take it in honour to his capital. However, the elephant carrying it turned away from Chiang Mai and went towards Lamphun, where the king, believing that was where the Buddha wished to be, built a special temple for it. However, a few years later the Lan Na king, King Tilokaracha (1442–1487), had it brought to Chiang Mai.

It was from there that either Chao Phothisarath, or a year or two later Chao Setthathirath, took the Emerald Buddha to Xieng Thong promising that it would be returned. By some accounts they also took the Buddha rupa, the Phra Saekkham, but this may already have been in Xieng Thong still standing beside the Prabang.

It was in 1550, two years after his departure from Chiang Mai, that Chao Phothisarath arrived back in Xieng Thong. Some idea of his involvement in foreign affairs may be judged from the fact that there were fifteen delegations from abroad waiting to meet him. In addition to these, the mission from Burma had also arrived in the hope of signing the treaty against Siam.

The Death of Chao Phothisarath

PHOTHISARATH DECIDED TO hold a grand audience and invited all the delegations to a large stockaded field where the wild elephants were trained. Here he mounted his elephant, *Nang Kai*, and rode into the middle of the herd of wild elephants and lassoed one of them. Unfortunately, the one he chose was over excited and managed to pull *Nang Kai* over so that she fell, crushing Phothisarath into the ground.

He was rescued and carried to the palace, and although mortally wounded, he arranged to thank the delegates and asked them to return to their countries. Seven days later he died.

One wishes that one knew more about this enigmatic person. Although he was a devout Buddhist, he did not hesitate to take his country into war. Although a seemingly able administrator, he was not content, as his father had been, merely to see his country get rich, but felt he had to concern himself with the affairs of neighbouring countries.

When considering his relationship with Ayudhya and other neighbouring states, one is very much aware that one can neither explain, nor even assess, the course of his foreign policy throughout his reign. There is so very much that remains hidden in the character of this great, but enigmatic, king.

CHAPTER FIVE

Wars and Invasions

AT THE TIME of his father's death Chao Setthathirath was king of Lan Na, but he probably lived in Chiang Saen, a town that he seems to have preferred to anywhere else. He had assumed that he would automatically be recognised as the successor to his father, but a faction in the Vang Na, the Oupahat's palace, favoured his two younger brothers, Chao Tha Heua, also known as Chao Voravongso, and Chao Lanchan, who was Governor of the important province of Pak Houei Luang, just south of Vientiane.

The two of them decided to divide the kingdom into two parts: the northern part to belong to Chao Tha Heua and the southern, to Chao Lanchan. However, Chao Setthathirath had sufficient support, including his mandarins in the south, and the two were arrested. Some of their relatives, who had been actively involved in the coup, were executed, but both Chao Tha Heua and Chao Lanchan were pardoned.

Chao Setthathirath tricked by his Mandarins

POSSIBLY AS A result of this, the Sena, the Council of Ministers of Lan Xang, requested Chao Setthathirath to leave Chiang Saen and to take up residence in Xieng Thong. The king's reply was unambiguous. He told them quite plainly that he disliked Xieng Thong, it was, he said, all peaks and mountains and there was not a bit of flat space to be seen. If, he said, the land of Chiang Saen should float down the Mekong to Xieng Thong, then he would come and rule there.

After the attempted coup the Sena decided there would never be stability while Chao Setthathirath ruled from a distance. They regretfully decided that he would never listen to reason, even though his present course of action was an invitation to civil war. The mandarins concluded that if reason would not be successful, they would have to devise a stratagem, regardless of the danger to themselves, and trick the King into moving back to Xieng Thong.

They finally decided on a very imaginative subterfuge that they could deploy during the annual pirogue races in Luang Prabang. They had built for the king a bamboo raft, which they covered with soil from Chiang Saen. On this they built a temporary palace and, when the king was on board watching the races, they cut the lines holding the raft so that it began to float downstream. Then, prostrating themselves before him, they told him that indeed the soil of Chiang Saen was floating down the Mekong and he was bound by his word to leave Chiang Saen. Chao Setthathirath was not pleased, but he was an honourable man and agreed that he was bound by his promise.

When Chao Setthathirath (1550–1571) announced that he would not be residing in Lan Na, he sent an order that Princess Chiraprapha should rule in his place. But it was too late. Either before this, or on hearing of his change of purpose, the Lan Na mandarins had sent a message to the Shan ruler of Mong Nai, who was temporarily a monk, asking him to unfrock and take the throne. His name was Chao Mekuti, or Mae Ku, and he was descended from Mangrai, the founder of the Chiang Mai dynasty. For once the majority of the mandarins in Chiang Mai were in agreement. On 22 December 1551, Chao Mekuti (1551–1564) was crowned King of Lan Na.

When Chao Setthathirath learnt of this, he became extremely angry but at that moment there was nothing he could do about it. Two years later he gave his brother, Chao Lanchan, command of an army to recapture Chiang Mai. Chiang Mai resisted and the Lan Xang army was repulsed. The Sena was unwilling to support a war that might tempt their king away again and refused to give any further support to the small army under Chao Lanchan. There was nothing Chao Setthathirath could do. For the time being he had to accept defeat.

Bayinnaung becomes King of Burma

BY THAT TIME there had been major changes in the balance of power in the region. In 1551, King Tabinshwehti of Burma was assassinated by his Mon courtiers and his half-brother Bayinnaung (1551–1581) having assumed the crown was faced with the task of recapturing all of the Burma that had previously been a part of the kingdom of Toungoo. In doing so, he made his new capital at Pegu. In 1555, he recaptured the ancient capital of

Ava, and began to campaign in Upper Burma, first subduing Manipur in modern India, then turning eastwards to the Shan states.

In the same year as Bayinnaung took Ava, Chao Setthathirath decided to recapture Chiang Mai. He had managed to overrule the Sena and had amassed a large army. He began the slow process of moving it northwards from Xieng Thong. He reached Namtha in the northwest and from there despatched part of his army against Chiang Saen in what was to be the northern half of a pincer movement against Chiang Mai town. However, treachery within the Lan Xang command brought disaster. The Lan Xang army was destroyed and Chiang Saen was able to hold out. It was at this point that Setthathirath chose one of his father's favourite ministers, Phagna Nhote Lukien, to lead a fresh army against Chiang Saen.

Phagna Nhot Lukien had been born in Nong Khai in 1511 with the name, Chane Tian. His father had been the Chief of the town and had sent him to Xieng Thong to better himself. Here he had come to the notice of Chao Phothisarath who had ennobled him under the name Phagna Nhot Lukien. He was then appointed Governor of Pak Houei Luang. From there he had returned to Xieng Thong and was appointed a general in Chao Setthathirath's army.

He captured Chiang Saen and Setthathirath was so impressed he gave him the title Sen Soulintha Luxai, *Luxai* being *Victory*. The title has never been conferred on any other person since. Phagna Sen Soulintha was gradually given more responsibilities until he became Chao Setthathirath's Chief Minister. Later, at the height of his powers, Sen Soulintha was to offer the King his daughter and, out of this union was born a son, Chao No Muong, who was to reign under the name Nokeo Koumane.

Although Chiang Saen had been recaptured, Setthathirath soon found that all the neighbouring muongs had allied themselves with Chiang Mai against him. The most important were Chiang Rai, and Fang, as well as Mong Nai and all of the Shan states who were gradually being brought under the influence of Burma. Realising that to continue the war would almost certainly result in disaster, Chao Setthathirath announced that he still maintained his legal right to the throne of Lan Na, but he withdrew his army and returned to Xieng Thong.

Setthathirath learns from Burmese military tactics

IN ONLY A few years Burma's military thinking had changed. Before, like all its neighbouring kingdoms, it had had a massive unskilled army that was held together by a few trained soldiers. Now, instead of relying on mass, it became a first class military power with a far smaller army that was built around a nucleus of a highly skilled, professional and resolute core of professional soldiers. As a result, its fighting power was greater than any other two of the Tai kingdoms put together.

Sen Soulintha was to show Chao Setthathirath how to imitate, and eventually better, the new Burmese way of fighting.

The Burmese king, Bayinnaung, possessed a burning hatred of the Tai peoples. When he had completed his conquest of Upper Burma, he advanced into the Shan states. Towards the end of March 1556, he reached Mong Nai. The ruler of Mong Nai immediately sent a message to his brother, King Mekuti of Chiang Mai, telling him that a Burmese army of 4,000 men was approaching and asked him to send an army, well-armed with arrows and snares to be used against the foot soldiers, horses and elephants. Mekuti foolishly ignored the request and did not send any troops.

As soon as Bayinnaung had taken Mong Nai he sent a message to Mekuti with the hardly veiled threat that the ruler of Mong Nai, his wives, children and people had submitted to him and were alive. He ordered King Mekuti to do the same. On 2 April, with no allies at hand, Chiang Mai opened its gates to Bayinnaung. Five days later, Mekuti was reinstated as a vassal king of Pegu. He was also provided with a Burmese military garrison to ensure his loyalty.

Bayinnaung then returned to Pegu. Before leaving he was struck by Chiang Mai's artistic richness. He forcibly transported back to Burma a whole colony of lacquer workers who were to set up the famous lacquer work to be found in Burma today. Linguistic studies among the present Burmese lacquer workers seem to point to their being directly descended from those living in Chiang Mai today.

In the Shan State of Yawnghwe today, the weavers have one special set of patterns that are called *zimme*, which is the Burmese name for Chiang Mai. They are similar to patterns found in modern Chiang Mai. The weavers who had brought the patterns across may have been among those deported by Bayinnaung.

The loss of Lan Na greatly increased Chao Setthathirath's dislike for life in Xieng Thong. He continued to complain that there were no flat spaces between the mountains and peaks and in 1559 he ordered the princely families to come with him and build themselves new palaces in Vientiane.

As Saveng notes, the course of the Mekong is plagued by rapids and is not a good means of communication, nor the unifying factor it appears if one were to judge merely by looking at a map. Maps, however, show that the mountain ridges run in a west to east direction, so dividing the country into the north, around Xieng Thong, the centre dominated by Vientiane, and the south under Champasak. Especially in those days of poor communications, the region where the king resided felt his strongest influence and his power diminished as the distance from his throne increased. As his father King Phothisarath had realised, Vientiane was the natural power centre of Lan Xang.

Vientiane becomes capital of Lan Xang

KING SETTHATHIRATH, LIKE his father, Chao Phothisarath, had always been fond of Vientiane. The king felt that by comparison with Xieng Thong, Vientiane was the ideal site for a capital. It lay in a broad, fertile valley that would permit its population to increase without restriction. As well as being surrounded by good agricultural land, it lay on the commercial routes between the Bay of Bengal, the Menam Chaophraya Valley, Vietnam's eastern coastline, and the South China Sea.

He placed the city of Xieng Thong in the hands of the chief monks and left for Vientiane. He took all his personal property, which included both the Emerald Buddha and the Phra Saekkham, but he left with the Sangharaja, the head of the Buddhist Sangha, the Prabang statue, which was accepted as the palladium of the realm. A little time later, in 1560, when Vientiane had been proclaimed capital, the name of the royal city of Xieng Thong was changed to Luang Prabang.

Setthathirath built a solid brick wall as a defence around Vientiane and strengthened all its fortifications. He also began to think how he could restore the ties between Ayudhya and Lan Xang that he and his father had, with such careless indifference, broken.

Setthathirath asks for Nang Thep Kasatti's hand

WHILST PLANNING THIS renewal of their traditional ties, Chao Setthathirath learnt that the eldest daughter of the Siamese king, Nang Thep Kasatti, was unmarried. She had a reputation for indomitable courage as well as for her beauty. In the Burmese attack on Ayudhya in 1549, she was said to have dressed in soldier's clothes and ridden out of the city to lead a counter attack against the Burmese army. Greatly attracted by her reputed beauty and courage, Chao Setthathirath sent a mission to King Chakraphat (1548–1569) proposing that Nang Thep Kasatti should become his First Queen to the mutual advantage of both countries.

The mandarins of Ayudhya agreed that Burma was an irrevocable enemy and a firm alliance with Lan Xang would be to their mutual advantage. But for some reason that we do know, King Chakraphat was reluctant to let Nang Thep Kasatti go since he thought he could obtain the same advantage by giving away a younger daughter. She was called Princess Keo Yot Fa.

When the Lan Xang Mission arrived at Ayudhya, they were told that Nang Thep Kasatti was too ill to travel and the King was sending Princess Keo Yot Fa with a large suite and many valuable presents. The Lan Xang Mission accepted the change and started back to Vientiane.

King Setthathirath with his mandarins and Court had come part of the way to meet his new bride. When he was told that another daughter had been sent, he became very upset. He sent a message to King Chakraphat reminding him that Chakraphat had promised him Nang Thep Kasatti and, he said, were his other daughters a thousand times more beautiful, he would not wish to exchange Nang Thep Kasatti for them. He left the Siamese king in no doubt that he was extremely angry and that he considered king Chakraphat guilty of a breach of faith. Princess Keo Fa and her retinue were returned to Ayudhya with the clear understanding that there would not be a treaty until he was married to Nang Thep Kasatti.

In some accounts this journey to meet Nang Thep Kasatti is wrongly tied to the first Burmese capture of Vientiane in 1564, when the Burmese held the city until August 1565 and retreated taking prisoners with them. One must reserve judgement whether any Lan Na personality, as we are about to describe below, ever fled to Vientiane pursued by the Burmese. However the Chiang Mai Chronicles give the following account and a minor incident similar to this may have occurred at some other time. Saveng comments that there is no mention in the Luang Prabang Chronicles of any dignitary from Lan Na taking refuge in Lan Xang

Burmese troops enter Vientiane

THE CHIANG MAI Chronicles recount how, unknown to King Setthathirath, two of the mandarins who had been installed by the Burmese to rule in Chiang Mai chose this moment to flee to Lan Xang. They were chased by the Burmese troops of the Chiang Mai garrison under the command of Bayinnaung's son, Immale, as far as Vientiane where they were given refuge. Some treacherous ministers allowed the Burmese troops to take over Vientiane.

Setthathirath returned from what had proved to be a fruitless journey to meet Nang Thep Kasatti to find his capital held by the enemy. However, his army and the townspeople remained faithful and he was able to dislodge the few Burmese soldiers and he executed the traitors. The Chiang Mai chronicles appear alone in this account, it may be possible that some ministers did flee from Chiang Mai to Lan Xang, but it is not certain that they reached Vientiane.

During the first attack on Ayudhya by Tabinshwehti, the Burmese had only been able to make a safe retreat from their disastrous siege through the good fortune of having captured the king's son, Ramesuen, and one of his chief ministers, Maha Thammaracha who, on his father's side, was descended from the kings of Sukhothai. In 1534, Maha Thammaracha had been an officer in the Palace Guard and chief conspirator in the palace coup that had placed King Chakraphat on the throne. As a reward he had acquired the powers of a Viceroy and had been given all the northern provinces of Siam to govern, with Phitsanulok as his capital.

From that time on, the Burmese had maintained close contact with him. Perhaps jealous of the king he had helped to create, he had over the years frequently sided with the Burmese against his own people. Now, possibly fearing he would no longer be so powerful if Lan Xang and Ayudhya were allied, Thammaracha betrayed the route that Nang Thep Kasatti was taking and a small Burmese force were able to intercept the party and kidnap her, taking her back to Burma: successfully bringing an end to any hopes for a formal alliance.

White Elephants provide an excuse for Bayinnaung

By 1563 Bayinnaung had conquered the whole of Burma and the Shan states and was looking for an excuse to launch an attack against the Tai states of the Menam Chaophraya Valley. The excuse he chose was extremely tenuous. The possession of one, or more, of the so-called 'White Elephants' brought immense prestige to a kingdom. There were numerous Buddhist legends attached to these elephants as they were believed to bring great magical benefits. In more practical terms, they were thought to attract foreign merchants, whose trade greatly enriched the king and members of his Court.

Bayinnaung had learnt that King Chakraphat had seven White Elephants more than he had. He sent a request that the Siamese king might give him one. Just as he had expected King Chakraphat refused his request. At the end of the 1563 monsoon, Bayinnaung's army was mobilised and he decided that King Chakraphat's refusal to give him a White Elephant provided all the excuse he needed to settle matters with the Tai once and for all.

He gathered an immense army in the Shan states and using the new vassal state of Chiang Mai as a base, he marched south through Kamphaeng Phet and Sukhothai. He gained the support of Maha Thammaracha and together with his vastly more experienced Burmese army they moved down to attack Ayudhya. It was obvious that this was no repetition of the 1549 debacle. Bayinnaung was determined to achieve his revenge.

Ayudhya was surrounded and the Portugese mercenaries began firing their cannons. As before they were too light to do the walls any great damage, but the people were already frightened and the constant battering at their walls seemed to spell their doom. As well, the Burmese, probably through Maha Thammaracha, had managed to create an anti war faction at the Court.

King Chakraphat, who was no great general, decided to listen to them and began to negotiate with Bayinnaung. Whatever the terms of the surrender, Bayinnaung must have broken the terms of the agreement, as no one would have accepted peace at the price his Siamese subjects were called on to pay.

The First Burmese capture of Ayudhya

THE SIAMESE SURRENDERED. King Chakraphat and most of his Court were made captive and taken back to Burma. Unusually, the noble prisoners were treated relatively well. King Chakraphat when he reached Burma was given permission to take the robe and he became a monk. His eldest son, Ramesuen was given an army command and was to be killed helping a Burmese army put down a rebellion in Lan Na.

It was a very different matter for the ordinary people. For them it was to be the beginning of a saga of horror. Thousands were strung together in long columns with wooden yokes around their necks and led away to Pegu and slavery. Many hundreds must have died on the journey. Among those taken away were actors and actresses whose traditional dances and songs are still performed and are known as *Yodaya*, Ayudhya, in Burma today. Bayinnaung also took three of the White Elephants.

Bayinnaung placed Phya Mahin, King Chakraphat's son, on the throne as a vassal king under the watchful eye of Maha Thammaracha and left a Burmese garrison of 3,000 men to ensure their loyalty.

Having taken Ayudhya, Bayinnaung turned his army against Chao Setthathirath. The Burmese had proved themselves far more skilful than either the Siamese, or the Lao. They were adept at changing their strategy to suit the terrain. They used ambushes, false retreats and other stratagems to lure the enemy into indefensible positions.

Realising that they could never hold Vientiane, Setthathirath and his army retired from Vientiane leaving it undefended and marched some 75 kilometres northeast to make camp near the mouth of the Nam Ngum. He had left behind three of his queens and some 20 concubines. What is more important, he made one of his younger brothers Regent. It was probably Chao Tha Heua who was his Oupahat and had earlier tried to seize the throne on the death of King Phothisarath.

The Burmese army entered a city to discover that it had been denuded of supplies, and, as Setthathirath had intended, they soon found themselves dependent on provisions brought in from the countryside. This too was part of Chao Setthathirath's strategy. His army working from guerrilla bases, harassed the foraging parties so successfully that by the monsoon of the next year, 1565, the Burmese army was suffering from malnutrition and disease. They had no other choice than to make an humiliating retreat. They took with them the Oupahat, and Chao Setthathirath's queens and concubines.

As soon as the last of the Burmese army had left, King Setthathirath returned to Vientiane. It was still a triumph, even though the city had been ravaged and the king had suffered the personal loss of his queens and younger brother. He had become the only Tai king to have forced the new Burmese war machine into an ignominious retreat.

Lan Na becomes a Burmese Vassal

AT THE SAME time as this, King Mekuti of Lan Na was implicated in a plot against the Burmese and was taken away to Burma. He was replaced by Queen Wisutthithewi, who, as Queen Chiraprapha, had been Regent for Setthathirath. Bayinnaung took the precaution of marrying her so that in the people's eyes she ruled as a Burmese Queen. Despite her wisdom and experience, in her fourteen years' reign (1564 – 1578), she could do little to alleviate the hardships Lan Na suffered, being ruthlessly treated as a subjugated nation. Lan Na was also invaded a number of times by the Shan from the north and it was probably as a result of the constant fighting that it suffered a devastating three year famine.

Lan Xang and Siam attack Phitsanulok

PRINCE MAHIN BECAME increasingly disillusioned by his role as Regent of Siam and deeply resented the Burmese policy and the dominance they had given his brother-in-law, Maha Thammaracha. In desperation, he invited Chao Setthathirath to help him attack Maha Thammaracha in Phitsanulok and to win independence from the Burmese. Chao Setthathirath agreed.

In the second month of 1567, Maha Thammaracha learnt that a Lan Xang army was approaching Phitsanulok. Not knowing Prince Mahin's real feelings, he immediately sent a message to Ayudhya asking for help. Prince Mahin saw this as an opportunity to take Maha Thammaracha prisoner and he sent a group of nobles to tell him that an Ayudhyan fleet was on its way. He then gave them secret instructions that, as soon as the Lan Xang army arrived, they should take the governor of Phitsanulok prisoner. However, the secret was not well kept and Maha Thammaracha soon knew about the plan. He immediately sent a secret message to Bayinnaung asking for help.

In the hope of disguising his real intentions, Chao Setthathirath sent one of his armies on a diversionary attack against Muong Khem in the north, while he himself marched against Phitsanulok with an army of 200,000 men, and 2,500 elephants. He surrounded the city, but before the Ayudhyan fleet had arrived, a Burmese force of 10,000 men appeared, broke through the Lan Xang lines, and entered the city.

Soon after, Setthathirath learnt that the Siamese fleet had been destroyed and he was without the support he had expected. He waited twenty days for Prince Mahin to send other troops, but when these did not materialise, he may have feared treachery on the part of the Siamese. Whatever the reason, he raised the siege and began to retreat.

Profiting by his knowledge of Bayinnaung's new strategies, he realised that the Burmese would undoubtedly try to attack his rearguard. As soon as the terrain allowed it, he set an ambush for the advancing enemy. In it five Burmese generals were killed, or wounded, and some thirteen of Maha Thammaracha's officers. The Burmese force was routed and fled back to Burma. Uncertain of the true situation, Setthathirath continued his retreat.

It was little consolation that the Lan Xang generals had successfully captured Muong Khem, as all that had been achieved was that Maha Thammaracha was now openly committed to the Burmese side, who appeared to be in an even stronger position than before.

In the same year, 1567, Bayinnaung, who was being plagued by petty rebellions throughout his Shan and Tai dependencies, decided to grant a request by King Chakraphat that he be allowed, as a monk, to make a pilgrimage to Ayudhya. Once there, King Chakraphat took off the robe and resumed his throne and declared Siam independent. Taking advantage of Maha Thammaracha's absence in Burma, he and Prince Mahin attacked Phitsanulok

King Chakraphat had never been a good military commander and he was by then old and tired. The campaign achieved nothing. He captured Phitsanulok, but failed to take Kamphaeng Phet, which controlled the all important route south from Chiang Mai and Burma. Tired and disillusioned, he retired back to Ayudhya.

The Second Burmese Invasion

INEVITABLY THIS BROUGHT about a second Burmese invasion. As soon as the 1568 monsoon was over Bayinnaung with an enormous army swelled by numerous Mon, Shan, Lu, Lao and Lan Na levies swept down upon Ayudhya via Tak and Kamphaeng Phet. Bayinnaung was joined by Maha Thammaracha with his Phitsanulok army.

King Chakraphat worn out by his last campaign had abdicated in favour of his son, Mahin, and died in January 1564 as the Burmese army approached the capital. Prince Mahin (1569) proved to be even more ineffectual than his father. In February, he sent a message to Vientiane asking for help. Chao Setthathirath responded by leading an army towards Phitsanulok. On hearing of this, Bayinnaung decided to mislead him and arranged for Setthathirath to be informed that there was only a weak Burmese detachment near Saraburi. Receiving this false message, the Lan Xang armies changed the direction of their march.

Just outside Saraburi, Setthathirath's army fell into the planned ambush. But the Lao generals were able to gain the advantage, and after a two day battle they defeated the Burmese at Pa Sak Valley near Phetchabun.

The advantage was lost, however, as Chao Setthathirath's two most senior and ambitious generals disagreed over the best course to follow. Sen Soulintha argued against attacking the Burmese while Phagna Nakhon felt that the success should be followed up immediately. When Sen Soulintha refused to join in the attack, Phagna Nakhon took his troops towards Ayudhya alone. He was outnumbered and had to retreat, bringing after him a Burmese army.

King Setthathirath decided to retreat and the Burmese harassed him all the way back to Vientiane. As a result, the Lao suffered heavy casualties.

Ayudhya was on its own. The dry season was coming to an end. The Burmese tried to make their way across the river and the moats surrounding the town. But the defences were too strong and they were unsuccessful. With the coming of the rains, they gave up any hope of obtaining victory through force and, instead, turned to guile. They were able to buy support from within the town and a party of Burmese were secretly let into the city. Both the siege and the war were over.

The Second Capture of Ayudhya and of Vientiane

THE CITY FELL on 8 August 1569. Bayinnaung took King Mahin captive, but the king died on the march back to Burma. Bayinnaung rewarded Maha Thammaracha (1569–1590) for his treachery making him the vassal king of Siam.

Once Bayinnaung had captured Ayudhya he was free to turn his attention to an attack against the only other large Tai nation: Lan Xang. He waited until the end of the rains and then in October marched his army to Phitsanulok where he left the sick and took only the best of his troops. He kept the main body with him on the bank opposite Vientiane, while others were sent across to take the Lan Xang army in the rear.

Even though he had strengthened his defences, Chao Setthathirath realised he could never defeat Bayinnaung's immense army. On Sen Soulintha's advice he once again ordered the complete evacuation of the people before they could be trapped in the town by the encircling army. Once again the Burmese entered Vientiane but this time to find only an empty town.

When Bayinnaung arrived, he made the mistake of letting his troops rest for a week before setting off in pursuit of the Lao army. He compounded his error by believing the Lao were thoroughly beaten, and when he decided to return to Burma, he left only a small force to mop up what he thought were the Lao survivors.

However, Setthathirath's army was still intact. They again retired behind the Nam Ngum River and from there were able to carry out marauding attacks on the Burmese troops whenever they left the walls of Vientiane in search of food. Just as in 1564, the Burmese troops fell prey to hunger and disease.

The rains in 1570 were the final straw. Bayinnaung at last acknowledged that the starving garrison were in desperate straits and ordered them back to Burma. When Chao Setthathirath saw that Bayinnaung had taken the main Burmese army away, he brought his army within striking distance of Vientiane. As soon as the Burmese began their evacuation, the Lao attacked and more than 30,000 garrison troops were taken prisoner. Among the booty captured were over 100 elephants and 2,300 ivories.

For the time being the war against the Burmese was over, but there were still many problems to be faced by Chao Setthathirath.

The mysterious death of King Setthathirath

THE MOVE TO Vientiane had not been accepted by everyone. Those who had remained in Luang Prabang were no longer at the seat of power. While those small principalities around Vientiane and in the south on the Korat plateau suddenly found that the king was now closer and their freedom to act was therefore more restricted.

In 1571, Phagna Nakhon, the general who had not been supported by Sen Soulintha in his attack against the Burmese, persuaded Chao Setthathirath to mount an operation against the mountain peoples in southern Laos, telling him that the ruler of Muong Ong Kan had died and his two daughters wished to offer their submission to him personally.

Chao Setthathirath decided to lead the army himself. As they approached the Annamite chain in southern Laos, his main body fell into an ambush and was largely destroyed. Chao Setthathirath managed to reach the army's base camp and there he was persuaded by Phagna Nakhon to take refuge with him in the jungle.

From that moment on, nothing is known of what became of Chao Setthathirath. It is possible that Phagna Nakhon murdered him. But neither the site of the battle nor the enemy can be determined. By some accounts, Setthathirath was defeated in the hills near Attopeu, by others, it was during a major, but ill-fated expedition against the Khmer near Angkor.

Sen Soulintha survived the battle and as we shall see became for a while Regent. Lan Xang was about to enter another period of internal strife and unsuccessful war.

So in 1571, Chao Setthathirath died, murdered by one of his own generals. He was one of the greatest generals of his times. He alone stood up to Bayinnaung and was never conquered by him. He learnt from his enemy and turned his enemy's strategies and tactics successfully against him.

His reign had not been a complete triumph. He and his father had seen with some trepidation the expansionist aims of Ayudhya and, as a result, had let their former good relationship turn into enmity. He, however, had the statesmanship to realise that the only hope for the two kingdoms was to combine against the Burmese. King Chakraphat was slower to see how dangerous a threat the Burmese posed. Had he allowed the marriage of Nang Thep Kasatti to take place, Maha Thammaracha might have thought twice before throwing in his lot with the Burmese and Ayudhya, without a pro-Burmese party, might have survived, and even turned the Burmese invasions back on themselves.

But all these are suppositions and did not happen. Instead, King Setthathirath made the most that he could of an impossible situation and, despite his failures, left Lan Xang even greater in glory than when he was crowned. He had proved to be a proud enemy of an implacable Burma.

CHAPTER SIX

Seventy years of Anarchy

THE STRANGE DISAPPEARANCE, and probable murder, of King Setthathirath was the beginning of nearly seventy years of anarchy and misrule that permeated every part of the country. The hardships were at their worst in those years when the Burmese army was able to capture Vientiane and dominate large parts of Lan Xang, including Luang Prabang at times.

Sen Soulintha, whose role in the disappearance of Chao Setthathirath cannot be known for certain, returned from the battlefield in the south and tried to take over Vientiane. But the aristocracy had not forgotten his humble origins. For more than thirty years they had watched this favourite of two kings be promoted from nothing to the most trusted general and from that to the most senior minister of the realm.

It is always possible that the reason for King Setthathirath's death was in some way connected with the hatred felt in some quarters for Sen Soulintha. Nor is it known whether Chao Setthathirath's death was planned by some of the Court to provide an opportunity to settle old scores. Certainly on his return Sen Soulintha found there was strong opposition to his becoming the regent for Chao Setthathirath's four year old son, Chao No Muong, despite the fact that the prince was his own grandson.

The strongest contender for the Regency was Chao Chantha Siharath, who with his powerful supporters was determined to bring an end to Sen Soulintha's power. For four months, the Sangha managed to prevent civil war, but neither side was willing to surrender to the other party, the chance of ruling the country.

Civil War

ACCORDING TO SOME accounts, Sen Soulintha disobeyed the wishes of the Sangha, in their search for a peaceful solution. He secretly instructed some

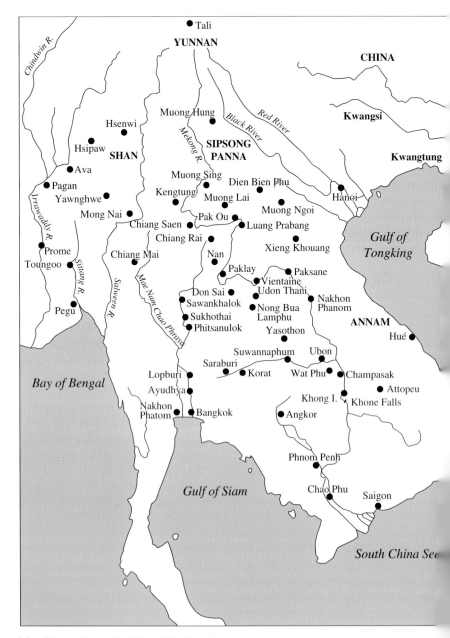

MAP 3 Indochina in the 16th to 18th Centuries

of his followers to take an army against Chao Chantha Siharath and kill him. Chao Chantha died nobly, fighting from the platform above his war elephant. In other accounts he was murdered on Sen Soulintha's orders. Whichever it was, the Sangha and people realised that there was nothing they could do to stop this ambitious minister and agreed to his becoming regent.

The death of his rival had not, however, solved his problems. At all levels, there was opposition to his rule. Possibly hoping to overcome this, in 1572 Sen Soulintha announced that he was taking the throne under the regnal name of Sumangkhala Ayako Photisad. Few, except his closest supporters, were willing to accept him. For whatever reason, he had failed to win the respect of those about him. To the Court and people he was known by the unflattering term, *Chao Pu Lan*, the *Royal Grandfather*.

The Coronation of Sen Soulintha

AFTER THE CORONATION of Sen Soulintha (1572–1574) a number of vassal principalities refused to accept his suzerainty, and, in an attempt to assert his rule, he began a series of ruthless executions of those who opposed him. Suddenly, no one felt safe. A mass exodus started from the Vientiane region with whole families leaving for the South: they fled to the Korat Plateau, especially around modern Roi Et, to Champasak and even to Khmer territories. Maha Sila describes it as the third greatest migration in Lao history.

The widespread discontent came to the notice of Bayinnaung, who still had ambitions to add Lan Xang to his empire. About the year 1573 Bayinnaung sent an ambassador demanding that Sen Soulintha abdicate. Sen Soulintha merely executed the ambassador and the members of his mission. He was later able to repulse a small Burmese army that came to revenge their deaths.

Third Burmese Capture of Vientiane

BAYINNAUNG COULD NOT let this go unpunished. In the next year, 1574, the Burmese king collected a massive army which he led himself against Vientiane. Sen Soulintha hoped to follow the strategy he had recommended to King Setthathirath and, by retiring into the jungle, to rely on hunger and disease to win the battle, as they had done in 1570. But he, unlike Chao Setthathirath, did not have the support of his people.

They refused to leave the comfort of their homes for the hardships of life in the jungle. Equally important, a large part of his army, feeling little loyalty towards him, deserted as soon as he ordered them to evacuate the city.

Bayinnaung had no difficulty in entering Vientiane. He had brought with him the former Oupahat who had been taken a prisoner in 1565 when the Burmese had first captured Vientiane. The Vientiane Annals, and most other sources, refer to him only as the 'Oupahat' or as a 'younger brother of Chao Setthathirath', possibly embarrassed by the role he was to play as a Burmese puppet. But the Luang Prabang Annals state quite clearly that the Oupahat was Chao Tha Heua, also known as Voravangso, one of Chao Setthathirath's two brothers. He was the elder of the two younger brothers, who had tried to usurp the northern part of the kingdom on the death of their father, King Phothisarath.

Tha Heua becomes a vassal king of Burma

BAYINNAUNG LEFT CHAO Tha Heua (1575–1579) as a vassal king, but he took back to Burma as a captive and hostage, King Setthathirath's son by Sen Soulintha's daughter, Chao No Muong. Chao No Muong would later take the regnal name Nokeo Koumane. Bayinnaung left a Burmese garrison in Vientiane and it was not long before they captured Sen Soulintha, who was then sent back to Pegu as a prisoner.

King Tha Heua was to reign for four years. His life at the Burmese Court had made him very favourable to the Burmese, an attitude that soon lost him the support of his ministers and the people. Things became worse when an impostor from the region of Attopeu, where King Setthathirath may have disappeared, claimed to be the reincarnation of Chao Setthathirath. As proof, he claimed to remember the names of many of the dead king's favourite animals, as well pretending to know many details of his personal life.

The imposter gathered a group of discontented people around him and marched on Vientiane. Bayinnaung sent one of his sons to put down the revolt. This Burmese prince found life in Vientiane so uncongenial that he returned to Burma as soon as peace had been restored. He left behind him a discontented Court few of whose mandarins favoured Burmese rule.

Bayinnaung found himself facing a host of problems, both internal and external, and he had little time for Chao Tha Heua. The King finding himself unsupported by the Burmese in whom he had trusted became

ILLUSTRATION 11 Mural, scenes from the Life of the Buddha

increasingly isolated and ignored. Finally, terrified that he would be killed, he fled from Vientiane. Taking a fleet of pirogues, he and his family tried to make their way back to Burma. However, probably at the rapids of Keng Chan, some 30 kilometres upstream from Vientiane, the pirogues overturned and he and all with him were drowned.

The Return of Sen Soulintha

BAYINNAUNG DECIDED THAT his best course now was to send Sen Soulintha (1580–1582) back to Vientiane, where, lacking Lao support, he would be dependent on the favour of the Burmese. It proved to be a temporary solution, Sen Soulintha was by then an old man and he managed to survive for only two years before he died in 1582, throwing open, once again, the vexed issue of who should be king. The Burmese decided, against Lao wishes, that he should be succeeded by his son, Nakhon Noi (1582–1583).

The year before this Bayinnaung had died and his son Nandabayin (1581–1599) had claimed the throne. However, Bayinnaung's wars had created great hardship within Burma and it was no longer the strong and united country it appeared to be on the surface. His accession was opposed by an uncle who had behind him a very powerful coalition of the principalities and minor states of Upper Burma whose loyalty had been worn thin by the constant demands for more men for Bayinnaung's armies. Nandabayin marched north and was only acknowledged king as, watched by the two armies, he overcame his uncle in a personal combat.

From then on, Nandabayin tried to maintain the hold that his father had exerted over the Tai states. His proved to be an ever diminishing power. With all his domestic problems, Nandabayin had no resources he could use to support his puppet king in Vientiane and his other Tai vassal rulers. Nakhon Noi proved to be no more popular than his father, Sen Soulintha, had been and, within a year, the Court sent him back to Burma.

Anarchy before Chao Nokeo Koumane returns

FOR LAN XANG, 1583 to 1591 were eight terrible years of anarchy. No single faction had the power to place its own contender on the throne. This lawlessness and bloodshed continued until the Sangha sent a mission to Burma and obtained the agreement from Nandabayin that Chao No Muong, King Setthathirath's son, should be allowed back to Lan Xang as king. He had been a prisoner in Burma for some sixteen years and was by then aged twenty. Nandabayin facing a number of petty rebellions throughout his empire was only too glad to buy peace with Lan Xang at so cheap a price.

The young king taking the regnal name of Chao Nokeo Koumane (1591–1596) was to bring new life and hope to Lan Xang. Once back and accepted by his people in Vientiane, he collected a military force and marched on Luang Prabang which had ceased to acknowledge Vientiane's position as capital. He entered it without fighting and northern Lan Xang was formally reunited with Vientiane. Soon after, he renounced any allegiance to Burma declaring his country free and independent.

Muong Phoueune and Lan Xang

To STRENGTHEN THE kingdom still further, Chao Nokeo proposed to Muong Phoueune that they resume their traditional relationship. With the Burmese capture of Vientiane, Muong Phoueune had been forced to accept Burmese suzerainty and was only too glad to regain its freedom once again. As a landlocked principality between Lan Xang on the west and south, Vietnam on the east, and the unruly hill tribes along its northern borders, it was under constant threat.

As a result, Muong Phoueune only paid tribute when Lan Xang was strong enough to give it protection. The payment was largely symbolic, and certainly not onerous, being a triennial payment of four branches of flowers made from gold, with 1,400 swords, lances, knives, spades and pickaxes made from silver.

Looking further afield, Chao Nokeo Koumane began to make plans to reimpose his suzerainty over Lan Na. In 1578, the great Queen Chiraprapha had died. She had ruled skilfully, the first being in the 1540's as a regent before the arrival of Chao Setthathirath. She probably had a large say in his government as Chao Setthathirath was only a fourteen year old boy prince when his father, King Phothisarath, left him to rule Lan Na on his own. Later, when his Ministers forced him to go back to Lan Xang to rule, Chao Setthathirath had again placed the regency in her hands. On that occasion, her rule had been ended by the coronation of King Mekuti.

Later, in 1565, when Mekuti plotted against the Burmese, she once again became the ruler. In the years that followed her skill and diplomacy had lessened the hardships for her subjects imposed by both the Burmese and Siamese suzerainties. On her death, there had not been an heir whom Bayinnaung could trust, so he had placed one of his sons, Tharrawaddy Min (1578–1595), on the throne. Bayinnaung had also tried to ensure her loyalty by making her one of his queens.

Chao Nokeo re-opens the war with Ayudhya

Two YEARS AFTER his accession, in 1593, Chao Nokeo felt strong enough to launch an attack against Lan Na. Tharrawaddy Min had maintained his rule with the power of Burma behind him. When he learnt of Chao Nokeo's advance, he immediately sent a message to his brother asking for help. But Nandabayin was, as usual, beset by a host of domestic and economic problems and could do nothing to help him.

In desperation Tharrawaddy Min sent a message to the king of Ayudhya, King Naresuen (1590–1605), or as he had been known in his youth, *The Black Prince*. His father, Maha Thammaracha, was the former ruler of Phitsanulok who had betrayed King Chakraphat and after the fall of Ayudhya in 1569 had been made a vassal king of the Burmese. King Naresuen had spent some time at the Court of Burma and had grown up with Tharrawaddy Min before the latter was made king of Lan Na by Bayinnaung, his father.

However, King Naresuen did not let his past friendship with Tharrawaddy Min stand in his way. Seizing the opportunity he demanded that Tharrawaddy Min accept his suzerainty and that Lan Na be returned to him as a vassal state of Siam. Unable to fight alone, Tharrawaddy Min was forced to accept. When he learnt this, Chao Nokeo in Vientiane, realised that with his base in Lan Xang being so far away, he would have no hope of beating the combined armies of Siam and Lan Na. He wisely gave up the idea of re-conquering his former realm.

It was one of the last actions of Chao Nokeo. In 1596 he died at the early age of twenty-five. Sadly, he left no heir to continue, and extend, his many achievements that had brought unity and peace to his country. Once again the Vientiane Court was divided. Finally, agreement was reached that the crown should go to a young prince called Voravongsa. Who Voravongsa was is still not clear, but he could have been a nephew of Chao Nokeo. If not, he may have been his cousin, whose mother, it has been suggested, was Nang Kham Khai, a sister of King Setthathirath.

Phra Vorapita becomes Regent

THE BURMESE OBJECTED to his selection claiming that at thirteen years he was still too young to be crowned. They accepted, however, that his father known only by the Sanskrit-derived term, Phra Vorapita (1596–1603), *Father of Vora*, should become Regent. There is some doubt over the date that he assumed the Regency, but it was in either 1596, or 1598.

The expansionist policies of both Bayinnaung and Nandabayin may appear to have been a time of glorious empire and prosperity for Burma, but in reality they had brought nothing but hardship, at times starvation, and constant terror. This was not merely true for the other peoples in

Indochina, but also for those in Burma itself, whose villages were depleted of the young men, and often women, to meet the kings' constant demands for soldiers and porters for the hungry armies.

Neither Bayinnaung nor Nandabayin had been able to exert direct control over any part of the country they called Burma, except that is, for the rich delta lands of the Irrawaddy and the Salween. They had farmed out the rest of the country to princelings and warlords, who were aptly known by the Burmese term *Myosa*, meaning *Eaters of Towns*. In return for their privileges they were expected to produce men and supplies for the king. It was not a very good bargain for either the rulers, or the people. The Myosas were motivated purely by private profit, and neither their contributions to the royal exchequer, nor their care for the people under them, could be relied on.

As Bayinnaung and Nandabayin continued in their endless endeavour to extend, or at least to maintain, their empires, they had constantly to conscribe men and supplies from the Delta, the only part of the country under their control. The result was that the once rice basket of the country, became depopulated. Without peasants to work the fields, those villagers who remained were hard pressed even to feed themselves.

Worse still, the Burmese had failed to replace the kingdoms and principalities they had conquered with anything better than the Myosa system of their own country. As a result, their reigns were devoted to suppressing the continuing rebellions that sprang up as soon as their armies returned to Burma. This was especially so in the Tai states.

The Sack of Pegu

BY 1599, THE Burmese Sangha decided that a change had to be made and they gave their authority to anyone who would depose Nandabayin. One of Nandabayin's relations, the Prince of Toungoo proposed to the Arakanese ruler that together they should mount a joint operation against the capital, Pegu. This they did. Nandabayin was taken prisoner and the Prince of Toungoo carried him and vast quantities of booty back to his home country, leaving the Arakanese to ransack and finally burn down Pegu.

When King Naresuen, the Siamese king, heard of this, he immediately mounted an army, but he arrived at Pegu only to find it apparently deserted and nothing more than smouldering ruins. He was unaware that the Arakanese force had hidden in the jungles as soon as they had learnt of his approach. They remained there while his army searched the ruins and he left Pegu still ignorant of their presence and the threat they posed to his communications.

He marched on to Toungoo and demanded Nandabayin be handed over to him. When this was refused, he settled down to lay siege to the city. However, as soon as he had left Pegu, the Arakanese came out of the jungle and began to raid his supply columns. Short of supplies, King Naresuen gave up any idea of conquering Burma and wisely decided to retire back to his capital, Ayudhya.

Escape of the Lao Hostages

TAKING ADVANTAGE OF the disarray of the administration at this time, a number of Lao hostages who had been forcibly deported to Burma decided to return to Lan Xang. Instead of making them temple slaves, a possibly hard, but humane existence under the eye of the Sangha, Bayinnaung had sent many of them to the Kyaukse area where they had been forced to build a canal and other public works that had resulted in many of them dying.

When the Lao families reached Chiang Mai, Tharrawaddy Min tried to send them back to Burma. However, the news of their escape had reached Vorapita, the Regent, who ordered an army to be sent to help them back to Laos. He also gave orders that the army should attack and capture Chiang Mai. Although his army managed to subdue Chiang Rai, and some other smaller towns in Lan Na, it found Chiang Mai too well fortified to capture easily. Running out of supplies, it decided to return to Vientiane.

Vorapita, angry at the army's failure to take Chiang Mai, refused to allow it to enter Vientiane. For four months, they argued back and forth, with the army becoming increasingly angry. Finally, it demanded that Vorapita abdicate and allow his son to ascend the throne. Unable to resist the army any longer, Vorapita agreed and his family were fortunate enough to be allowed to find a home in the south. His son, Voravongsa, became king in 1603 with the regnal name of Thammikarath (1603–1622).

Chao Thammikarath brings peace

MORE THAN ANYTHING else, Lan Xang needed time to recover. Except for a minor campaign against Ayudhya in 1612, Chao Thammikarath gave it the respite it required. His eldest son, Chao Oupagnouvarath, as soon as he became an adult showed a great interest and skill in the administration and very soon, being popular with the king's ministers, he took over many of King Thammikarath's responsibilities.

His father became jealous of this popularity and when, in 1621, on a visit with his chief queen to Luang Prabang, he was told that his son was plotting to overthrow him, he immediately ordered his arrest and execution, without trying to find out whether the accusation was the truth or not.

Chao Oupagnouvarath gathered an army together in Vientiane and marched northwards. The king was able to send an army to meet his advance, but after a bloody battle that ended in defeat for the king's army, his ministers who were with him in Luang Prabang gradually turned against him. Chao Thammikarath was captured and, three months later, along with the rest of his family and many of his supporters, was executed on the orders of his son.

Chao Oupagnouvarath (1622–1623) did not enjoy his newly found power for long. Within a year he died, possibly murdered. Once again, there was no obvious claimant for the crown and, as before, the Court divided into different factions, each struggling to place its own pretender on the throne. It was to be yet another time of anarchy as, for the next fifteen years, one dynastic struggle was to be followed by another.

As a successor to Chao Oupagnouvarath, some of the mandarins sent for a son of Sen Soulintha, who was then the ruler of Sikothabong, modern Khammouan. He took the regnal name of Phothisarath II (1623–1627) and ruled for four years. He left no heir that was recognised by the Court.

About 1627, the throne was offered to Phra Mon Keo (c.1627), a brother of Oupagnouvarath, who had been his strong supporter in the fight against their father, King Thammikarath. But he was not popular within the Court and a new struggle for power ensued. It is impossible to determine the dates of the different reigns in the ten years that followed.

Chao Mone Keo was followed by two of his sons. The first Chao Tone Kham and on his death, possibly in 1633, he was succeeded by his younger brother, Chao Vichai. Fortunately for Lan Xang both Burma and Ayudhya had their own internal problems, so that weak and split by dissension as she was, Lan Xang did not have to defend herself against her enemies.

Following the death of Chao Vichai, Chao Souligna Vongsa, a great grand nephew of Chao Thammikarath was declared king, or declared himself king, in 1637. It was to prove to be a momentous event. For Lan Xang was about to experience sixty years of rule under one of her greatest kings. Chao Souligna Vongsa was to bring Lan Xang to the very apex of her power and greatness.

CHAPTER SEVEN

A New Golden Age

THE KINGDOM OF Lan Xang was about to enter a Golden Age that was to last some fifty-five years. It was to be the culmination of the kingdom's history, possibly never to be repeated again. The beginning, however, was not auspicious. As today, succession is not an automatic right of the eldest son. The only condition attached to kinghood is that the prince must be of royal blood. The only constitutional exception is that should the mother of a claimant be a commoner, she must have been publicly recognised by the king as a full member of the royal family. Within this framework, the senior members of the family, with any powerful mandarins they chose to nominate, are at liberty to name whoever they think best suited to be king.

Chao Tone Kham had three sons. When the members of the family gathered to discuss the succession, it soon became obvious that the relatives of Chao Souligna Vongsa, the youngest son, far outnumbered the supporters of the other claimants and he was duly elected. At the time, it seemed a happy escape from the turmoil that had preceded each coronation for the last few decades. But when nearly sixty years later Chao Souligna Vongsa died at the height of his glory, the price that had to be paid for that decision was to be the complete destruction of Lan Xang as a kingdom.

Chao Souligna Vongsa (1637–1694) was then aged about thirty-four and, with the foresight based on the previous years of dynastic struggle, he immediately exiled his two brothers and his two cousins. His eldest brother, Chao Som Phu went to the Court of Annam at Hué where he had a son, Chao Sai Ong Hue, named after his birthplace. His other brother, Chao Boun Sou, decided to become a monk and probably chose to live in Lan Na.

With peace assured at his Court, Chao Souligna Vongsa set about the re-creation of a truly great Lao nation. He encouraged the growth of Buddhism and ensured that its teachings were disseminated throughout the country. He was a liberal man and encouraged people to express their thoughts and ideas. So under him grew up a nation of great thinkers, of poets and writers. They searched for and transcribed many of the oral legends and poems that otherwise would have been lost. Their interests in the works of art of the past brought a new richness to life both at Court and in all the major towns in Lan Xang.

King Souligna Vongsa also codified the laws and more importantly created a system of justice that administered the laws with equal rigour for the rich and powerful as for the poor and unknown. They were sometimes severe laws. For the crime of adultery, the death sentence was obligatory and for the sake of this one ideal, morally correct as it was, Chao Souligna Vongsa was to bring catastrophe and desolation on his country: a desolation such as it had never known, even in the times of the Maha Devi. At one stroke he was to undo all Chao Fa Ngum had created and to make himself the last king to rule over Lan Xang.

This was doubly tragic in a reign full of so many achievements. He was the first king to develop a real foreign policy. He maintained regular contacts with not only his neighbours, but all the major Asian powers, as well as those from Europe. The first European visitor in his reign, and possibly the very first to visit Laos, was a Jesuit priest, Father Jean-Marie Leria who came about 1639 or 1640. Little is known about the Father beyond the fact that he was in Laos for a number of years.

Laos was a rich country and as well as its gold and ivories, it was especially known for its silks, its gumlac and benzoin, a resinous substance like frankincense. Both of these last were in great demand throughout Asia and Europe.

The First Europeans

IT WAS IN search of these that in 1641 the Dutch East India Company sent an agent, Gerritt van Wuysthoff with letters to King Souligna Vongsa from the Governor General of Batavia, (Java and Sumatra), asking permission to set up permanent trading arrangements. Van Wuysthoff kept a diary of the 109 day journey up the Mekong from Phnom Penh to Vientiane and of his stay there.

It was a dangerous journey on a raft that was probably nothing more than two long pirogues strapped together. To make them somewhat safer they were supported on each side with bundles of bamboo that provided some extra flotation if the pirogues took on water. The whole was covered with matting strapped to semicircular bamboo supports.

The journey was made in numerous short stages, sometimes as little as a few miles at a time. The boatmen were Lao whose entire life was spent navigating boats between the Khmer kingdom, modern Cambodia and Lan Xang. They were legally responsible for the behaviour of their passengers and had to ensure that they complied with the different regulations at the ports of call. The Dutchmen were reported to the Lao officials at each stop and when they reached Pak Houei Luang, modern Phon Phisai across the Mekong in Thailand, they were held while messages were sent to Vientiane requesting instructions.

Van Wuysthoff remarks that Pak Houei Luang was the main centre for all Laotian products and for those that came down from the countries to the north, including China. Pak Houei Luang was famous for the clothes it made from silk, and it was a collecting point for the gold, and other products going south.

Chao Souligna Vongsa sent instructions that the foreigners should be brought to Vientiane and Van Wuysthoff notes that they were very fortunate to be received so quickly. He remarks that it was usual in Asia to keep ambassadors waiting in a special tented village, sometimes for months. He comments that when some ambassadors did eventually have an audience, they could find that they were then dismissed and told to return to their own countries empty handed, the king having decided to send a reply by his own ambassadors.

However, all was not plain sailing. There were complaints from one of the king's uncles, who had been given the responsibility of presenting van Wuysthoff to the king, that the presents the Dutchmen had offered were not sufficiently valuable. So, additions were made, both to those for the king and for the king's uncle.

When that had been arranged satisfactorily, van Wuysthoff was asked to produce his credentials so that they could be translated. At first he refused to do this saying that in some countries courtiers who, for one reason or another, were opposed to the visit would get the translators to use unsuitable language, or even to insert insults that were not in the original. He was eventually persuaded to hand the letter over, accepting the assurances that this would not be allowed to happen. He was then asked whether he had any messages for the King, as these would be passed on to him. Van Wuysthoff, with his knowledge of the behaviour of other kings, asked that the King would give him permission to leave when he wished and that he would not be kept against his will. He was assured that there would not be any danger of that.

The Tevinia Lankan, the title of the king's uncle who was responsible for him, then told van Wuysthoff that by custom anyone granted an

audience with the king had to hold two wax candles in his hands and bow
deeply three times in front of the king. The candles would then be taken
away and the audience would begin. Van Wuysthoff assured the Tevinia
Lankan that he would be happy to follow any of the Court's customs. The
minister then questioned him closely about Batavia, modern Java. Its size
astonished him and he asked van Wuysthoff for the description to be put in
writing.

The Splendour of the Court

EARLY ON THE morning of the 16 November 1641, six elephants arrived to
carry van Wuysthoff's letter, which had by then been translated. It was
placed in a gold box on the first elephant and the entourage mounted the
other elephants, including van Wuysthoff with his presents.

The Dutchman found the journey on the elephant to be enthralling. He
says that as he was high up on the back of an elephant he could view the
town easily. It was surrounded by a ditch that was wider than the range of a
musket, but probably as a result of the years of peace, it was full of refuse
and filth that had been thrown into it and it was covered in rank weeds.

ILLUSTRATION 12 The That Luang, Vientiane, one of the holiest shrines in Laos; said to
hold a relic of the Buddha sent by Aśoka, Emperor of India, third century BC.

97

The procession made its way to the That Luang that Chao Setthathirath had turned into one of the most beautiful and sacred shrines in Lan Xang. Earlier this century, it had become marked by lichen and the weather and it is difficult to imagine the splendour it must then have presented with its spire proudly gilded and surrounded by beautiful wats. Van Wuysthoff leaves no doubt about the magnificence and colour of the scene that greeted them on arrival.

Van Wuysthoff and his two colleagues were taken to a tent to await the audience. They were surrounded by the temporary quarters of the grandees of the Court, with soldiers, war elephants and horses gathered all about them. He comments that there was so much noise that one would have thought one was surrounded by the army of his own ruler, the Prince of Orange.

Finally the king, mounted on an elephant, arrived from his palace in Vientiane. Before him marched 300 soldiers with lances and rifles, then came elephants carrying armed men, then more elephants carrying musicians. Behind these came 200 soldiers and 16 elephants that carried his five wives.

At four o'clock they were called to the audience and, after making all the proper obeisances, they were invited to sit on a mat some seven or eight feet from the King. Having asked after the health of the Governor-General the king said he wished to send an ambassador back with them to propose an annual exchange of letters so as to ensure the continued maintenance of good relations.

The King's Graciousness

THERE IS A telling glimpse of the personality of Chao Souligna Vongsa. Most kings would expect any visitors to do exactly as they chose. But this was plainly not in Chao Souligna Vongsa's character. Instead he told them he had arranged some entertainments and he asked them whether they would like to attend, or, since the night was coming on, whether they would like to return to their own place. They assured him that it would be a great honour to attend.

Immediately some boxers appeared, followed by acrobats, and then as night had fallen, blazing torches were brought and the King's four youngest wives performed a dance that lasted for over an hour. Van Wuysthoff records that the four royal wives were followed by a dancer with the tail feathers of a peacock in each hand.

They were escorted back to their tents and were informed that it was a very long time since the King had granted such honours to visitors. Only two months before the Siamese ambassador had not been allowed to sit under the dome of the building as they had. As well, he had been made to sit on the bare ground without a mat.

At about half past eleven that night, another Minister called on them to ask when they wished to leave as the king would be sending an ambassador with them. They replied that they had to leave within a few days as otherwise the level of the Mekong would be too low to negotiate the rapids. If that was so, they were told, it would not be possible to send the ambassador with them as the King had ordered the collection of the finest benzoin and other products and these would not arrive for at least forty days.

For the next two days they did not see the king, but on 20 November he sent them a message saying that he had arranged a fireworks display and he invited them to attend. That evening they were taken to his palace by the Mekong. A square platform of bamboo had been moored in the river for the fireworks and when night fell 200 boats carrying candles floated down in front of them. They were followed by three large boats, each carrying a pyramid of lighted candles creating an impression that the river was made of fire and light.

This was the last of their audiences with the king. They moved downstream to Muong Kuk for a month but maintained contact with the mandarins of the court. Then they returned to Pak Houei Luang. According to Garnier, van Wuysthoff left his two assistants to accompany the Lan Xang ambassador on his mission to deliver the presents to the Governor-General. Van Wuysthoff set off on 26 December, 1641 for a journey that would not get him back to Phnom Penh until 11 April 1642. He and the Dutch East India Company were pleased by his reception and for many years, the Company was to maintain its connection with Lan Xang, but largely through the trading posts in the south.

Vientiane had by then become the centre of Lan Xang and about the time of van Wuysthoff's visit, Luang Prabang was a deserted town. An epidemic of cholera had been so severe that most of its inhabitants had fled, many of them to Vientiane and the other neighbouring trading centres along the Mekong.

The Pearl of Tran Ninh

IN 1651, SOME ten years after van Wuysthoff's visit, Chao Souligna Vongsa heard that the King of Muong Phoueune, Chao Kham Sanh, had a daughter, Princess Nang Ken Chan, who was renowned for her beauty and wisdom. So beautiful was she that she was known as the 'Pearl of Tran Ninh'. Inflamed by the descriptions he had received, he sent a message to his vassal ruler, asking for her hand in marriage.

To his extreme annoyance, Chao Kham Sanh replied that his daughter's hand was not free and he must decline the honour of such an alliance. Chao Souligna Vongsa pretending not to understand the reply, sent the princess very valuable presents. But by return Chao Kham Sanh sent another refusal. Angered by this, the king of Lan Xang despatched a small armed detachment to bring back the princess. It was ambushed and the whole force made prisoner.

The people of Muong Phoueune realising that worse was to follow began work on new fortifications for their capital, Xieng Khouang. Before they were finished, the Vientiane army of 2,000 men arrived. They brushed past the incomplete works, threw a bridge across the ramparts of the city and made the king a prisoner in his own palace.

He had no choice but to surrender and the Princess became a wife of Chao Souligna Vongsa. In revenge for their earlier defeat the Vientiane troops devastated the country and deported 500 families from Xieng Khouang to Vientiane. In modern times, there are still descendants of these people living in Vientiane who are referred to by their neighbours as the 'former P'uon'.

As well, Vientiane exacted new and harsher tribute, so that the former good relations with Xieng Khouang were replaced by hatred.

Alliance with the Sipsong Panna

TO THE NORTH in the Sipsong Panna were the Tai Lu, a people who retained all the fierceness of the original Tai. They made frequent raids against their neighbouring states and around 1673, they attacked the principality of Chiang Hung, which bordered the Mekong to the north of the present frontiers of Burma.

The ruler, Chao Intha Kumman and his sister, Princess Chanta Kummaly, fled and Chao Souligna Vongsa took them under his protection in Vientiane. Princess Chanta Kummaly married Chao Souligna Vongsa's only son, the Chao Rajaput, and she gave him two sons. These were Chao Kingkitsarat and Chao Inthasom. Her brother, Chao Intha Kumman, also married Nang Kham, one of the princesses of the Court, and by her he had a son, Chao Ong Nok.

It was soon after the birth of his second son, that the Chao Rajaput, Souligna Vongsa's only male heir, committed adultery with one of the

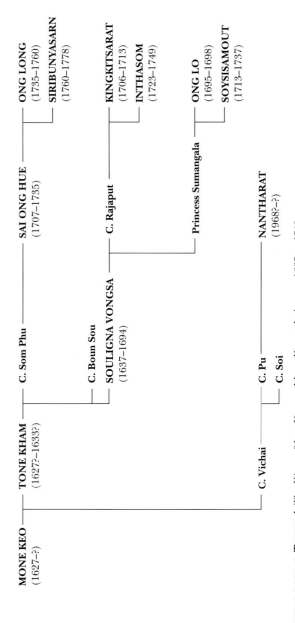

GENEALOGICAL TABLE 4 The Kings of Lan Xang – Mone Keo to Inthasom, 1627 to 1749

wives of a palace attendant. Her husband, Thao Ko, found out and lodged a complaint with the King in his capacity as Chief Justice. The king found his only son guilty and with his determination that justice must be respected by all levels of society, whatever the price to himself, he had his only son executed. With that one blow, he set in motion the terrible events that were to ensure the end of the kingdom of Lan Xang.

The Death of Souligna Vongsa

EXCEPT FOR THE expedition against Xieng Khouang, King Souligna Vongsa's reign was peaceful and brought much prosperity and cultural richness to the kingdom. He died between 1690 and 1694, aged about eighty or slightly more. He had not had another son after the Chao Rajaput so his only direct heirs were his two daughters, Nang Kumar and Nang Sumangala, and his two grandsons, Chao Kingkitsarat and Chao Inthasom. The grandsons were too young to accede and neither of the two daughters appears to have married a high-ranking noble as there is no mention of their being considered as queen consorts.

Hall wrote: 'this reign of the greatest of Laotian sovereigns was mainly distinguished by notable achievements in the traditional culture of the country. Music, architecture, sculpture, paintings, gold and silver work, basket work and weaving all flourished.'

Six claimants to the throne came forward and, taking advantage of the lack of any central authority, one of the most senior mandarins, known by the title of Phagna Muong Chan, or Tian Thala (1694), proclaimed himself king. To legitimise this act, he proposed marriage to Nang Sumangala, who may have been the younger of Chao Souligna Vongsa's two daughters.

Her husband, whose name is not known, had just died, or possibly had been killed on the orders of Phagna Muong Chan himself. Nang Sumangala angrily refused him. She had already had one son, Chao Ong Lo, by her husband and was bearing his second child. She therefore had good reason to refuse, but, with so much at stake, Phagna Muong Chan decided that so long as she was alive she was a threat to him and decided to have her killed.

If the Champasak Annals, as well as current beliefs in the South, are to be believed, he had an even stronger reason, since they say she was one of Chao Souligna Vongsa's wives. If this was so her elder son, Chao Ong Lo, would have had a very clear right to the throne.

The Flight of Princess Sumangala

In 1956, we were in Champasak and Chao Siromé gave us the southern version of these events. In this account King Souligna Vongsa was killed fighting the 'Chinese'. They were probably not ethnic Chinese, but mountain tribes from the Sipsong Panna and southern China. In this southern version, Nang Sumangala instead of being Chao Souligna Vongsa's daughter is his queen and she is befriended by the Abbot of Wat Phon Samet, *the wat on the small hill beside the samet tree*, in Vientiane. In this account the Abbot is referred to by the name of his Wat, although his real name was probably Phra Kru Nhot Keo. Phagna Muong Chan is not referred to by name, but is said to be a Chaomuong. There are other accounts but we thought the following narrative of Chao Siromé's had the engaging viewpoint of Lao oral tradition.

Here is Chao Siromé's account.

It appears that once in Vientiane there was a monk who could read men's minds. He was called Chao Phra Tan Prahon Khonsamik or more simply Phra Kon Ki Hom.

The kingdom was happy and contented. Perhaps the gods were jealous, so a great disaster came to it. The king of Vientiane was killed while fighting with his army against the Chinese. It happened that the widowed queen was in the very early stage of pregnancy and the Phra knew this. The king on his departure, had left one of the Chaomuongs, a commoner, as Regent and when the king was killed the Chaomuong, wishing to prolong his rule, asked the Queen to marry him.

However, as he was not of royal blood the queen refused. Soon after she found that she was with child. As soon as she knew, she told the Chaomuong that she intended to rule with the help of a Council until such time as her son, for the Phra had told her it would be a son, was old enough to rule by himself. She thought that the Chaomuong would then give up any ideas of his own blood forming a new dynasty.

But the Chaomuong was not going to give in so easily. Although he said he accepted the Queen's command, he began to spread a story at Court that the child the queen was carrying was not by the king, but by the Phra.

The Phra could read all the thoughts in the Chaomuong's mind, so being a man of peace he persuaded the queen with two hundred families to retire to a village in the south called Vang Vieng, *the fortified town*. There is no indication where this town was, but it is unlikely to be the modern town of Vang Vieng on the road to Luang Prabang.

The Phra stayed with the queen and her retinue until the son had been born. He then told the queen that he was going in search of a kingdom for her son and she must on no account leave the village until he returned.

In Search of a new kingdom

THE PHRA WITH some hermits began walking to the south. Wherever they came to a place that seemed to promise well as a future kingdom they stayed and meditated to discover whether it were truly auspicious or not. But nowhere proved suitable, so they travelled further and further south until they reached Phnom Penh. The new kingdom they sought was as far from discovery as ever. The Phra decided that they must return to the north by the Mekong and tell the queen that his mission had failed.

So they walked to the great falls of Khone and here, at last, they thought they had found the wished-for site. But after many months the Phra came to understand that it was not suitable and regretfully they began their journey upstream. By this time seven years had passed since they had left the queen.

As they were sailing along the Right Bank of the river, they came close to Champasak and stopped for a while. Here they found the queen who was reigning was unmarried. She was very strict, especially on matters pertaining to morality and had some years before promulgated a law that any unmarried girl who had an illegitimate child should be put to death, as well as the man responsible if he could be found.

Unfortunately for the queen the year before the Phra arrived she had invited the Prince of Thakhek to a state visit. The celebrations had both been magnificent and prolonged.

Perhaps the prince was exceptionally charming, or the weight of chastity and sovereignty proved too much. It may even be, that the prince was something of a bounder. But certainly within a few weeks of his departure the queen had to face the dawning consequences of his stay. She was by her own law condemned to death.

Collecting together only the most trusted of her maids-in-waiting she announced that she was going into a lengthy retreat. There in secret, the child, a girl, was born. Although this had been kept a secret from all her subjects, the Phra as soon as he saw the queen knew what had happened and realised immediately that it offered a solution to his problem. So he remained in Champasak and his wise advice soon won him the position of the queen's most trusted councillor.

The Beginnings of modern Champasak

ONE DAY THE queen offered him the whole country to make as his own. But the Phra refused and told her that he knew of the daughter she had kept secret. He suggested that, if he were to bring his Queen (Sumangala) and the young prince, her son, to Champasak, the prince and princess could be married. Perhaps the queen took a great deal of persuading, but, whatever the reason, it was another seven years before the Phra eventually left to return to the village near Vang Vieng to find his queen and her son.

So far the story is clear, even if historically parts of it are doubtful, but at this point tradition becomes vague and lacunal. Nang Sumangala, her son, the Phra and all her retinue came down to Champasak. Her son, who was by this time fifteen years old, immediately became king, but he never married the daughter of the Queen of Champasak.

Both she and her daughter are dropped from the story, leaving to history only the shadowy memories of the early part of their lives. Even their name is said to be forgotten, though one family still living in Champasak claims direct descent from the queen. The young king from whom the present House of Champasak is descended took the regnal name Chao Soysisamout. An account of King Soysisamout's reign is given in a later chapter.

The Overthrow of the Muong Chan

In Vientiane, Phagna Muong Chan soon found that he had little support, either at Court or abroad. People were frightened by his ruthless attacks on his opponents. The two grandsons of Souligna Vongsa, Chao Kingkitsarat and Chao Inthasom, left Vientiane secretly, either just before, or immediately after, he assumed the regency. They fled to Luang Prabang where they were safe for a while.

Phagna Muong Chan's days were, however, numbered, even though the different factions as usual found it impossible to unite behind a single candidate. Princess Sumangala posed no threat as she was safely out of the kingdom, but her elder son was not far from Vientiane having been hidden in the south, probably near to Nakhon Phanom. A majority of the nobles began to see him as their future king and within six months of Phagna Muong Chan usurping the throne, forces loyal to the young Prince Ong Lo had marched against Vientiane. They captured and executed Phagna Muong Chan and placed Chao Ong Lo (1694–1698) on the throne.

However, Chao Ong Lo failed to build up any substantial support and after only four years he was challenged by a Chao Nantharat. His army was defeated and he either committed suicide by taking poison, or was executed.

His successor, Chao Nantharat (1698) was the son of Chao Pu, a cousin of Chao Souligna Vongsa. Chao Pu had been among those exiled when

King Souligna Vongsa came to the throne. Chao Nantharat based his claim on his grandfather who was King Vichai, an uncle of Chao Souligna Vongsa. It was certainly a valid claim, but once again it did not have the support that would legitimise it. Within a short time, he was attacked and beaten by yet another descendant of the relatives who had been exiled by Souligna Vongsa. He was Chao Sai Ong Hue who, as we shall see, was to formally sign away the kingdom of Lan Xang.

CHAPTER EIGHT

The End of Lan Xang

THE NEW KING was Chao Sai Ong Hue (1698–1735). His father, Chao Som Phu, had been a brother of Chao Souligna Vongsa who had sent him into exile in Vietnam. He had finally chosen to live at the Court of Hué, where his son had grown up. It was from this capital city of central Vietnam that his son had taken his name. Chao Sai Ong Hue, tempted by the dynastic struggles in Vientiane, persuaded the Annamite king to give him an army of 9,000 men to capture the throne for himself. In exchange, he promised to recognise Annamite suzerainty over Lan Xang and to pay an annual tribute.

In 1698 Chao Sai Ong Hue reached an agreement with the king of Muong Phoueune that he might make use of his territory to launch his attack on Vientiane. He made camp at Xieng Khouang and waited for a propitious moment. When his soothsayers told him it had come, he marched down on Vientiane. He took Nantharat prisoner and executed him. He chose the name of Setthathirath II, but his reign was so undistinguished, unlike King Setthathirath's, that he is seldom, if ever, referred to by his regnal name. He remains in history as Chao Sai Ong Hue.

He appointed his half-brother, Chao Nong, as Oupahat of Luang Prabang. Chao Nong was the son of Chao Som Phu's widow who had remarried one of the loyal ministers who had accompanied him into exile. When the young grandchildren, Chao Souligna Vongsa's apparent heirs, learnt of the appointment of Chao Nong, they were afraid that the king would want to have them killed. Chao Kingkitsarat fled from Luang Prabang, with his supporters, to Muong Phong in the Sipsong Panna, while Chao Inthasom decided to look for safety in Muong Phrae, a place that has not been identified. It was probably also in the Sipsong Panna, but was not the large town in northeastern Thailand of that name today.

At first it seemed as though stability had at last returned to Lan Xang. But it soon became apparent that few of the principalities gave Chao Sai

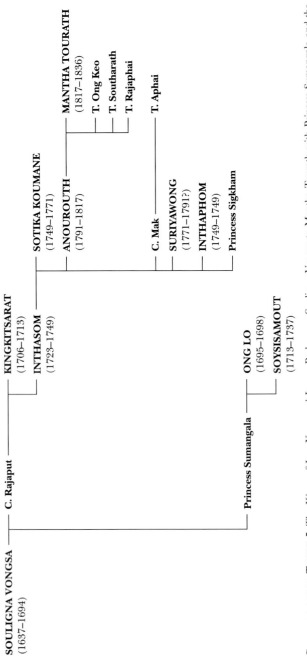

GENEALOGICAL TABLE 5 The Kings of Lan Xang and Luang Prabang – Souligna Vongsa to Mantha Tourath with Princess Sumangala and the beginning of the House of Champasak, 1637 to 1836

Ong Hue their wholehearted allegiance and, most of them went so far as to hate him for his vassalage to Vietnam. Much as this outside support might have made him unpopular, it was the power of Vietnam that made him secure on his throne. In 1705, he instructed his half-brother, Chao Nong, to send the Prabang statue and the Emerald Buddha by river from Luang Prabang to Vientiane where they were placed in Wat Pasak.

While he could control the South, Luang Prabang and other provinces in the north were a different matter. The next year, 1706, Chao Kingkitsarat obtained an army from the King of the Sipsong Panna and advanced on Luang Prabang. As soon as Chao Nong, the Oupahat, learnt of its approach, he fled to Vientiane leaving Luang Prabang undefended to be taken over by Chao Kingkitsarat (1706–1713). Encouraged by this sign of weakness, Chao Kingkitsarat decided to march on Vientiane and take the throne from his cousin.

Lan Xang is divided

THERE ARE TWO very different accounts of what happened next. The generally accepted version is that Chao Kingkitsarat was able to surround Vientiane but was not strong enough to capture it immediately. King Sai Ong Hue realised that he could not hold out for ever and sent a message secretly to the Siamese king, King Phetracha (1688–1703) to help him.

Lan Xang had for centuries been a rival to Ayudhya and King Phetracha astutely decided that he was being presented with the means to solve the problem for all time. He brought a large army to Vientiane, so strong that neither Chao Sai Ong Hue, nor Chao Kingkitsarat could individually be certain of repulsing it. King Phetracha then proposed that Lan Xang be divided into two kingdoms: those of Vientiane and Luang Prabang. Neither Lao king had the means to object and Chao Fa Ngum's mighty nation came to a sad and inglorious end. However there are serious discrepancies in this account as by 1707 King Phetracha, a usurper, was no longer on the throne and the Siamese king was then King Prachao Sua (1703–1709).

The Luang Prabang Annals give a very different account of how the country came to be divided. According to these, Chao Kingkitsarat wrote to Chao Sai Ong Hue pointing out that they were, after all, relatives and if either tried to take over the whole kingdom they would have to go to war, which would cause a great deal of deal of hardship for themselves and for their subjects. He therefore proposed that they divide Lan Xang between them. Chao Sai Ong Hue agreed and the final terms were that the north

ILLUSTRATION 13 Carved Doorway from a Wat in Luang Prabang

© Peter & Sanda Simms

and western frontier of Vientiane would be at the mouth of the Nam Heuang on the Right Bank of the Mekong, which is exactly where the Sayaboury frontier lies with modern Thailand today. The Left Bank, which is the northern side, was a few kilometres closer to Vientiane at the mouth of the Nam Mi, opposite present-day Nam Khan.

Vientiane demands Muong Phoueune pay tribute

IT WAS ALSO agreed that all the northern principalities, including Muong Phoueune, would owe allegiance to Luang Prabang and not to Vientiane. At that time the ties with Vientiane had grown so very tenuous as to be nonexistent. In fact, Muong Phoueune was considered by the Vietnamese as one of its prefectures and had taken the name, Tran Ninh, that is still used at times today.

This is according to the Luang Prabang Annals, but evidently Chao Sai Ong Hue did not accept that Muong Phoueune should pay tribute to Luang Prabang and, when it later refused to pay its tribute to Vientiane, he sent an army to enforce its payment.

As we have seen, the payment and receipt of tribute were a complex matter. In its grossest form it was a tax, often collected by troops from the sovereign state who were garrisoned there to ensure loyalty. However, when the sovereign power found its resources stretched, it would often confer the governorship on the king, or ruler, of the principality and the tribute might be reduced to more symbolic, but valuable objects. If the vassal kingdom were strong enough, the tribute would be called a formal gift between the two rulers.

The payment of tribute, or the giving of presents, was seldom, if ever, connected with a willing allegiance. Most allegiance existed only through fear of punishment if it were not given, or because it appeared to be in the vassal states' best interests. By the middle of the eighteenth century, the individual Lao kingdoms were simultaneously paying tribute, or sending gifts, to Burma, China, Siam and Vietnam.

Trouble from the South

FOR VIENTIANE TROUBLE did not only lie to the north. In the legendary days of Khun Boulom his sixth son, Chao Kom, had been given the land around present day Nakhon Phanom on the river bank opposite Thakhek. Here Chao Kom had founded his kingdom and from this, it has been said, came the name Khammouan, Chao *Kom's Muong.*

As we have seen, Chao Sai Ong Hue's assumption of the throne was not welcomed by the southern states. In 1709 the ruler of Nakhon Phanom, Phra Boulom Raja, rebelled and refused to send his tribute to Vientiane. Believing Vientiane to be too weak to resist his army, he marched against Vientiane and captured the two neighbouring towns of Vieng Kuk and Muong Say Fong, to the south and east of Vientiane on the banks of the Mekong.

The Boulom Raja's army was driven off but Chao Sai Ong Hue did not put down the rebellion until six years later in 1715 when he attacked and took Nakhon Phanom. Phra Boulom Raja was captured and died soon after. Vientiane appointed Khamsing, the son-in-law of the deceased ruler, as the Governor of the kingdom. Phra Boulom Raja's son, Chao Kukeo, afraid for his life, fled to the newly created kingdom of Champasak, where for many years he was to be a thorn in the side of Vientiane as he plotted to win back his father's throne.

Chao Ong Kham the new King of Luang Prabang

IN THOSE UNHAPPY days, it was not only Vientiane that suffered. In Luang Prabang, Chao Kingkitsarat died in 1713 and he was succeeded by his cousin, Chao Ong Kham (1713–1723), whose father was the uncle of the late King Kingkitsarat and Chao Inthasom. They had grown up together in the Sipsong Panna and were very close, the three of them were more like brothers than cousins. However when the news of Chao Kingkitsarat's death reached Chao Inthasom, he felt he had the stronger claim to his brother's throne. He collected an army and marched towards Luang Prabang. According to the Luang Prabang annals he stopped at Muong Ngoi on the Nam Ou. From there he sent an ultimatum demanding Chao Ong Kham renounce any claim. The fact that he had collected his army in the north would seem to prove that the Muong Phrae where he had taken refuge was in the Sipsong Panna, and was not the Muong Phrae in present-day Thailand

Chao Ong Kham was persuaded by his mandarins that he should not spill the blood of his cousin. So he went to Muong Ngoi and proposed to Chao Inthasom that they should share the throne of Luang Prabang. Chao Inthasom agreed and for ten years they managed to live together without trouble.

But then in 1723, Chao Inthasom was persuaded by some of his supporters that he with his greater claim should take over the kingdom. King Ong Kham was very fond of hunting turtle doves and Chao Inthasom chose a day when his cousin was out hunting. He had the gates of the city of Luang Prabang closed and proclaimed himself king.

Chao Inthasom declares himself king (1723–1749)

A VERY VIVID picture of this event has come down to us. Chao Ong Kham as he approached the city could hear a great deal of noise and shouting so he asked some people nearby what was happening. He was told that Chao Inthasom had declared himself king and that he had been locked out of the city. An impetuous person, his anger was so great that he crumpled up a gold cup he was holding in his hand. Then he turned away from Luang Prabang and told his courtiers that they could make up their own minds, either to stay with him or to return to the city.

Chao Ong Kham first went to a monastery some 80 kilometres on the way to Lan Na where he stayed for some years. He appears to have left his wives in Luang Prabang and at least three of his sons. Later, having become a monk he moved to Chiang Mai, which had an uneasy relationship with Burma and still had a Burmese governor to ensure its loyalty. When the King of Chiang Mai died, a Lao named Thep Sin who had gained a reputation as a holy man possessing supernatural powers, assassinated the Burmese governor and usurped the throne. He was very autocratic, and was particularly harsh against the Burmese residents.

The mandarins approached Chao Ong Kham, who had also acquired a reputation for having special powers, and asked him what he would do, were he king, about the Burmese residents and troops who were camped outside the city. He surprised them all by saying that he would do nothing as the Burmese would leave the next day. Impossible as it seemed, the next morning the Burmese were seen to break camp and march off. Chao Ong Kham (1727–1759) was thereupon made king of Lan Na where he reigned for some thirty-two years before dying.

Following Chao Ong Kham's departure, King Inthasom continued what was to be a largely peaceful reign. At some time, three of the sons of Chao Ong Kham, who had remained in Luang Prabang, tried to stage a coup against their uncle, but their plot was discovered and they were executed. Other than this, very little has been recorded about his reign. King Inthasom had fifteen children, four of whom were to become kings of Luang Prabang.

Luang Prabang sends Mission to China

IN THE 1690s China had become worried by the increasing influence of Burma on her border states and had mounted an operation against the Tai Lu of the Sipsong Panna to remind them who was their master. In 1723, the year of King Inthasom's accession, the king of the Sipsong Panna recommended to Chao Inthasom that he send a mission to China. This was a wise insurance policy as, in Chinese eyes, any mission sent to them was a tacit admission of China's suzerainty. As a vassal, the country would then be entitled to protection, if such protection were in China's interests.

Chao Inthasom seems to have believed that in any dispute with Burma China would, therefore, be willing to mediate on his behalf and be of help to Luang Prabang. Some ten years later, in 1734, Chao Inthasom sent a second mission to Peking in the hope of maintaining friendly relations.

China's concern over her southwest frontier was to be fully justified when in the 1750s Burma experienced a resurgence of military power under King Alaungpaya (1752–1760), a simple village headmen who became possessed by a determination to rebuild the former Burmese empire.

In the year of King Inthasom's death, an Annamite army advanced on Luang Prabang. His ninth son, Chao Inthaphom (1749), was given command of the Lan Xang army and in a successful battle scattered the Vietnamese invaders to the winds. On his return to Luang Prabang, he was offered the throne as a reward for saving the country. But for reasons that are not known, possibly under pressure by a faction within his family, he abdicated after only eight months in favour of his eldest brother, who took the regnal name Chao Sotika Koumane (1749–1771).

In 1735, Chao Sai Ong Hue, the King of Vientiane, died. He had never been a popular king and there were few regrets at his passing. He was succeeded by his son, Chao Ong Long (1735–1760). There is very little recorded of the events in Chao Ong Long's reign. Le Boulanger comments that the annals of Vientiane for the eighteenth and early nineteenth centuries were completely destroyed when the Siamese sacked the town in 1828. To make matters worse, then, and again later, its people were split up and taken away in captivity, so destroying any oral history that might otherwise have been preserved.

The Champasak Dynasty

CHAO FA NGUM had reduced the southern principalities to vassalage but the people remained a mixture of races of which the Lao formed only a small part. Champasak is first mentioned in AD 157 when it was a part of Champa and then Chenla. The town goes back more than 2,000 years. The oldest surviving buildings are to be found at nearby Wat Phu, where the ruins of a stone castle, wats, buildings and beautiful carvings can still be seen.

The first king of the new dynasty, King Soysisamout, died in 1737 and his son succeeded him as King Sayakoummane (1737–1780). Any previous ties to Vientiane through his grandmother, Princess Sumangala, had long been forgotten in the succession of kings, including his murdered uncle Chao Ong Lo, who had been enthroned in Vientiane.

Despite his distant relationship to the kings of Vientiane, Sayakoummane did not see himself as a vassal and, in the years to come, the failure of Chao Siribunyasarn as king of Vientiane to ensure binding ties with his, the Lao ruling family of Champasak, was eventually to lead Vientiane and Champasak into a number of confrontations that would destroy them both.

Siribunyasarn: Vientiane's new King

IN VIENTIANE, CHAO Ong Long was succeeded by his son, Chao Ong Boun, who took the name Chao Siribunyasarn (1760–1778). Within four years, he was faced with a rebellion in Nakhon Phanom as the troubles that his grandfather, Chao Sai Ong Hue, thought he had solved in 1715, flared up once again some 49 years later.

In 1764, Chao Kukeo who had been living in exile in Champasak collected together an army of 3,000 men and marched on Nakhon Phanom to win back his father's kingdom that had been given to Chao Khamsing to rule as a vassal king. Chao Khamsing immediately called for help from Annam and the Annamite king, never averse to mixing into Lao affairs, sent an army.

However, neither he nor Chao Khamsing was prepared for the wily Chao Kukeo. Taking his small army with him, Chao Kukeo went out to meet the Annamite army and convinced the Annamite general that *he*, Chao Kukeo, was the person the Vietnamese army had been sent to help. Together the 3,000 men belonging to Chao Kukeo with the 6,000 Vietnamese marched on Nakhon Phanom and took the city.

Belatedly, Chao Khamsing called on Vientiane for help. The Lao army arrived to find the Annamite troops, who having placed Chao Kukeo on the throne were returning victorious to Vietnam, in the act of crossing a river valley by a suspension bridge. Chao Siribunyasarn's troops managed to cut the bridge and so split the enemy army into two parts, which they then destroyed piecemeal. Only a few of the Vietnamese troops found their way back to Annam.

Chao Siribunyasarn realised that if he were to put his protégé, Chao Khamsing, back on the throne of Nakhon Phanom, he would have to garrison an army in the south. If he did this, he would not be able to

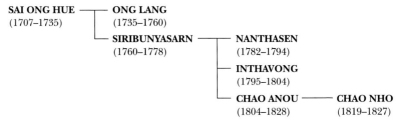

GENEALOGICAL TABLE 6 The Kings of Vientiane – Sai Ong Hue to Chao Anou with Chao Nho, King of Champasak, 1707 to 1828

continue his fight against his hated rival in Luang Prabang. He, therefore, decided to confirm Chao Kukeo as the ruler of Nakhon Phanom and brought Chao Khamsing and 3,500 of his followers back to Vientiane.

This was a wise move so far as Nakhon Phanom was concerned, but all that Chao Siribunyasarn gained by creating a peaceful solution in the south, was thrown away by his continuing war against Luang Prabang.

Even before Nandabayin died in 1599, the Burmese empire had been coming apart. One principality after another had rebelled and thrown off the Burmese rule. From the seventeenth century until the middle of the eighteenth century, Burma was too weak to present any threat to Lan Xang or Siam.

However, in 1752, a young man of good family from Shwebo named Alaungpaya rebelled against the Mon rulers and by the time of his death only eight years later he had reunited the whole of Burma under his rule. His son, Naungdawgyi (1760–1763) continued the consolidation of their rule until his death only three years later. It was not until he was succeeded by his brother, Hsinbyushin (1763–1776), that the new Burmese military machine was forged. With Burma united behind him, Hsinbyushin began to plan the re-creation of the former empire of Bayinnaung and the complete subjugation of the Tai world.

A fresh Burmese Invasion

BY THE BEGINNING of 1764, he had sent one army southwards to the Tavoy area, and in March he formed a new army composed of 100 elephants, 20,000 men and ten squadrons of cavalry of 1,000 horses. He sent this army under General Thihapate northwards first to Chiang Mai, which it entered before the rains set in. It remained there during the rainy season while it prepared for the invasion of Luang Prabang.

By this time the army had been considerably enlarged. The usual Burmese practice was to conscribe the strongest men, the best elephants and horses from each town or village they passed through. Each town had also to pay a levy to help maintain the army on the march. This system had the double advantage of bringing fresh men into the Burmese army, and, since it was the fittest local men who were chosen, only the old or unfit were left to form any resistance. In this way, only quite small garrisons had to be left behind to guard the lines of communication.

By November of that year, 1764, General Thihapate had two Burmese armies under his command, one of 25 regiments and one of 10 regiments. He ordered them both to march on Luang Prabang. King Sotika Koumane had fortified Luang Prabang and led a force of 1,000 elephants, 2,000 horses and 50,000 men in an attempt to drive away the Burmese.

It was in vain, the Lao army had to retire after suffering heavy losses. The Burmese claimed they had killed or captured more than 10,000 men. They executed them all and, cutting off the heads, made them into an horrendous pile and heaped them in front of the walls to terrify the inhabitants.

The capture of Luang Prabang

THE BURMESE FORCED their way across the Nam Khan, which formed one of the boundaries of the city, and, having built gun platforms, they shelled the town day and night. Even so, King Sotika Koumane and his people managed to hold out. However, Hsinbyushin had ordered his generals to take Ayudhya before the next monsoon and they could not start on the campaign against Ayudhya until they had captured Luang Prabang. Knowing what the penalty they each would pay if they failed to take Ayudhya on time, they decided to gamble everything on an all-out attack on Luang Prabang.

For this they ordered all thirty-five regiments to start building 'tortoises', which were sheds mounted on wheels with strongly reinforced roofs that they could push right up under the walls. Protected by these, they began to dig away at the foundations. Others brought up ladders ready to swarm into the town as soon as the defences fell.

Their efforts were successful and they managed to enter and capture half of the town and, bringing forward their guns, mounted them on the highest parts so that the rest of the town was under constant shell fire.

By March 1765, after nearly five months of siege, the short range and deadly fire had done so much damage and killed so many people, that

King Sotika Koumane sued for peace and offered to accept Burmese suzerainty. Also as was customary, he offered the royal princesses for King Hsinbyushin as a guarantee of peace.

The Burmese general, General Thihapate, administered the oath of allegiance to the King and took away the princesses. They were accompanied by the daughters of the principal ministers as maids-of-honour, and as well more than 1,000 slave attendants were taken. General Thihapate also seized more than 300 kgs. of silver, 75 kgs. of gold, 500 canons, 1,000 rifles, 100 elephants, 500 boxes and 500 ornamental coverings for elephants and horses.

Not content with the royal princesses, the Burmese also took into captivity the king's brother, who would later reign as King Suriyawong. There was never any doubt that the capture of Luang Prabang had been suggested by the king of Vientiane, King Siribunyasarn, and it was even possible that Vientiane troops had taken part in the siege. From this time on, Chao Suriyawong and the nobles of Luang Prabang detested Vientiane with a bitter hatred at their betrayal and were determined that, when the opportunity came, they would assist in the destruction of Vientiane.

Three Burmese Armies march on Ayudhya

THE MONSOON WAS approaching as three Burmese armies, one through Chiang Mai, the second through the Three Pagodas Pass, and the third from Tavoy, marched on Ayudhya. It was late in the year 1765 when they began to encircle the city.

By February 1766, Ayudhya was surrounded and the siege began in earnest. Even when the rains came, there was no respite for the Siamese. The Burmese had a large number of boats and kept themselves supplied without difficulty.

The siege dragged on and in 1767, the Burmese offered an honourable surrender, but wisely or not the Siamese king, Boromoracha V (1758–1767) refused. By this time General Taksin, a brilliant young Sino–Tai general, and some of his colleagues were completely opposed to the king's strategy for the war. Seeing disaster ahead, General Taksin decided to take 500 of his followers and break out through the Burmese lines. He was successful and established himself at Rayong where he became what today would be called the leader of a resistance movement.

Not long after Taksin's breakout, the Burmese attacked Ayudhya and in the final assault the unfortunate King Boromoracha disappeared and was never heard of again. Ayudhya was put to the sword. Anything worth plundering was taken, the palaces and houses were then burnt to the ground and the people led away to repopulate the villages of Burma. Some of the royal family survived, but they were so discredited by the ill-fated reign of Boromoraja that there was no popular support to reinstate them.

General Taksin rebuilds Siam

IN JUNE, TAKSIN captured Chanthaburi, some 250 kms to the southeast of today's Bangkok. In the anarchy that prevailed, thousands came to join his army. In October he was strong enough to sail up the Menam Chaophraya and recapture Dhonburi, the city opposite modern Bangkok. He considered advancing on Ayudhya, but his few resources seemed too small to risk recapturing what was only a collection of ruins.

Instead, General Taksin (1767–1782) decided to create a new capital and had himself crowned king in Dhonburi, which remained the capital until his death, when a new capital, today's Bangkok, was built on the other side of the river. General Taksin then embarked on what was to be a ten year war before the Burmese had been completely driven out of Siam.

In Vientiane, Chao Siribunyasarn watched Taksin gradually recovering the territory the Siamese had earlier lost to the Burmese. He decided that Taksin would be a useful ally, but as in all other matters, he made the great mistake of choosing the least possible action rather than committing himself to a consistent policy.

In 1770 the king began a correspondence with King Taksin, who promptly offered him an alliance against the Burmese. At the time when his help would have been of incalculable benefit to Taksin, Chao Siribunyasarn not merely withheld it, but, worse, still dallied with the Burmese, who were, if he could only have seen it, his and Taksin's only dangerous enemies. King Taksin who had welcomed an alliance with Vientiane, gradually lost faith in king Siribunyasarn's integrity and was later to refuse him help when it was most needed it.

The Return of Chao Suriyawong

ABOUT THIS TIME, the Burmese decided to entrust to their former prisoner Chao Suriyawong and his 600 followers with an army to pacify some of the Sipsong Panna muongs. As soon as it was possible, Chao Suriyawong and his followers slipped away from the Burmese army, and entering the Sipsong Chau Tai, made their base in Muong Thene, modern

Dien Bien Phu. It was from there that Khun Boulom had first started his sons on their journeys to found the Tai nations.

From there Chao Suriyawong sent a letter to his brother, King Sotika Koumane asking permission to return to Luang Prabang. The King brusquely refused, so Chao Suriyawong and his nobles formed an army from the local people and came down secretly to Luang Prabang. They scaled the walls one night and took over the city.

The King managed to flee to Pak Lay, downstream on the Mekong from Luang Prabang. According to the Luang Prabang annals, Princess Sigam Kham, a sister of both the King and Chao Suriyawong stayed behind and made her rebel brother swear an oath that he would not hurt his brother, the king. When she was satisfied, she told King Sotika that he should return and resume the throne, but it is not certain whether he did and, if he did, for how long. What is known is that in 1771 he abdicated in favour of Chao Suriyawong (1771–1779).

Once crowned king, Chao Suriyawong had only one objective: to avenge himself on Vientiane for the instigating the Burmese capture of the capital in 1765 and for the wasted years he had spent as a prisoner in Burma.

Within a year, Chao Suriyawong had mounted an army and marched on Vientiane. Looking for help in the wrong direction, Chao Siribunyasarn asked the Burmese to come to his rescue. Hsinbyushin sent an army and Chao Suriyawong retreated to Luang Prabang. Vientiane was saved for the moment, but King Taksin became suspicious of Chao Siribunyasarn's true motives and from then on was more conscious of his refusal to act against the Burmese, than of his protestations of friendship.

King Siribunyasarn faces a Revolt

BUT BEFORE CONTINUING, we have to return to the very beginning of King Siribunyasarn's reign. Since an eldest son does not have a right to succeed his father, but can only be enthroned by the consent of his family in concert with the important nobles, a new king often discovered that after accepting the crown he was expected to repay his obligations to those who had helped him to the throne. King Siribunyasarn found himself in just this predicament. Two nobles named Phra Vorarat and Phra Ta believed that it was only through their support that Chao Siribunyasarn had obtained the throne. They, therefore, expected high office and large rewards. When Chao Siribunyasarn gave his half brother, Chao Khuang Na, the highest office as Oupahat, and they were not offered anything they thought worthy of the help they had given, they became intensely angry.

They left Vientiane and within six years they had created an autonomous state near modern Udorn Thani in territory that Vientiane considered its own. This angered Chao Siribunyasarn and he sent an army to attack them. After three long years of battle Phra Vorarat and Phra Ta realised they could not hold out much longer and they asked the Burmese to send an army to help them.

King Siribunyasarn heard of this, and being on friendly terms with the Burmese king was able to persuade him not to help the rebels. In the meantime, Phra Ta was killed in the fighting and Phra Vorarat's army was defeated.

Phra Vorarat with his son and three of Phra Ta's sons fled to a muong near Champasak. They asked for asylum from Chao Sayakoummane (1738–1778), the Champasak king, who saw no reason why he should withhold his protection from them. They settled down and in two years, by 1768, they had built a new capital and once again Phra Vorarat proclaimed himself an independent ruler.

Annoyed by this, King Siribunyasarn entered into an alliance with the ruler of Nakhon Ratchasima, modern Korat, which was then under the suzerainty of Ayudhya. A combined army from Ratchasima and Vientiane attacked Phra Vorarat who, unable to defend his capital, fled to Don Mote Daeng in the province of modern Ubol Ratchathani. He once again asked for protection and accepted the suzerainty of Champasak.

For the moment there was a stalemate, then in 1771 Chao Siribunyasarn sent an army to capture Vorarat, but King Sayakoummane sent out his Champasak army with a letter to Chao Siribunyasarn asking him to spare Phra Vorarat. Chao Siribunyasarn not wishing to fight Champasak, agreed to leave Phra Vorarat alone.

King Sayakoummane enlarges his Capital

ABOUT 1777, CHAO Sayakoummane started to extend and beautify his capital and Vorarat who had some skill as an architect came to Champasak to help. His contribution was to rebuild the walls of the city. A great festival was held to celebrate the new magnificence of the capital. Phra Vorarat was tactless enough to ask King Sayakoummane whether he did not think the wall he had built was better than the audience hall another had built. When the king said that while each had its purpose, he and his court could use the audience hall for their amusement, so if he had to choose between the two, he preferred the audience hall.

121

Phra Vorarat, ever his own worst enemy, was overwhelmed by rage and left Champasak and returned to his new capital. From there he sent his son, Thao Kan, to pledge allegiance to King Taksin, the Siamese king, and enemy of Champasak.

When Chao Siribunyasarn heard of the split with Champasak, he ordered Vorarat to be attacked. Not surprisingly when King Sayakoummane was asked for help by Vorarat, he refused. Chao Siribunyasarn's army captured Vorarat and executed him. His son was fortunate enough to escape capture by Chao Siribunyasarn's army. Wishing to cause trouble and confusion, he sent messages to King Taksin claiming his protection and informing him that the King of Vientiane was plotting with the Burmese against him.

King Taksin loses his patience with King Siribunyasarn

KING TAKSIN WAS glad to have an excuse to pick a fight with Chao Siribunyasarn. Having reconquered his own country, he saw no reason why he should not extend his boundaries to include those of his northern Tai neighbours.

In 1778, the Siamese advanced into Champasak and the Vientiane general, who had captured Chao Vorarat's capital, retreated northwards with his army. Chao Sayakoummane was deposed by the Siamese and sent to Bangkok until peace was restored.

King Taksin then decided on a two pronged attack. General Chakri mobilised his army around Nakhon Ratchasima and marched directly against Vientiane, while General Surasi leaving a garrison in Champasak used a flotilla of boats on the Mekong as support for his land army in its march northwards to Vientiane.

Nakhon Phanom was captured followed by all the river ports to Nong Khai. Muong Pak Ho and Vieng Kuk both resisted until Chaophraya Surasi beheaded a large number of his prisoners and, placing the heads on rafts, he had them floated down to rest on the river banks before the two towns. The terrified inhabitants decided to surrender. Vientiane, however, was made of tougher material and prepared itself for a long siege.

Luang Prabang joins Siam in attack on Vientiane

BY 1779, THE Siamese had encircled Vientiane helped by a Luang Prabang army sent by King Suriyawong, who the year before had become an ally of Siam against Vientiane.

Vientiane managed to hold out for four months when, for no reason that is known, King Siribunyasarn with two of his sons and some other members of the Royal Family fled the city.

His son, Chao Nanthasen, who had been in charge of the defences was so demoralised that he opened the gates of the city and let the Siamese army in. This act of surrender did not mitigate the horrors that were then wreaked on the kingdom. Chao Nanthasen, his sister Nang Keo Nhot Fa Kanlayani, whom Chao Siribunyasarn had at one time offered in marriage to Taksin, and other members of the Royal Family, as well as most of the Court, were taken as prisoners to Bangkok. Following the capture of Vientiane, there may well have been an interregnum (1778 to 1781) while it was administered by a Siamese governor.

According to contemporary accounts, the sacking of Ayudhya by the Burmese was nothing compared to what was done to Vientiane. A Siamese Governor was installed and the Prabang and the Emerald Buddha were immediately taken across the river and then sent down to Bangkok. All the citizens and thousands of those in the Vientiane region were linked together by plaited bamboos threaded through the palms of their hands. They were led across the river and taken down to the plateau lands around Korat. Here they became part of the Lao Isarn community that still live there today.

General Taksin, having achieved his major objectives of subduing Champasak and Vientiane, could not resist extending his frontiers even further. Although King Suriyawong had been an ally, he demanded that he acknowledge Bangkok's suzerainty and become a vassal king. Faced by the large Siamese army, Chao Suriyawong was forced to accept.

Luang Prabang and Vientiane become Siamese vassals

GENERAL TAKSIN'S SUCCESS in battle continued. By 1776, he had driven the Burmese out of Siam and conquered their only remaining areas of influence: Vientiane and Luang Prabang. For King Taksin his conquests came too late for him to enjoy them. Within two years, 1778, he began to suffer from bouts of madness. When this happened no one was safe, so that those around him became afraid that they might be accused of being a traitor and be executed.

General Taksin will always be honoured as the saviour of the country after the fall of Ayudhya, but he was not a member of the Siamese aristocracy and it was only to be expected that when his mental powers began to fail, the Court would look for a Siamese to replace him.

On 6 April 1782, General Chakri, was offered the throne. He took the regnal name Rama I (1782–1809) and was the founder of the present Chakri dynasty. Officially, General Taksin died in 1782, but in some secret accounts, it is said that out of respect for his great achievements a beautiful palace was built for him in the Isthmus of Kra and he was kept there in comfort until he died at the beginning of nineteenth century.

Chao Siribunyasarn was allowed to return to Vientiane in 1780, probably without any powers. He died the next year and in 1781 the Siamese allowed his son, Chao Nanthasen, to return to Vientiane with the Prabang, which General Taksin thought had brought Siam bad luck. The Emerald Buddha remained in Bangkok and is there to this day. Chao Nanthasen (1781–1794) was enthroned and ruled for twelve years in Vientiane. At the same time (1781) King Sayakoummane was sent back to Champasak as a vassal king.

Siamese agree to Chao Anourouth becoming King

In 1791, THE year Chao Suriyawong died, the Sena (King's Council) of Luang Prabang went to Bangkok to request permission for the crown to be given to Chao Anourouth (1791–1817), who was the second son of King Inthasom. This was agreed by Rama I. A year later in 1792, Chao Nanthasen, King of Vientiane was able to persuade Rama I that Chao Anourouth had been treating with the Burmese and obtained permission to attack Luang Prabang.

Chao Nanthasen resorted to treachery to achieve his objective. He secretly had a letter taken to the Queen Mother, Nang Taen Kham, the widow of King Suriyawong, saying that if she would open the gates he would give her the crown of Luang Prabang. She sent a message back that arrangements had been made for the South Gate to be opened as soon as his troops attacked after dark. This happened as planned and Luang Prabang fell within fifteen days of the Vientiane troops' arrival.

King Anourouth, Chao Mak, the Oupahat and Chao Mantha Tourath, the Rajavong with their families were sent as prisoners to Bangkok, where they were to remain for four years. At the same time, Rama I ordered the recruitment of thousands of Lao to be brought to work on the building of the canals that were to earn Bangkok the title of the 'Venice of the East'. The work was hard and the Lao were not well fed so that very many of them died.

Vengeance leads to Destruction of the two Kingdoms

ONLY TWO YEARS later, Chao Nanthasen, in his turn, with the ruler of Nakhon Phanom which was a Siamese vassal state, was accused of treachery. He was called to Bangkok where he remained a prisoner for the last year of his life.

He was succeeded by his brother Chao Inthavong (1795–1804), who had fled with his father King Siribunyasarn just before Vientiane surrendered to the Siamese in 1782. In both 1797 and in 1802, the Burmese sent large armies into Siam, but Rama I managed to fight them off, aided by Vientiane and some of the principalities in the north. He also helped the Siamese in their attempt to win control of the Sipsong Chau Tai, especially around Muong Thene, Dien Bien Phu. In these battles the third son of King Siribunyasarn, Chao Anou, played a conspicuous part on the Siamese side and won a name for himself as a general

To strengthen the alliance, Chao Inthavong gave a daughter to Rama I as one of his queens. This family alliance may be one reason for the close affinity between Rama II and Chao Anou when he became king. It may also have been one of the contributing factors in the disagreements between Rama III and Chao Anou. Saveng remarks that according to Vietnamese chronicles, Chao Anou may have believed that one of his grandsons who was living at the Bangkok Court was assassinated in the power struggle after Rama II's death.

Chao Anou was to be the last king of Vientiane and has, in this century, become something of a folk hero. Tiao Souphanouvong, who joined the procommunist independence party in 1945, called his second son after him. Chao Anou's attempts to retrieve the fortunes of his kingdom, form the greater part of the next chapter.

CHAPTER NINE

The rise of Nationalism

ALTHOUGH IT WAS not apparent at the time, the last decade of the eighteenth century saw the end of a way of life founded on customs, traditions and the concepts of monarchy that went back to the times of Chao Fa Ngum. In European terms, the transition was comparable to that experienced when the Tudor and Caroline Ages slowly and painfully developed into the beginnings of modern Europe.

From the times of Chao Fa Ngum the Tai kingdoms of Lan Xang, Lan Na, and Siam were political entities in name only. Each kingdom was, in reality, a group of independent Tai muongs, joined together partly by force and partly by any temporary advantages they might derive from an alliance. The primary loyalties of the muongs were always to themselves. They had no intention of giving up their independence permanently. Even in the times of the strong kings such as Chao Fa Ngum, Lan Xang was still only a loose conglomeration bound together by a mixture of force and self interest. The individual chiefs never doubted their unquestionable right to give, or rescind, their allegiance as it suited them.

It must also be remembered that the innumerable wars over the centuries were not usually started in order to gain territory. The Burmese and Tai regions were generally underpopulated and probably the most important objectives of a war were either to repatriate people who had been forcibly taken away, or to deport the inhabitants of towns and villages with the dual purpose of augmenting your own population and by taking people away to reduce its strength of your enemy. Strategically, the greatest achievement was to depopulate whole regions, leaving only a waste land along the borders.

To this basic need for increased manpower, another factor, unrecognised as such, had become a part of eighteenth century politics. This was the growth of a new form of nationalism and racial antagonism. It was a development that in many respects may be equated with the spontaneous postwar creation of the two superpowers: America and Russia.

The culmination came in 1787, with the Burmese capture of Ayudhya, and the complete devastation of the capital. It destroyed the old royal family as an entity, it razed their capital, removed its entire population, shattered its administration and demolished its position as a centre of power. So complete was the destruction that when the Siamese began to recover they found that they had to start from scratch. The former capital was not worth rebuilding, the former dynasty comprised only distant relatives whose claims would have the subject of countless disputes, the former army had melted away except for the five hundred men that had broken out of Ayudhya under General Taksin. The old order had been obliterated.

It was General Taksin, a Chinese mercenary, and his 500 followers who were to rebuild the country from the very roots up. He set about re-conquering the territory seized by the Burmese, who in 1766 without any previous warning had to bring a large part of their armies back to Burma to protect their country against an invasion by China. In reinstating their control over their southwestern frontiers, the Chinese had decided to reduce Burma once again to a vassal state.

During the first invasion, the Chinese were within thirty miles of Ava. However, the Burmese were able to turn them back and, thanks to the jealousies between the Chinese generals, they inflicted a number of defeats on the two Chinese armies. By December 1769, the Chinese had agreed to sign a treaty with Burma. Hsinbyushin only survived that crisis to be faced with very serious internal problems. As a result, he could not divert sufficient resources to prevent General Taksin's gradually recovering all of the lost Siamese territory.

General Taksin set out to achieve what is still one of the main pillars of Thai policy today: the welding of the Tai peoples into one nation under Siamese rule. The Burmese had failed to dominate Ayudhya, Lan Na and Lan Xang. General Taksin was determined he would at last achieve this evanescent Siamese dream.

General Taksin's new form of nationalism was to be based not only on armed conquest, but what is more important, on a much greater centralised control of the newly captured territories. It was to take the remaining years of the eighteenth century and the death of King Taksin before Siam had the ability to begin turning itself into the regional superpower.

The Rebuilding of the Kingdom of Vientiane

SUCH A CONCEPT was not, could not possibly have been, obvious to the new king of Vientiane, King Anouvong (1804–1828). Unknowingly, he had

ILLUSTRATION 14 Wat Prakeo, Vientiane

entered a new power game for which the rules were only gradually being evolved. It was, and would be for the next century, in Bangkok where the rules were decided and only by Bangkok that they were enforced.

The Vientiane king who was to find himself enmeshed in this new, undeclared game was the third son of King Siribunyasarn. As a young man it was obvious that he was intensely ambitious, but this fault was tempered by his bravery and his success as a battle-tried general. He had also been trained to rule. His elder brother, King Inthavong had made him his Maha Oupahat and, following tradition, had given him command of his armies. In the nine years of his brother's reign Chao Anou extended the boundaries of the Vientiane kingdom and brought peace and stability to the country. He had just completed a successful campaign against Chiang Saen when his brother died. He returned triumphantly to Vientiane to be given the throne by the Siamese king, Rama I (1782–1809). It should be remembered that Vientiane was still a vassal state and Lao victories were ultimately victories on the behalf of Bangkok.

As king, Chao Anouvong's ambitions reached beyond the mere command of armies. In his first year, 1805, he built a new palace in

128

Vientiane and began the creation of a revitalised religious, artistic and commercial life for his people. At that time, the kingdom of Vientiane, Sisatanakhanahud, comprised some seventy-nine different principalities and Anouvong was determined to bind them together, not merely by force of arms, but by creating joint interests brought about through the fostering of trade, the building of bridges, and improving the roads.

In 1816, as part of his determination to demonstrate the greatness of his kingdom, he presided over the inaugural ceremonies for the Temple of the Emerald Buddha and its library that he had built in Vientiane.

Chao Anou and Rama II: a special relationship

HIS ACUMEN GAINED him the respect of the Siamese king, Rama II (1809–1824), who took particular care of the palace in Bangkok that he had assigned to Anouvong. Rama II personally ensured that everything about the palace was worthy of a vassal king of the great Siamese nation. He was responsible for having a lake within the grounds of the palace enlarged, cleaned, and stocked with fish. In 1820 he was pleased to write to Chao Anou telling him about how the lake and the palace grounds were being improved.

In 1818, Chao Anou put down a rebellion in the kingdom of Champasak that, as a frontier state with Annam, was of considerable importance to Siam. When peace had been restored, he asked Rama II for permission to install his son, Chao Nho as King of Champasak, and his nephew, Chao Khampom, as Oupahat. There was very considerable opposition to this in the Court at Bangkok.

Some of the nobles argued that it gave too much power to Vientiane. They pointed out that it was extremely dangerous for any vassal state to have such power. With his son and nephew as rulers, Chao Anou would control two of the three most important of Siam's frontiers. They were especially important as both Cambodia and Annam were unfriendly states.

Rama II, placing his trust in his friendship with Chao Anouvong, overruled this Court faction. While Rama II lived, they were silenced, but they were not convinced. Later when the opportunity came they took their revenge and were able to humiliate King Anou so greatly that his tempestuous character found it impossible to accept the indignity they imposed on him.

In 1825 Rama II died. The result was to prove catastrophic for Chao Anou. It was at about this date that a series of natural disasters struck Vientiane. They became so closely associated in people's minds with the death of Rama II that it is now impossible to determine whether they took place at the time of his death, or during the two succeeding years. Whichever it was, they were to be auguries of misfortune for both the king of Vientiane and his realm.

Vientiane Warned

THE FIRST DISASTER was a violent storm that caused great damage to the whole of Vientiane and, most sinisterly, broke the summit of the newly constructed temple of the Emerald Buddha. A month later this was followed by a second terrible storm that damaged the royal palace. As though this were not enough, two months later an earthquake shook the capital.

During 1825, Chao Anou and several hundred members of his Court were invited to attend the funeral of Rama II. When Chao Anou arrived it was to find a very different atmosphere to the one he had known during the reign of Rama II. No longer was the new Siamese king anxious to see that Chao Anou had the best of everything, nor that his palace was maintained at the height of excellence. Instead, during the year long ceremonies, Rama III (1824–1851) demanded that King Anou employ his Lao retinue on public works that were turning Bangkok into a great city. Not without reason, Chao Anou thought these were undignified activities for those accompanying his mission.

To escape further indignities, using the excuse that the rainy season was approaching, Chao Anou requested permission from Rama III to return to Vientiane. He also made three additional requests: that Rama III allow him to take with him the dancing girls and artists that had been provided for his palace, secondly that a Princess Duang Kham, who was of Lao origin might return to Vientiane with her entourage and, thirdly, that the Lao families who had earlier been brought forcibly to the town of Saraburi, be allowed to return with him.

Custom of taking the robe on the death of a sovereing monarch

WHILE RAMA III was undoubtedly to prove at fault, Chao Anou was not blameless. On the death of a sovereign king, it was the custom for the vassal kings to behave as though their own father had died. This entailed taking the robe, that is to say to become a Buddhist monk, for a period that might be anything from a few days to a month or a year. So far as a vassal king was concerned this act had subtle, but important, consequences. No monk may also be simultaneously a king and a monk. So behaving as though a sovereign king was one's father entailed giving up the crown whilst a monk. But, on returning to lay life, as a vassal king, one could not take back one's crown without the permission of one's new sovereign. So the whole procedure entailed first of all surrendering the recognition that one was the vassal king and then accepting the crown back from the new king with any new conditions he might demand. Chao Anou had not done this.

In considering Chao Anou's requests, Rama III may have compared his behaviour with that of King Mantha Tourath of Luang Prabang (1817–1836). Before leaving Luang Prabang, Chao Mantha Tourath had handed over the administration of the kingdom to a council. This was an indication that he would be away for a considerable time and had temporarily given up his royal power to his Oupahat, or to his Sena. On arrival in Bangkok, he had sought permission to be ordained a monk for a year and offered the merit for this act to the dead king, Rama II.

At the end of the ceremonies, Chao Mantha Tourath probably wished to leave just as much as Chao Anou did, but he could see the political advantages of remaining and he was to stay for an additional year. He only sought permission to return in late 1826 when an epidemic that had broken out in Luang Prabang provided him with a good reason. Further, as a pledge for his future good behaviour, he left behind one of his sons, Chao Pho Nua Thong, to be trained as an official in the Siamese administration.

Chao Anou plans war against Siam

WHETHER IT WAS the unfavourable impression created by Chao Anou compared with that of King Mantha Tourath, or the faction at the Siamese Court who had opposed his son becoming King of Champasak, all of Chao Anou's requests, except to return to Vientiane, were refused. Chao Anou left not merely regretting the loss of his former patron Rama II, but also nursing a bitter grievance against his new overlord.

Once back in Vientiane he called a council of his Ministers and some of the rulers from his seventy-nine principalities. He told them that he had observed while in Bangkok that Rama III had very few experienced leaders in his government. As well, he did not believe that the Siamese army would be very effective. He therefore proposed that Lan Xang attack and capture Bangkok and take over the government.

At the time, the ruler of Nakhon Ratchasima, a major town on the route to Bangkok, was leading an expedition on behalf of Rama III against

Khmer rebels was not at the meeting so his opinion was not known. However, other rulers whose states were also on the planned invasion route were not at all pleased by the suggestion.

Even Anou's half-brother and Maha Oupahat, Chao Titsah, was against the plan saying that Bangkok was so large that they would never be able to control it, even if they defeated the Siamese army.

Chao Anou, however, was not to be held back. He was prepared to consider this a possibility, but pointed out that if they were unable to control Bangkok, the Lao army could always retreat back to Vientiane. As the route back over the Korat plateau was dominated by a series of narrow passes, the Lao could ambush any Siamese army that tried to follow them and so harass the Siamese that their forces would have to give up their pursuit.

Undeterred by the inauspicious auguries that had only recently struck Vientiane, King Anou began to lay out a vast plan of attack that would encompass the whole of the south of Laos and the Siamese territory to the north of Bangkok.

The area of operation he had chosen was the Korat plateau, which covered an area of more than 60,000 square miles, being approximately 250 miles wide by 250 miles deep. In the Northwest corner, on the northern side of the Mekong river lies Vientiane. The Mekong forms the northern boundary before turning south separating the plateau from the principality of Khammouan and the furthest south of the Lao territories, the kingdom of Champasak. The southern edge of the plateau is formed by a range of mountains that mark the frontiers of Cambodia.

To the west of the plateau is another range of mountains that runs parallel to the Siamese river valley system. In the very southwest corner lies the main pass that joins the plateau to Saraburi only 75 miles, as the crow flies, from Bangkok.

The centre and eastern parts of the Korat Plateau are called the Pak Isarn and from this has come the name *Lao Isarn* given to the hundreds of thousands of Lao who formed, as do their descendants today, the majority of the population. They came to live originally either as colonisers of the Lan Xang empire, or they had been forcibly deported there by the Siamese in the previous century.

The Pak Isarn, or Korat Plateau, is a bare, level laterite plain whose poor soil is difficult to farm. On the whole it provides only a bare level of sustenance to the villages scattered across it. Most of the Pak Isarn was under the nominal rule of Vientiane, with Champasak forming its eastern flank and the rebellious Khmer to the south, Chao Anou's experience as a military commander told him it was the best base for his peremptory strike against Bangkok.

Order of Battle for the three Lao Armies

CHAO ANOU ASSIGNED the whole of the middle region of the Korat plateau to his half brother Chao Titsah, the Maha Oupahat, who was to raise an army and then join the main force at Nakhon Ratchasima. At this stage Chao Anou had not realised, or had decided to ignore, the very strong feelings that Chao Titsah held over the whole question of invading Siam.

The southern region Chao Anou gave to his son Chao Nho, King of Champasak. Starting from Champasak, Chao Nho was to march northwards collecting troops in the Khammouan on the east bank of the Mekong up to the Vientiane region. From there he was to turn south and march down to join Chao Titsah in Nakhon Ratchasima.

As soon as these plans were under way, Chao Anou sent fifty officials to King Mantha Tourath in Luang Prabang proposing he join in what would be a war for independence for the two kingdoms. Chao Mantha Tourath was fifty-two years old and no longer youthful. He had decided on a policy of conciliation with Bangkok and had no intention of changing this at the request of his traditional enemy, Vientiane. He chose prudence, promising King Anou's delegation that he would be willing to join him, but as soon as the delegation had left he sent his son, Chao Soukhaseum, to Bangkok to warn Rama III of the impending attack. A warning that Rama III appears to have ignored.

Chao Anou leaves Vientiane for the battle

ON 17 FEBRUARY 1827, Chao Anou joined his army of 8,000 men across the Mekong at Ban Phan Phao where he held manoeuvres and waited for the auspicious moment to depart. Ban Phan Pao, the village of a *Thousand Coconut Trees*, should have been an auspicious starting point as it was the village where the legendary Naga of Seven Heads, told Prince Desartha that he and his followers should cross the river and found a city that would be of great renown. This they did and the city later became Vientiane.

Chao Anou sent his younger son Chao Ngao with 3,000 men as an advance guard to secure Nakhon Ratchasima. The ruler of Nakhon Ratchasima was still absent, fighting the Khmer rebels, so Chao Ngao was able to take command of the city. His first action was to order the evacuation of the townspeople to Vientiane, which it is said was completed in the amazingly short period of four days.

Chao Anou arrived with his army and once again sent his son, Chao Ngao, ahead of him, this time to Saraburi to inform the Siamese officials that the British were advancing on Bangkok and that Chao Anou had come to the defence of Rama III and they should send all their Lao people to Vientiane.

That Chao Anou's deception worked can only mean that Chao Mantha Tourath's warning had not been believed by Rama III and surprise was still on the side of Chao Anou. But this was not to last for long.

The Maha Oupahat deceives Chao Anou

CHAO TITSAH, CHAO Anou's half brother and Maha Oupahat, despite his reservations about the war, had raised an army and marched to Suwannaphum one of the towns on the eastern edge of the Korat plateau. Here by chance he met a Siamese noble, Suriya Phakdi, who was taking a census for Rama III. Chao Titsah, foreseeing probable defeat ahead, decided that he might become king of Vientiane if he were to secretly change sides. He confided in Suriya Phakdi all his brother's plans and, providing him with a safe-conduct, sent him off to Bangkok.

Suriya Phakdi had to pass through Nakhon Ratchasima. There, possibly at the suggestion of Chao Titsah, he asked to see the King. He said he wanted to take his family to Vientiane and begged to be allowed to go on to Bangkok to collect them. Chao Anou accepted his story. Suriya Phakdi was told to assure Rama III that the ruler of Nakhon Ratchasima had oppressed his people and that he, King Anou, was only there to redress their complaints.

However when Suriya Phakdi reached Dong Phagna Fai, near Saraburi, he was taken to Chao Ngao, King Anou's son, who wished to arrest him immediately. Unfortunately for the future of Vientiane, his officials persuaded him that his father, the king, would see such an action as impeaching his royal decision. Reluctantly, Chao Ngao allowed Suriya Phakdi to continue his journey and who was then able to inform Rama III of the real intentions of the Lao.

The plight of the displaced Lao families

MUONG DONG PHAGNA Fai is an example that has come down to us of the terrible suffering the people of Laos have been through. Chao Ngao reported that he had found in the whole muong only ten Siamese families, some twenty Chinese, and ten thousand Lao people. The ten thousand may be an overestimate, but there is no doubt that the vast majority of the population were Lao. Since it had never been part of Lan Xang, they must have been among those who had earlier been deported by the Siamese. Chao Ngao organised their evacuation and they were sent back to Nakhon Ratchasima to await an escort for their journey to Vientiane.

If the first blow to Chao Anou's plans had been the treachery of his half-brother, the Maha Oupahat, the second and fatal blow came from the complexity of his plans and the great length of time required to bring his three large armies together. In an age not noted for individual loyalty, it was virtually impossible that he could have directed so massive an attack against Bangkok without news being passed to Rama III. It was only amazing that the covert preparations apparently remained secret for so long.

From the arrival of Phya Suriya Phakdi in Bangkok, Chao Anou's plans began to fall apart. Either the ruler of Nakhon Ratchasima, or his Oupahat, returned to the city to find that he was about to be stripped of the major part of his population and, therefore, his power. Realising that he was completely at the mercy of Chao Anou, he chose to dissimulate his real feelings and begged to be allowed to supervise the evacuation. This was granted and he set off towards Vientiane in charge of the people being repatriated.

As soon as he was safely beyond the immediate reach of Chao Anou's army, he had the Lao guards drugged and killed. He then armed his people and went into hiding. A few of the Lao escort managed to escape and they went back to Chao Anou, who sent fifty soldiers to investigate.

When they did not return, Chao Anou sent 3,000 more under the command of his youngest son, Chao Suthisan, but they were so vigorously attacked that Chao Suthisan thought that the Nakhon Ratchasima army had returned from its campaign and he decided to retreat.

On the 3 March, Rama III sent a detachment of troops forward to Saraburi to await the arrival of the main Siamese army that was finally being prepared. Looking back, it is difficult to understand why Chao Anou, a respected general of many years, conceived a battle plan in which his armies were to be so scattered. One reason for this may have been that instead of joining Chao Anou, Chao Titsah intentionally kept his army back so as not to have to fight.

The first Battles

By the end of March, Chao Anou had left Ratchasima and he was with his main army at Nong Bua Lamphu. General Phagna Supho in

Champasak had an army of 3,000, other troops were at Sanom, and Chao Titsah still remained unmoving in Suwannaphum. By the end of April, Rama III's army had reached Nakhon Ratchasima and felt themselves strong enough to send a detachment in the direction Champasak. This Siamese force met some of Chao Anou's troops who retreated to Suwannaphum.

The Siamese general then sent a message to Chao Titsah thanking him for the help he had already given and asked him to fall back on Vientiane. This Chao Titsah did, at the same time sending a message to Chao Anou that clearly implied his treachery. This left Chao Anou considerably mystified about what was happening. Even so, despite this he decided to continue his attack against the Siamese.

By this time Rama III had collected together five other Siamese armies. One by one, the scattered Lao armies were surrounded. Chao Anou ordered his armies to fight on, but taking his two sons, he fled back to Vientiane. His soldiers fought bravely. One General Phagna Narindh, although his army was surrounded and himself taken a prisoner, refused to order his men to surrender. The Siamese had him trampled to death by an elephant. At one time, three of the Lao armies counterattacked and managed to surround the Siamese armies. But Rama III sent reinforcements and the Lao were caught in a pincer movement and had to scatter to save themselves.

On 13 May, the Lao army pulled out of Khao San Pass, the last of the passes onto the Korat plateau. When Chao Anou, who was safely back in Vientiane, learnt of this, he took his family by boat down the Mekong and then made his way overland to the Annamite kingdom of Hué.

The Siamese enter Vientiane

THE SIAMESE ADVANCED on Vientiane. Five days after Chao Anou's flight they entered the city. The destruction by their army far exceeded anything that had happened to Vientiane in the past. They first ransacked the city. Then set about destroying it. They forced the people to pull down the city walls, to demolish the monuments, and to cut down all the fruit trees. After this they set fire to everything. The people were rounded up and held in preparation for being sent on what would be for many a death march towards Pak Isarn and the Menam Chaophraya Valley.

By the end of May, the Siamese General Phraya Ratchasuphawadi, later to become Chaophraya Bodindecha, felt sufficiently in control to move his army southwards and attack Champasak. When Chao Nho, the

King and son of Chao Anou, heard this he tried to defend Ubol, but the townspeople turned against him and he was forced to march his small detachment on to Champasak. Here, however, a Chao Houy, the son of a former Champasak Oupahat, persuaded the people to close the gates, forcing him and his men to take refuge on the far side of the Mekong. Chao Houy probably did not feel any loyalty to Chao Nho, even though he was his king. Chao Nho was, after all, an outsider imposed by Chao Anou from Vientiane, while he, Chao Houy, was a member of the royal family of Champasak.

When the Siamese troops arrived, Chao Houy opened the gates to them. He then sent his men across to track down and capture Chao Nho, who with his followers were soon made prisoners and were handed over to the Siamese who sent them to Bangkok.

General Ratchasuphawadi depopulates Vientiane

GENERAL RATCHASUPHAWADI THEN moved eastwards to take Nakhon Phanom before returning to his base at Phan Phao. The treacherous Chao Titsah on hearing that Chao Anou had fled handed over himself and his army to Ratchasuphawadi and was put in charge of regrouping all the Lao families. These included some 20,000 soldiers and their families from the northern states including Luang Prabang, who had fought as allies of the Siamese. But their fate was no different. They were all ordered to report to Phan Phao before being sent to repopulate the south.

General Ratchasuphawadi explained this action in a letter to Rama III saying that even those from Luang Prabang were not to be trusted and had only appeared after the fall of Vientiane. He added that Luang Prabang was weak and, presumably, would not complain at the loss of its soldiers.

He continued his report by saying that he had had some difficulty rounding up all the Vientiane people, some of whom had fled as far away as Chiang Mai. From his descriptions it is clear the hardships for the Vientiane people must have been appalling. One group had counter-attacked and he had managed to surround between 200 and 300 men who were hiding together. When the Siamese wanted to move them, they found only 10 were strong enough to walk.

Maha Sila quotes from General Ratchasuphawadi's letter to Rama III, 'I will endeavour to the best of my ability to deal with the conquered people in the best interests of our kingdom. I have planned to transfer the people of the area to cities near Bangkok itself. *I know one thing for sure, that the people of the Lao and Khmer princedoms and the same goes for the rulers' families, the officials' families etc. have either died or been separated from each other to the extent that it would be difficult to determine who is who and where they are.'* (Our italics).

He explained that if he sent small armed companies to find those who were in hiding and the party was outnumbered by the Lao they would be ambushed and attacked. When on the other hand he sent out large detachments, the Lao would be warned and melt away.

He estimated that the number of physically fit males in Vientiane to be about 20,000. He thought that later it would be possible to recruit eight to ten thousand for the army. He pointed out that there was a shortage of food in the areas where there had been fighting and in some places people were starving. Later he would bring 10,000 physically fit males to Bangkok, which, with their families, would total 50,000 in all. He intended to leave 500 to 1,000 officials in Vientiane to run the affairs. He would make arrangements to clear up 'resistance nests' and he expected to be able to send back the main Siamese army about the middle of July.

He was unable at the moment to estimate how much wealth had been collected, but it would be presented to Rama III, with the names of those by whom the gold and silver were obtained. It was possible that the 110 elephants he had already sent to Bangkok were not very suitable for palace use as they had been used to transport goods. He expected to secure at least 2,000 more elephants. There were, he added, too few horses to be worth collecting. It is interesting to see that there must have been some sort of armaments industry in Vientiane as he said the cannons and guns he had captured were of the most obsolete types and not worth sending to Bangkok, but, he added, he would endeavour to have new ones made.

Of the Buddhist statues he had found only eight. Out of which only one, Phra Serm, was worth bringing back. Some others were too large to move. He intended to build shrines to house all those left behind. The main shrine would be called *The Shrine of the Quelling of the Vientiane Rebellion.* This highly provocative name was one day to drive Chao Anou into a fit of rage and, against all reason, to start a new revolt.

Departure of the Siamese Army

By July the same year, 1827, the main Siamese army left and General Ratchasuphawadi was in charge. He placed the senior Lao administrator, the Phya Muong Chan, in charge of Vientiane, which by then held only a few poor Lao peasants, while Chao Titsah, having served his traitorous purpose, was taken to Bangkok.

No mercy had been shown to anyone. When a contingent of hostages arrived from Muong Yasothon, someone told Ratchasuphawadi that the brother of the Chief Minister had hidden some of the Vientiane refugees. Ratchasuphawadi ordered him executed, but his brother, the Chief Minister, said that if his brother were to be executed, he, as Chief Minister, also should be executed. This plea for mercy, far from arousing Ratchasuphawadi's pity, resulted in his immediately ordering the whole family, which with the children totalled more than 100 persons, to be brought and placed in a cage and he then had them burnt alive.

By February of the next year, 1828, General Ratchasuphawadi decided that he had cleaned out all the 'resistance nests' and that the punishment of Vientiane was sufficient. The town had been razed, so he left a small government of Lao officials with the main Siamese garrison in Nong Khai on the opposite bank of the Mekong, and returned to Bangkok.

However, Rama III was not satisfied. He wanted Vientiane completely eliminated as he was afraid that it might revive either under the Vietnamese, or the Black Tai, or Xieng Khouang. Rama III then sent Ratchasuphawadi back to Vientiane with orders to reduce it to ashes. Meanwhile, in Bangkok, the Prabang was housed in Wat Chakkawat. Chao Titsah was placed in the prison-like palace that had been built for Chao Anou when he was captured. The Vientiane families were dispersed around Lopburi, Saraburi, Suphanburi and Nakhon Chaisi, while those from Nakhon Phanom were sent to Phanat Nikhom.

Chao Anou returns to negotiate

ON 27 JULY, Chao Ngao sent a message to Vientiane saying that the Vietnamese were sending Chao Anou back and that they were five days march away. This message was forwarded to Ratchasuphawadi. On 31 July, Ratchasuphawadi led his troops out of Udorn Thani and reached Phan Phao on 1 August, the same day that Chao Anou with 1,000 men arrived in Vientiane. Word was sent from Vientiane that Chao Anou would come to Phan Phao the next day.

When Chao Anou crossed to Phan Pao with his Vietnamese advisers, it was the Vietnamese who did all the talking. They explained that Vietnam was like the 'Mother' to Chao Anou and Siam the 'Father'. The 'Mother' had a responsibility to make peace in the family. Some form of agreement was reached and Chao Anou returned to Vientiane.

On his way back he was told of the *Shrine of the Quelling of the Vientiane Rebellion*, where Ratchasuphawadi had placed the Buddhas he had not sent to Bangkok. Chao Anou was also told that at the shrine he was referred to in a very insulting manner. He was so enraged by this that he decided to take his revenge on the nearest Siamese. These happened to be 300 soldiers stationed at Wat Kang near Vientiane, whom he ordered killed. Only 40 managed to escape and they fled across the river to Phan Pao.

Ratchasuphawadi decided that it was too risky with his small force to remain in what had once again become enemy territory and he decided to move further south that same night. When Chao Anou heard this, he crossed the Mekong and destroyed the *Shrine of Quelling the Vientiane revolt* and took back the Phra Serm to Vientiane.

Two weeks later Chao Anou sent Chao Ngao in pursuit of Ratchasuphawadi. He caught up with the Siamese and a hand-to-hand battle ensued. Chao Ngao managed to wound General Ratchasuphawadi, but was himself hit by a bullet and his troops decided to retire taking him with them.

In September 1828, the Annamite Emperor, Minh Mang (1820–1841), sent two letters to Rama III apologising on Chao Anou's behalf and suggesting Rama III agree to Chao Anou's presenting himself in Bangkok. But Rama III would not agree.

Chao Anou flees from the Siamese for the second time

By MID-OCTOBER Chao Ngao was able to persuade his father that the fight was hopeless and Chao Anou once again fled from Vientiane. Ratchasuphawadi had not sufficiently recovered to march with his troops but sent 600 men to Vientiane in the hope of capturing him. Chao Anou had already left. However, a large part of his family, including his son, Chao Suthisan, had stayed on and they were taken prisoner and a few days later were sent to Bangkok.

Chao Anou's luck had finally run out. His slow progress was reported as his party made its way through Xieng Khouang territory along the foot of the Annamite Chain on the road to safety at the Court of the Emperor Minh Mang in Hué.

Some years earlier, Chao Anou had had Chao Noi (1804–1828) the king Xieng Khouang arrested and held captive for three years in Vientiane. He had made a deadly enemy of Chao Noi who from then on wanted nothing more than his revenge on Chao Anou and his freedom from the suzerainty of Vientiane.

Chao Anou's flight offered the chance to achieve both these objectives. Chao Noi sent a message to the Siamese in Vientiane saying that if they

140

agreed not to invade Xieng Khouang he would arrange the capture of Chao Anou. Chao Noi was not the only one who wished to take revenge on Chao Anou. King Mantha Tourath also sent a message from Luang Prabang offering to assist in his capture.

The capture of Chao Anou

ONCE GENERAL RATCHASUPHAWADI had agreed to the terms, Chao Noi sent out hunting parties to look for the Vientiane king. Chao Anou's pathetic group, which included some of his sisters, was finally discovered at the foot of the Khao Kai Mountain, the *White Buffalo Mountain*, and were taken back as captives to Vientiane, which they reached on 21 December 1828.

Chao Anou, who only a year before had proudly led 8,000 soldiers across the Pak Isarn to overthrow the Rama III, was placed under a guard of 300 soldiers and escorted to Saraburi. Whatever the pains of the journey had been until then, they were nothing compared to the humiliation that was about to be inflicted on him and his family members. He was placed in a cage aboard a river boat with obscene and abusive placards tied to the bars. The boat was stopped at every village so that the villagers could gaze on this human beast who had dared to challenge their king.

In Bangkok he and his relatives were placed in cages in public view. They were tortured by sharp instruments placed in their cages, by boiling water and heated sand thrown on them and were attacked with spears and saws. They were taken out of their cages to be fed like animals in front of the spectators. After eight days the torment and suffering had their effect and Chao Anou died. His body was then stuck through with a pole and placed on exhibition. Evidently, Rama III was satisfied with this, as the rest of the family were released, if not to freedom, at least from the torment they had been through.

Rama III had achieved his objective. The kingdom of Vientiane had ceased to exist and would never again come back to life. When the French explorer Henri Mouhot passed by on the Mekong river in 1861, there was nothing to be seen but the roofless walls of some of the wats. The rest was trees and jungle. It was uninhabited except for a handful of peasants, who were so impoverished that they were prepared to risk living in such an ill-omened place.

But if Vientiane ceased to exist, its legacy lived on for almost another century. The Emperor Minh Mang had Chao Noi captured and executed for his part in betraying his overlord. Xieng Khouang itself was subjected to the humiliation of being forced to accept Annamite clothes, language, customs and behaviour until they were strong enough to win back their Lao independence once again.

As a last legacy, Siam and Annam were to be enemies for many decades ahead. Luang Prabang and Champasak as we shall see were to fare better, but they were not to throw off the suzerainty of Bangkok.

CHAPTER TEN

Siamese Dominance

Lan Xang has known many disasters in the course of its history, but they are as nothing compared to the consequences of Chao Anou's 'war of independence'. Despite the train of calamities and horrors that followed his defeat, there has been little attempt over the last century and three-quarters to make an historical assessment of why Chao Anou, against the advice of his family and Ministers, ever started the war with Siam.

The Annals and other sources give a large number of different reasons, but with most of the written records of Vientiane destroyed, and the oral traditions and folk histories scattered across Siam by the subsequent deportations, it is difficult, if not impossible to discover what reasons, if there were reasons and not merely sheer anger, that drove him to such a disastrous decision.

He appears to have felt that in three different ways he had been insupportably humiliated. The first concerned the forced labour, or what perhaps King Rama III saw as obligatory duties, that one of his sons and all of his Court had been made to perform during their stay in Bangkok. Exactly what these exactions were is not clear.

The second humiliation had been when he had complained to Rama III that the tribute, or taxes, paid to Siam were too large, as Vientiane had the onerous responsibility of maintaining the first line of defence against the Vietnamese.

The third humiliation was Rama III's refusal to allow the return of the tens of thousands of Lao who had been deported to Siam after the capture of Vientiane in 1778. Associated with this was the Siamese refusal to let him take back the dancers and other entertainers who had been provided for his entertainment while in Bangkok.

Most of the Siamese sources explain his actions by saying that he was ungrateful! While those at the Siamese Court who had been against allowing his son Chao Nho to become king of Champasak, merely said

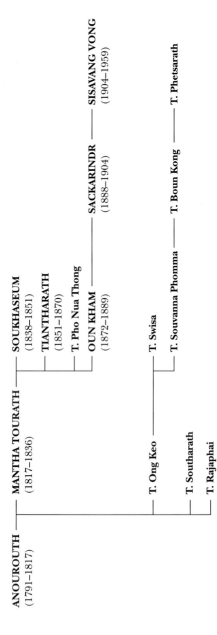

GENEALOGICAL TABLE 7 The Kings of Luang Prabang – Anourouth to Savang Vatthana, 1791 to 1905

144

that his behaviour was exactly what they had always feared. Neither offers a satisfactory reason.

Saveng notes that in the Vietnamese annals, it is said that Chao Anou wished to revenge the murder of his grandson, who had been assassinated as a pretender to the Siamese throne. It is, however, difficult to identify who this grandchild might have been unless the reference is to the marriage arranged between Rama I and one of Chao Anou's sisters, Keo Yot Fah Kalayani.

Saveng comments, *the revolt by Chao Anou against Siam, which resulted in the destruction of Vientiane and the total decline of Lan Xang merits more than a mere annotation and deserves study in depth. Effectively it is considered by all Lao as a high point of their history and as a symbol of their struggle for their dignity and independence of their country, this dangerous rebellion mortgaged Lao Thai relations for over 150 years.* An academic study has, however, yet to be made.

A new Outlook

WITH THE FALL of Vientiane we see a fundamental change in the outlook of the Siamese. Whereas, in the past, wars had been largely of aggression for the spoils, especially manpower, that went to the victor. From the fall of Vientiane a new attitude had begun to develop. As an example, after the capture of Vientiane, Rama III had no hesitation in repaying his ally Luang Prabang by forcing her to become a vassal state and to form a part of what he planned to be a Greater Siam, comprising all the Tai states.

This was the new outlook, the gaining of political strength from war, rather than just the forcible appropriation of wealth and manpower.

Although he was to allow the Luang Prabang royal family to continue to rule, the official posts they held, and even who was made king, were completely under the authority of Bangkok, as was the entire administration of the kingdom.

Following the capture of Chao Anou and the total destruction of the kingdom of Vientiane, the Emperor Minh Mang of Vietnam sent his troops into Xieng Khouang, arrested Chao Noi, the ruler, for handing the Vientiane king over to the Siamese, and had him executed. In 1832 Muong Phoueune became the Vietnamese prefecture of Tran Ninh. The Vietnamese then instituted a reign of terror. Annamite dress became compulsory, the people were expected to learn the Vietnamese language and to follow the customs of their new rulers. The nation of Muong Phoueune was almost exterminated.

Xieng Khouang rebels against the Vietnamese

In 1834, THE people of Xieng Khouang were driven to revolt, but the rebellion was put down with such brutality that whole areas of the kingdom were depopulated. The Siamese promised asylum on the Right Bank of the Mekong, but when some 6,000 people crossed the river they learnt that they were to be deported to areas around Bangkok. 3,000 tried to return, but when they did so, they found in their old homelands only a desert patrolled by Vietnamese soldiers. Most of those who tried to return perished.

After the destruction of Vientiane, Mantha Tourath found himself isolated and completely at the mercy of the Siamese. In 1831 and 1833 he sent missions to the Emperor Minh Mang with the traditional tribute of gold and silver flowers as a token of his vassalage. He hoped that with the help of the Vietnamese he might throw off the Siamese yoke, but Minh Mang had his own problems and could not see any benefit to himself in antagonising the Siamese further. However, the messages King Mantha Tourath sent, and his offer of vassalage, were to be used by the French in the second half of the century as evidence that as the sovereign power of Vietnam they were also the overlords, by its own admission, of Luang Prabang.

The Three Siamese Administrative Regions

KING MANTHA TOURATH'S attempt to break away had failed. In 1829, the Siamese, in line with their new policy, set up three administrations. That in Luang Prabang had only a small garrison of Siamese troops and relied on King Mantha Tourath's army for support. It administered Luang Prabang, Namtha, the Sipsong Panna, the Sipsong Chau Tai in the Red River area and Houa Phan, today's Sam Neua.

The second administration covered the former kingdom of Vientiane and was based in Nong Khai. Many of the people in this region had come from the kingdom of Vientiane and had been forcibly deported under the harshest of conditions to found new villages in the muongs that were being created. This northeastern administration was nominally responsible for Xieng Khouang, as well as, more realistically Borikane, Nakhon Phanom and southwards to the borders of Champasak.

The third administration was based on Champasak, covering the areas down to Cochin China, Cambodia on the west, including some areas that were in dispute with the French, and the southeastern part of the Korat plateau.

The cooperation between the Siamese and King Mantha Tourath was to have severe repercussions in the Sipsong Chau Tai. In an attempt to lessened the effect of the Vietnamese takeover of Xieng Khouang, Siam and Luang Prabang began to move the p'uon peoples away from the Xieng Khouang borders.

At the same time, the Siamese started a policy of demanding the vassalage of the muongs in the Sipsong Chau Tai, who traditionally had maintained a state of independence, paying tribute to Vietnam, China or Luang Prabang only when compelled to do so.

Over the next three decades from the 1830s to the 1860s Siam demanded their complete vassalage and the repudiation of any treaties with Vietnam: a policy that was not well-received by these highly independent peoples. In 1835 there was the first of a number of revolts when both the Sipsong Chau Tai and Xieng Khouang refused to pay tribute to Luang Prabang. The Maha Oupahat, Chao Rajaphai a brother of the King Mantha Tourath, led a combined Lao and Siamese army. During the campaign he led part of the army into Xieng Khouang to attack the Vietnamese there. When the revolt had been put down, the Siamese army returned to Bangkok.

Dynastic disputes

THE NEXT YEAR King Mantha Tourath died and the Siamese Minister who was present at the ceremonies formally proclaimed the sovereign rights of Siam and let it be known that Bangkok would decide who would be the next king. Chao Soukhaseum, the eldest of King Mantha Tourath's sons, might have expected to be accepted by the Luang Prabang Court, but Chao Rajaphai, the Oupahat, objected to his succeeding.

In the meantime, Chao Oun Keo, who although an elder brother of Chao Rajaphai held the more junior post of Rajaput went to Bangkok carrying presents to Rama III and officially announced the death of King Mantha Tourath. Rama III promoted him to Rajavong, and made him responsible for all the affairs of the kingdom, so placing him above the Oupahat, who had been acting as Regent.

By 1836, both Chao Soukhaseum and Chao Rajaphai were in Bangkok pleading their special cases for the throne. Chao Soukhaseum accused Chao Rajaphai of having committed treason by sending presents to the Vietnamese when campaigning in Xieng Khouang. Rama III appears to have believed Chao Soukhaseum and Chao Rajaphai was given an honorific title and ordered to remain in Bangkok where he died the next year.

Chao Soukhaseum acknowledged king

IN 1838, CHAO Soukhaseum (1838–1850) returned to Luang Prabang as the future king with Chao Oun Keo as his Oupahat. His reign was generally peaceful and a time of stability.

In 1848, he was away in Bangkok when the ruler of Chiang Hung in the Sipsong Panna revolted against the Siamese rule. Immediately on his return to Luang Prabang, he once again sent Chao Oun Keo to put down the rebellion. The next year, 1849, Chao Oun Keo was sent to Bangkok with the tribute of gold and silver flowers. He remained there for some months and died in Bangkok in 1850, so bringing to a conclusion a lifetime of service to Luang Prabang.

He was to be soon followed by King Soukhaseum who died in the same year. Within a few months the great enemy of the former Lan Xang, Rama III, had also died and was succeeded by his son Rama IV (1851–1868), who is better known as King Mongkut.

King Mongkut's aim was to bring to Siam all that was best in different forms of government, especially those of Europe. He set in progress a complete overhaul of every aspect of the administration, from the system of laws and justice, to tax collecting and internal administration.

With the death of Rama III, no decision could be taken over who should be the king of Luang Prabang until Prince Mongkut had ascended the throne. His choice then fell on Chao Tiantharath, the next younger brother of Chao Soukhaseum.

The last Luang Prabang Mission to China

ONE OF THE first things King Tiantharath (1851–1870) did was to send a mission with the traditional tribute to Peking. When the mission arrived at the southern borders, they found the whole area in turmoil as the Taiping rebellion had spread throughout the region. They left their presents with the first Chaomuong they found and returned to Luang Prabang. It was to be the last tribute that Luang Prabang was to offer China.

In 1853, a joint Siamese-Lao expedition was mounted against Kengtung. The Burmese came to the assistance of the Shan, who were able to ward off the attack. In the fighting two sons of the former Oupahat Chao Oun Keo were lost: Chao Sivisa was killed in the fighting and Chao Khammao disappeared, never to be heard of again.

Two years later, Muong Phoueune revolted against the Vietnamese. Tu Duc, the emperor, had placed the eldest son of Chao Noi, the king who had betrayed Chao Anou, as ruler of Xieng Khouang with the title, *Imperial Mandatory Prince*. Chao Tiantharath immediately claimed that this constituted recognition of the existence of the former kingdom. As such, it owed Luang Prabang a triennial tribute. Emperor Tu Duc was too deeply involved with fighting off French incursions as they placed more and more of his territory under their protection that he made little protest against King Tiantharath's demands.

Sipsong Chau Tai and King Tiantharath

At the beginning of the 1860s Muong Thene (Dien Bien Phu) and Muong Lai, two of the Sipsong Chau Tai cantons went to war and Muong Lai lost. Kam Seng, the ruler of Muong Lai, complained to Chao Tiantharath as his nominal overlord. Chao Tiantharath persuaded Muong Thene to accept an indemnity in exchange for leaving Muong Lai in peace. This was agreed, but unfortunately Kam Seng did not have enough money to make the payment. Once again he appealed to Luang Prabang and Chao Tiantharath agreed to lend him the sum, provided his son Deo Van Tri, or to give him his Tai name, Kam Hom, came to live in a monastery as a surety.

After two years Kam Seng repaid the money and Deo Van Tri returned home. Kam Seng was by then getting old and he handed over the affairs of Muong Lai to Deo Van Tri. Soon after a rebel of Muong Lai fled to Muong Ngoi, which is on the Nam Ou and a part of Luang Prabang. Deo Van Tri sent one of his officials named Bac Mao and five soldiers to arrest the rebel there. Instead they themselves were arrested by the authorities for being illegally armed in the kingdom. They were taken to Luang Prabang and Bac Mao was put into prison. Three years later the prison caught fire and Bac Mao managed to escape. He made his way back to Muong Lai and this was the beginning of a quarrel between Deo Van Tri and Chao Oun Kham, who had by then become king of Luang Prabang.

The Ho Pirates and northern Laos

From the 1840s Peking had been trying to bring the hill peoples of southern China under their control and to make them pay taxes. The result was a gradual migration southwards that when the Chinese carried out punitive raids would become a great exodus of people. Most of them came down the Red and Black River valleys and there were constant minor battles as the inhabitants tried to prevent the newcomers taking over their land. These newcomers came to be known by the Siamese word 'Ho', the term used for a Chinese, although few if any were ethnic Chinese.

By the middle of the century, the number of landless Ho had increased to such an extent that there was no possibility of their finding land and settling down. Attacked by the frightened inhabitants wherever they went, they gradually coalesced into three large bandit groups. These became known by the banners they carried into battle. The first was the Yellow, or Stripped, Banners and the other two, the Red and Black Banners respectively.

Zasloff quotes from an anonymous French army commander who described the bands as mercenaries whose main goal was opium and smuggling, especially to and from the Tongking ports into southern China. He says that there were many Europeans, especially French, who on finishing their military service, or after deserting the French armies, joined these bands. It was said that after two or three trips on the Red River they could, if they avoided being killed, make 100,000 francs, ten million or more francs in modern terms. It was high-risk, with high returns. Many of the bands were well armed with the latest guns such as Winchesters, Remingtons and Martinis, others were far less well equipped, having little more than cutlasses and old-fashioned rifles. But all were utterly ruthless, whose only aim was plunder and rapine.

In 1872, some 3,000 Yellow Banners having ransacked the Sipsong Chau Tai moved into Houa Phan, the *Thousand Springs*, which is today's Sam Neua. Within two years the people of Houa Phan had been driven out and the Yellow Banners prepared to join up with the Red Banners who had been moving down the Nam Ou. Chao Khamsouk, a son of King Oun Kham, stopped them from approaching Luang Prabang, but they regrouped and with the other Ho bands first took Xieng Khouang and from there advanced on Vientiane where there was a handful of Siamese troops and some Lao.

The Siamese, who were administering the former kingdom from across the river in Nong Khai, had only a small detachment of troops and they had to send for reinforcements from Ubol. It was four months before these arrived and were able to drive out the Ho bandits. There was obviously nothing of value in the former capital, but the Ho thought that the inhabitants must have buried their treasure before the Siamese attack in 1828 and spent their time digging in the ruins looking for anything of value that might have been buried.

By 1880, the Ho bands were no longer a threat to Luang Prabang, but they still controlled Xieng Khouang, which Bangkok now considered a

150

part of the Siamese kingdom. In 1883, the Siamese and Luang Prabang armies attacked the Ho pirates in Xieng Khouang, but were badly beaten. They then decided on an all out attack on the Ho bases in the Sipsong Chau Tai. The Commander-in-Chief of the Siamese army was Meun Vai Voronat. However, the Siamese attempt to clear them out was a disaster and from that followed consequences that were to lead to the fall and destruction of Luang Prabang itself.

The Search for Xanadu

BEFORE ONE CAN look at this, it is necessary to turn back some twenty or more years. The high taxes and innumerable regulations imposed on trade at the Chinese ports made western businesses dream of finding a way to reach China's lucrative market by some overland route. The Mekong was at its southern end impossible to navigate, at least without a series of locks that could not be financed without the certainty of a market at the other end. There, therefore, began series of explorations, financed by commerce, but largely motivated by the desire for discovery. The ruins of Angkor, hidden for centuries beneath the Cambodian jungle had just been found. Might there not be other lost civilisations still undiscovered in the jungles and secret valleys of the north? Where did the great Mekong have its source? These and many other still unanswered questions were incentive enough.

In 1861, Henri Mouhot whose small group had started at Angkor and gradually made their way up the Mekong, finally reached Luang Prabang. Mouhot described it as 'a delicious little town' in a charming situation. It had, he said, about 8,000 inhabitants. They stayed for a few days before setting off north again. Sadly, they had hardly gone more than a day's travel upstream when Mouhot caught a fever and died.

Five years later Admiral de la Grandière ordered Captain Doudart de Lagrée, Francis Garnier, and others to explore the Mekong from Phnom Penh to Chiang Hung in the Sipsong Panna. The expedition reached Luang Prabang in April 1867 and from there went on to find Henri Mouhot's grave which they repaired. At the Chinese frontier, Lagrée died of exhaustion and Francis Garnier took over the leadership. He persuaded the group to continue and they managed to reach Talifu, the original homeland of the western Tai. Here, the Chinese authorities forbad them to continue their journey northwards, a journey Garnier had hoped would take them to the source of the Mekong. They had, however, learnt enough of the hazards of the Mekong which they realised was commercially unnavigable, so they returned along the Yangtze River to Shanghai.

MAP 4 Indochina in the 19th Century

However, if the Mekong in its entirety was unnavigable there were certainly stretches that could be used. If a route could be found from Luang Prabang overland through either the Sipsong Chau Tai, or through Xieng Khouang, to Hanoi, then the Mekong could be used for the last part of the journey to reach China to the north. The French began to turn their attention to exploration from Tongking westwards and from Luang Prabang eastwards.

The return of the Prabang

THIS CHANGE IN strategy came just at the time when King Chulalongkorn (1868–1910) had come to the throne and was anxious to extend his father's ideas for the administration of the country. In 1866, as a gesture of goodwill to the Lao he returned the Prabang to them.

At the same time, he set about the implementation of a more efficient system of government in the kingdoms and principalities that had become a part of Siam. The keystone of his policy was the use of his sons and immediate relatives who were appointed as Royal Commissioners with supreme powers in their own areas. However, while they were all-powerful in their administrative areas, they were strictly bound by the policies laid down in Bangkok. In this way, local needs could be met, laws and justice pursued, but the ultimate control lay with the King in Bangkok.

The lawlessness of the Ho bands made a mockery of Bangkok's claimed suzerainty over the northen regions, so Chulalongkorn sent two Royal Commissioners with General Vai Voronat to Luang Prabang in a determined effort to create stability and recognised rule in the Sipsong Chau Tai. This attempted extension of Siamese power upset the French for whom Laos was becoming increasingly important, both for the defence of Vietnam and as a stop to the extension of British rule in Asia.

Auguste Pavie

BY SOME FORTUNATE chance for the French, Auguste Pavie, an official of the Postal and Telegraph Service, came to the notice of the French Governor of Cochin China. He had recently supervised the installation of a telegraph line between Phnom Penh and Bangkok and had collected an immense amount of information on the peoples and their history, as well as the flora and fauna along the route. This he had published in a series of articles in Saigon.

ILLUSTRATION 15 Auguste Pavie with members of his Mission at Muong Nan, 1894

© Photothéque du Musée de l'Homme

The Governor, Le Myre de Vilers, found that Pavie was an expert linguist and, wherever he might be, took a deep interest in the local people. During the construction of the telegraph line, he had displayed considerable stamina and determination under very difficult conditions. De Vilers decided to send Pavie back to Paris to accompany a group of Cambodians who were to be the first students in a new colonial school for potential indigenous leaders. This gave the Quai d'Orsay, and other government ministries, an opportunity to assess his potential value to them as an agent of policy when he returned to Indochina.

Pavie lived up to the expectations of de Vilers and Paris appointed him vice-consul in Luang Prabang. It was 1885 and was to be the first year of France's intervention in Laotian affairs. This was the year of the British invasion of the Shan States and the threat that she would be able to extend across the Mekong up to the borders of China. At the same time Siam and France came close to war over the demarcation of the Vietnamese–Laotian border.

The 1885 Provisional Franco–Siamese Convention

IN THE MIDST of this Phra Vai Voronat arrived in Luang Prabang with the two Royal Commissioners. He had strict orders to consolidate the Siamese position in Luang Prabang and in Xieng Khouang. He left the two Commissioners in Luang Prabang and decided to lead a joint Lao–Siamese army into the Sipsong Chau Tai to bring the Ho under control before tackling them in Xieng Khouang.

This immediately caused deep concern among the French who saw it as extension of Siamese territory. They reacted by demanding a joint survey based in and working out of Luang Prabang as the best way to demarcate new frontiers and to confirm France's possessions along the valleys of the Red and Black rivers.

On 7 May 1885, a Provisional Franco–Siamese Convention was signed laying down new conditions for France in the Siamese territories. Among the provisions was permission to open a Vice-Consulate in Luang Prabang and to start work on the joint Franco–Siamese border survey.

When Pavie arrived in Bangkok, the Siamese put every possible bureaucratic obstacle in his path. They did not want him to reach Luang Prabang until Vai Voronat had managed to suppress the Ho and had completed the survey, since if the survey were finished before he arrived, the French would not have an opportunity to express their point of view on where the borders should be.

However, by sheer force of character Pavie cut himself free from the Siamese red tape and after a long journey on foot, by elephant and river, he managed to circumvent all the difficulties and reached Luang Prabang on 10 February, 1887.

Vai Voronat and his troops had already left Luang Prabang to follow out the Siamese king's orders to drive the Ho bands from the Black River region. The expedition was a dismal failure. The Ho wisely refused set battles. In true guerrilla style, they split up into small groups on the approach of the Siamese troops and reformed after their departure.

To compound his mistakes, Vai Voronat's overbearing behaviour infuriated the Tai rulers, who anyway felt no love for their Vietnamese suzerains. He demanded they exchange any treaties with the Vietnamese for identical treaties, naming in place of the Vietnamese emperor, the Siamese king as the sovereign power. In doing so, he merely switched their dislike of the Vietnamese to a burning resentment against their new Siamese masters.

However, as Pavie was to note, they were an easy-going people and all of the Sipsong Chau Tai rulers agreed, with the exception of Kam Seng. When Vai Voronat demanded Kam Seng's allegiance, he refused to give it, even though he was no longer the ruler, having some years before abdicated in favour of his eldest son, Deo Van Tri. By chance Deo Van Tri was away fighting the French, the enemies of the Siamese.

This, however, did nothing in Vai Voronat's eyes to mitigate the refusal. He foolishly arrested two of Kam Seng's sons and a son-in-law. They were placed in cages and he had them sent down the Nam Ou on their way to Bangkok. When the Luang Prabang soothsayers and monks learnt who were imprisoned in the cages, they warned the people that it was a bad omen, and something dreadful would soon happen to the kingdom.

Pavie on his arrival in Luang Prabang received a very cold reception from the Siamese Commissioners, but the king, Tiao Oun Kham (1872-1889), saw the French as a counterbalance against the Siamese and welcomed Pavie warmly. The Lao officials were ordered to find him a house and give him every assistance.

It seems that when Vai Voronat returned with his army to Luang Prabang, he purposely lied to Pavie, telling him that the Ho threat was ended, and it would be quite safe for him to travel on up the Nam Ou to explore the Black and River regions. There seems little doubt that he would have had no regrets if Pavie had been killed as a result. He also told him, quite untruthfully, that the survey had been completed and there was nothing he could do.

Pavie accepted his assurances and started off on what was his most immediate task: to see whether there was a route to Tongking by way of the Nam Ou. However, he had only gone a few days northwards when he was warned that the Ho were on the march and Luang Prabang was threatened. He immediately returned to the capital and informed the king. He and his Maha Oupahat, Tiao Souvanna Phomma, did have a small army, but the king who had been stripped of his powers found it almost impossible to act effectively without the concurrence of the Siamese Commissioners. Vai Voronat had taken the Siamese army with him, so that while they possessed nominal power were without the means to defend Luang Prabang.

If they believed Pavie that the Ho were marching against Luang Prabang they were acknowledging that Vai Voronat guilty of incompetence on two counts: the first for leaving the Ho unsubdued, and the second for depriving the Lao king of the armed forces needed to defend himself. Unfortunately for the Lao inhabitants, the Siamese Commissioners had neither the ability, nor the personal courage to meet the situation.

Deo Van Tri's Retaliation

PAVIE'S INFORMATION WAS correct. When Deo Van Tri had returned to Muong Lai and found that the Siamese had arrested his brothers, he immediately considered how best he could revenge himself. If he had had only the small resources of his muong, he would probably have accepted the situation and waited for an opportunity to attack the Siamese when they next sent troops into the Sipsong Chau Tai. But, by chance, there was a group of 600 Yellow Banner Ho encamped near Muong Lai who were terrorising his people.

Deo Van Tri decided to buy them off with money and, at the same time, offering them the added inducement of plundering Luang Prabang. In this way, he would remove the Ho from his state and exact revenge on both the Siamese and the Lao. The Ho bandits agreed to attack Luang Prabang and, with Deo Van Tri's faithful Bac Mao as guide, they descended the Nam Ou.

On 7 June 1887, just four months after Pavie's first arrival, they reached Luang Prabang. The Maha Oupahat, Chao Souvanna Phomma, showed great bravery, but he was unable to deploy his troops effectively against Deo Van Tri, even though his troops were trained and those of the Ho were poorly equipped and more like a rabble than an army.

One of the Siamese Commissioners left precipitately and the one who remained proved both incompetent and ineffective. The new Siamese policy of having all-powerful Commissioners had created a division of authority between King Oun Kham and the Commissioners that was to prove disastrous. The remaining Commissioner was responsible for policy, and the King was head of the Lao army. This unfortunate division between the King and the Commissioner deprived the Lao army of the decisive leadership it needed.

By the 9 June, the Ho bandits had persuaded the Siamese Commissioner to accept what they called a truce that allowed their men to enter Luang Prabang. It was a fatal decision. Once in, they began to pillage whatever they could lay their hands on and to shoot at any of the inhabitants who tried to prevent them.

Pavie sent his most trusted colleague, a Cambodian, to the king with orders that whatever happened he was not to leave the king's side and was to do everything possible to effect his escape.

Pavie himself tried to help other members of the Royal Family to get away and persuaded a number of them to leave by pirogue. He only agreed to leave when a party of the Ho appeared above him on the river bank and began shooting at him.

Death of Tiao Souvanna Phomma and the escape of the King

THE MAHA OUPAHAT, Tiao Souvanna Phomma, was killed in the fighting, but the king and a large part of his family with Pavie reached Pak Lay downstream from Luang Prabang. Here Pavie helped with the wounded and with the organization of food and shelter. He also sent a message to the French in Bangkok and to King Chulalongkorn telling them what had happened.

Nine days later a goldsmith from the Court also reached Pak Lay. He had hidden in the jungle and had stayed there watching what was happening. He reported that after plundering the town the Yellow Flags and Deo Van Tri had left on the 12th and 13th June.

The King, on the advice, of Pavie decided not to return to his devastated capital but with Pavie to make his way to Bangkok, where Chulalongkorn had invited him to stay. This placed Pavie in the position of chief adviser to the king and emphasised the terrible disaster that had come about through the Siamese failure to protect the King and his people.

They reached Bangkok in September and Vai Voronat was ordered to take an army back to pacify Deo Van Tri. His task was made easier by Pavie obtaining an agreement that Deo Van Tri's brothers should be released and sent ahead. Pavie made certain that the brothers knew that it was he who had obtained their freedom.

In October, the Siamese agreed to a Franco–Siamese Commission to study the frontiers. On the French side it comprised Pavie and two French officers. The French administration in Hanoi organised two columns led by Commandant Oudri and Colonel Pernot to advance along the Black River with the intention of meeting Pavie. In this way Pavie would be able to complete the journey he had earlier had to give up in when faced by the advance of the Ho bandits on Luang Prabang. Pavie left Bangkok for Luang Prabang on 22 October. With three elephants for the baggage and walking barefoot he reached there in November.

He left Luang Prabang at the end of January and reached the Sipsong Chau Tai without difficulty, but then came under attack by a band of Ho. By exceptional good fortune, Colonel Pernot's column heard the firing and went to investigate. He rescued Pavie and drove off the Ho. The link between Luang Prabang and Tongking had been made as planned.

The French decided to set up military posts in the region and to use persuasion rather than force to get the Sipsong Chau Tai rulers on their side.

The Beginning of the French Pacification

By this decision the French had taken over the task of pacification of the area. In December 1888, the local Siamese official in Muong Thene was instructed to meet Pavie and to formally renounce any Siamese claim to the Black and Red River areas.

By January 1889, Pavie was back in Luang Prabang. Despite all the travelling and his political negotiations, he had also found time to collect together a number of documents that he had transcribed. The originals he sent to Paris, where they are today and form an important historical collection. In the same month, King Oun Kham returned from Bangkok and about March the Siamese persuaded him that at 78 years he was too old and should abdicate. It is not clear when Chao Khamsouk, Chao Oun Kham's son came to the throne, but it seems probable that it was in 1894, by which time French influence had become dominant. Chao Khamsouk took the regnal name of Sackarindr (1894–1904).

In February, Pavie was called to Hanoi and from there to Paris where he was asked his opinion on the making of a topographical study of the Lao areas between the Left Bank of the Mekong and the Annamite Mountain Chain.

There were a number of reasons behind this proposal. The first was that France felt a need to protect the long flank of Vietnam and the best way of

ILLUSTRATION 16 King Oun Kham in the audience hall, Luang Prabang. The Crown Prince, the future King Sackarindr, at the table on the left, with Tiao Boun Khong, the Maha Oupahat, on the right, and Tiao Sisavang Vong, the grandson and future king, seated on a stool immediately in front of the King.

© Collection Prince Mangra Souvanna Phouma

doing this would be to take possession of the eastern part of Laos. The second was that they hoped to be able to show that Siam had no particular rights to the territory. Lastly, it was proposed to extend the survey to include the exploration of the commercial and mining potential of eastern Laos. Pavie, who had earlier visited the Khammouan, fully supported the proposal.

In April, Pavie was back in the Sipsong Chau Tai and went to meet Deo Van Tri and spent some time with him. He won his confidence, not least in Pavie's favour was his having had his brothers released by the Siamese. Pavie was successful and he obtained Deo Van Tri's submission.

Both of Pavie's trips to Sipsong Chau Tai had been successful, although the northeast was never to become the rich commercial route as the French had hoped. By then the French had far greater objectives than securing a new route to inland China. It was nothing less than taking over the whole of Laos, making its frontiers run with the British in the Shan States and with the Chinese to the north. In this they were to be successful, but only after using force whenever persuasion failed.

160

CHAPTER ELEVEN

An Overview of Champasak History

THE LAOTIAN CHARACTER embodies a very strong sense of personal identity. Nowhere is this stronger than in the south, where the people of Champasak, more especially those from the Island of Khong, have a passionate sense of their heritage that separates them from all other Lao. They believe that to have been born a native of Champasak is to have been brought up in a society of the intellectual elite that have preserved the finest customs and artistic traditions of the Lao people. Champasak today may be small and its modern history is only a little more than two hundred years long, but its traditions go back far beyond any history of the region and encompass the great states of Funan, Chenla, and Champa. The definitive account of Champasak history is by Archaimbault, who edited the most important versions of the Annals.

Eight kilometres to the southwest of Champasak is Wat Phu, *the Mountain Temple*, whose glorious stairway, naga entrance and temple buildings still live as memorials to the greatness of the Khmer empire and the inspiration that their architecture has left throughout southern Laos. The earliest parts of Wat Phu are, probably, from the Chenla periods between the sixth and ninth centuries. It continued to flourish as one of the great temple complexes of the Hindu world, first with a mixture of the old, sacrificial, religion and the different Hindu rites until the thirteenth century or fourteenth century. After the collapse of the Khmer empire, Wat Phu became a Buddhist temple.

Its recent history begins about 1550, when King Khajanam, or Kakanam, reigned. Little more is known of him except that he was succeeded by his son Phya Kamatha. The next named king is King Suthasaraja, or Sutsraja, who died in 1628. He had no heirs and his reign was followed by an eleven year interregnum. At the end of that period, the people chose a commoner, who was much respected for his justice and wisdom, as their king. When he died, he was succeeded by his beautiful daughter, who became Queen Phao (1641–?).

161

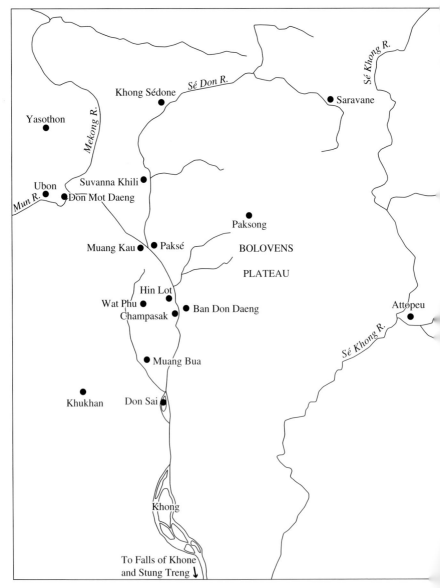

MAP 5 Champasak in the 18th and 19th Centuries

It was in August, or September 1641, that the Dutch East Indies representative, van Wuysthoff stopped in Champasak on his way to the Court of Chao Souligna Vongsa. He makes no mention of a Queen ruling the country and, in fact says, that it was under the control of a Tevinia, Minister, from Vientiane.

This does not exclude the possibility that Queen Phao existed, since the Tevinia may have been powerful enough to force her to stay in the background so that he could impress van Wuysthoff with the great size of Chao Souligna Vongsa's realm. It does, however, seem to rule out the possibility that Queen Phao in 1641 ruled over an independent Champasak.

Queen Phao and her Lover

TRADITION HAS IT that Queen Phao had an illicit affair with a visiting noble and to have borne him a daughter. It is very probable that this did happen and the young nobleman was called Thao Pang Kham, who had come from Nong Bua Lamphu on a hunting trip. Knowingly or not, he left Queen Phao pregnant and the daughter she bore was to succeed her as Queen Pheng.

By this account, Queen Pheng must have been born about 1642 and she would have been about seventy years old when Phra Kru Nhot Keo was regent of Champasak. With such a great difference in age, it is extremely unlikely that Princess Sumangala's son, who was only born about 1694 or 1695, could have been considered as her consort. In Chao Siromé's account, the suggestion is made by Phra Kru Nhot Keo, but nothing further is said about it.

It is not known when either of the Queens died, but it is recorded that Phra Kru Nhot Keo acted as Regent for five years (1708–1713), either during Queen Pheng's final years, or from her death until Princess Sumangala arrived with her son, who would be crowned King Soysisamout.

The Champasak Dynasty

THE GREATNESS OF modern Champasak dates from this time. King Soysisamout's reign (1713–1737) and his son's, who succeeded him, saw the glorious renaissance of a Champasak and the rebirth of an ancient line of kings going back into prehistory. One of Phra Kru Nhot Keo's earliest companions in his search for a kingdom for Princess Sumangala was a noble who was known as Achan, *Teacher*, Houat. He claimed descent from the royal line of the most ancient of the cities that became Vientiane. It was then known as *Krung Sri Sattanaganahut, The Sacred City of the Seven-Headed Naga* after the legend that it had been selected by a Naga as a place of future greatness.

Phra Kru Nhot Keo made Achan Houat Chaomuong of the island of Khong. At the time, it was nothing more than a guard post and trading centre, but in the coming years it was to be a position of the greatest importance for the kingdom of Champasak. The island of Khong controls the passage of the Mekong River and is the natural defensive base for the southern frontiers of Champasak.

Achan Houat is always referred to as the First Chaomuong of Khong. His importance in the realm of Champasak and that of his descendants can be seen by their being permitted to bear the title *Agna*. This was certainly the equivalent to the rank of Chao and was only marginally below that of the king. The title was only surrendered in 1946, when Champasak was finally united in what was the newly independent Laos. This chapter of history continues to the present day as some of the chief families of Khong trace their ancestry back to Achan Houat.

One of King Soysisamout's first acts on becoming king was to build a new capital on the island of Khong. He then immediately set about reorganising the administration. It is not clear how extensive Champasak was, a question that anyway in those days had little meaning. Some of the rulers and chaomuongs paid tribute to both Champasak and Vientiane and did not see themselves as 'belonging' to either country. They formed a part of the two spheres of influence of Champasak and Vientiane and they acknowledged as their first suzerain whichever was at the time the stronger.

However, Champasak's influence certainly extended quite a distance north, as Chao Soysisamout is recorded as giving Muong Manh, modern Saravane, a new capital.

When he died, he left to his son Chao Sayakoummane a fully functioning state with the new ideas and the new vitality that Princess Sumangala and the other families had brought with them from Vientiane.

King Sayakoummane: the Creator of a Nation

HIS SON, KING Sayakoummane (1738–1791) was a deeply religious man, and his determination to rule in accordance with the precepts of the Buddha was to invite open dissension, even rebellions. Despite this and the problems his nonviolence policy brought upon him and his people, he was to be the longest reigning monarch and the one who best succeeded in welding Champasak into a nation.

Sayakoummane was the eldest of four brothers, each of whom had the traditional right to be considered for the throne. When the decision was announced, the family and nobles chose Sayakoummane to be their king. His first act was to make his eldest brother, Chao Thammathevo, the Maha Oupahat or Viceroy of the new Champasak. Sayakoummane's next brother, Chao Phothisane he passed over in favour of the youngest of the brothers, Chao Soury Nho, whom he made Rajavong.

He seems to have found the island of Khong too restrictive, possibly because of the control exercised by Achan Houat's family, as he soon moved his capital to Nakhon Champanakhaburisi, near to the present day Champasak town. However, in leaving them alone as sole rulers of the island he allowed them even greater local importance. For the next hundred years, the Chaomuongs of Khong, were not far removed from the status of kings, with their own Court, a Court language, and poets and musicians each with a style and individuality that was distinctive of Khong.

For the first twenty years of Chao Sayakoummane's reign, the country was at peace under his benign rule, but in 1758 he and his brother, Chao Thammathevo, the Oupahat, had a serious disagreement. Sayakoummane then took the extraordinary action for those days of bringing a legal case against his own Oupahat. This probably meant that he placed the matters in dispute before his senior Ministers for their ruling.

Chao Thammathevo's immediate response was to seek the support of the Chaomuong of Khong. It is probable that in this year, 1758, Achan Houat died and his son, Thao Sithat (1718–1758) had become the Second Chaomuong of Khong. Together, Chao Thammathevo and he raised an army and marched on Sayakoummane's capital.

The King applies Buddhist Principles

The King, true to his Buddhist principles, refused to enter into a war and instead, taking his family, fled to the island of Don Mote Daeng near to today's Ubon Ratchathani where he obtained a pledge from the Sangha, the Buddhist church, to protect him.

As a result, Chao Thammathevo did not try to take his life and some form of reconciliation between the king and his Oupahat seems to have been achieved. However, two years later Chao Thammathevo and Thao Sithat, or his son, again raised an army and once again the King took

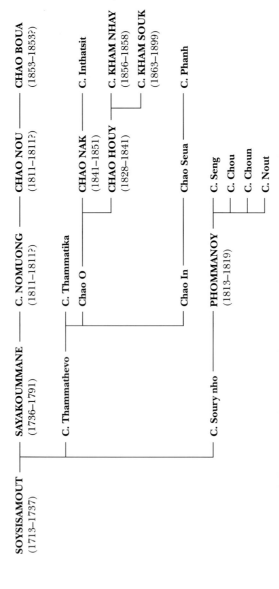

GENEALOGICAL TABLE 8 The Kings of Champasak – Soysisamout to Chao Kham Souk, 1713 to 1899

refuge in flight. However, on this occasion the Queen Mother begged Thammathevo to stop harassing his elder brother and warned him that she would not eat or sleep until there was peace between them.

She kept her word and her son, Chao Thammathevo, was forced to watch her gradually growing weaker and weaker, until, afraid of what would happen if he were seen to be responsible for his mother's death, he consulted his ministers and agreed that he had to submit to his brother. This he did and Sayakoummane returned to reign. In 1768 Chao Thammathevo died and with his death the opposition to the king was temporarily muted.

King Sayakoummane makes Enemies

CHAMPASAK WAS ABOUT to be drawn into the affairs of Vientiane and Siam. Phra Vorarat and Phra Ta Suvarnkut, the disaffected Ministers of Chao Siribunyasarn, King of Vientiane, had created for themselves an independent state at Nong Bua Lamphu near Udorn Thani. However, their state was only some 120 kilometres south of Vientiane, far too close to give them any protection. In 1768 Chao Siribunyasarn sent his Vientiane troops over and was able to capture their city. They fled south to Champasak and asked Sayakoummane for his protection. This was granted and as a result, Chao Siribunyasarn was very angry, declaring Champasak an enemy of Vientiane. In the Annals of Champasak the two former Ministers are known as Phawo (*Phra Vor*) and Patha (*Phra Ta*).

The two were given land and soon built themselves a new capital close to Champasak. But, some time later, about 1777, Phra Vorarat foolishly antagonised Chao Sayakoummane over the rebuilding of the Champasak capital and as a result found himself without a major ally in the South.

King Siribunyasarn was quick to send his Vientiane army against him. Phra Vor was killed in the battle, but his son, Thao Kham, managed to escape. He sent a message to King Taksin reminding him that his father had been a Siamese vassal, adding further that Chao Siribunyasarn was planning to join in a Burmese attack on Siam.

Siam punishes Chao Sayakoummane

THIS WAS AN opportunity King Taksin found too good to be missed. Taksin immediately mounted two armies: one against Champasak as punishment for not coming to the aid of Phra Vor, and a second to join it and together to march on Vientiane with orders to destroy the capital completely.

Chao Sayakoummane reacted to the Siamese advance as he had always done to any threat of violence. His fears that he expressed then give one a glimpse of the horrors of war of those times. He said he was refusing battle not only because of the death of the human beings that would take place, but equally because of the great massacre of the elephants and horses that always happened in battle. Rather than lead his army, he left secretly with his family for Don Sai, an island midway between Champasak and Khong. Here he was found by the Siamese and brought back to the capital in golden chains.

At the same time the Siamese commander, General Chakri, who as Rama I was to be the next king of Siam, called upon Fay Na and Kham Phong, the sons of Phra Ta, to collect their troops and join him in the assault on Vientiane.

Chao Sayakoummane had failed in his duty as an ally of Siam and was taken back to Bangkok where he remained for two years (1778–1780) before being allowed back to rule as a vassal king. In reality, 1778 was the last year of an independent kingdom of Champasak since from 1778 to 1893 it was a dependency of the Siamese and in 1893 Champasak came under French administration.

Although the Siamese had allowed Chao Sayakoummane to return to his throne both he and his successors were to be under increasing pressure to permit the actual administration of the country to be controlled by Bangkok. From 1809 Rama II (1809–1824) and his Ministers devoted every effort to creating a 'Tai land' made up of all the Tai people, of which Champasak, was a small, but important part.

Chao O and Chao In exceed their Powers

WHEN CHAO SAYAKOUMMANE was allowed to return to Champasak in 1780, he found a divided kingdom. During his absence, the Siamese had begun to make their own appointments. Among these were his nephews, Chao O and Chao In, who were the sons of his rebellious brother, Chao Thammathevo. Chao O was made the Oupahat, or Governor, and Chao In the Chaomuong of Attopeu a province to the east of Champasak on the border with Vietnam. This was a very sensitive appointment as the inhabitants were chiefly montagnards who did not always accept the authority of Champasak.

When Sayakoummane was told that Chao O and Chao In were oppressing the people and stirring up trouble, he ordered his grandsons,

Chao Nou and Chao Set to take an army to Attopeu and investigate. Unfortunately, with memories of the Thammathevo's rebellions fresh in their memories, they saw this as a chance to take revenge on the former Oupahat's family and immediately made plans to arrest and execute Chao O and Chao In.

Chao In learnt of their plans in time to take refuge in the forest, but Chao O took refuge in a wat, where he placed his arms around a Buddha figure claiming protection. But this was not sufficient to restrain the blood thirsty intentions of the Sayakoummane's two grandsons. As Chao O was torn from the Buddha figure, he begged to be allowed to at least perform the last rites before being killed.

This was granted. With his wife he prepared 100 fruits of the saba tree and filled them with powdered gold. Then as he began his offering to the monks he prayed that if he were innocent no descendant of Chao Nou or Chao Set should ever rule. It was a curse that would almost come true. In 1811, Chao Nou, his murderer, was to be king for three days before dying and Chao Nou's son, Chao Boua, died of a sudden illness before he could be crowned. Chao Set was never offered the crown. They were the last of Chao Sayakoummane's line. Thereafter, the crown passed to the descendants of Chao Thammathevo and continued in that line down to the last two kings of Champasak, Chao Rasadanay and his son, Chao Boun Oum.

When the Siamese general informed Bangkok of Chao O's assassination, Chulalongkorn ordered a Commissioner (*Kha luang*) to be sent as soon as possible to Champasak. The Commissioner decided that it was too serious a matter for him to deal with and ordered Chao Sayakoummane, and other members of the royal family to report to Bangkok where the Siamese king could decide what should be done. Sayakoummane, however, did not complete the journey. He became so ill that the Siamese Commissioner took pity on him and allowed him to return to Champasak to recover.

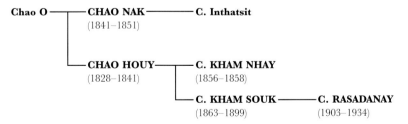

GENEALOGICAL TABLE 9 The Royal Line passes to Chao O's descendants

A Magician starts a Revolt

THE AFFAIR BLEW over and it was not until 1791, eleven years later, that new trouble arose. A man called Sieng Keu, claiming magical powers, was able to raise a revolt and marched on Champasak town. He and his followers overwhelmed the defences and Chao Sayakoummane learning of this new disaster had a stroke and died. Fay Na and Kham Phong, who had earlier raised an army to help the Siamese attack Vientiane, immediately took advantage of the situation and raising a new army they helped the Siamese commander from Yasothon to recapture Champasak. Sieng Keu was soon caught and executed.

Archaimbault notes that Western historians assess Chao Sayakoummane as a weak and indecisive king. He points out, however, that the Lao annalists saw him as a traditional Buddhist king, who deplored war and killing, whether of human beings, or of animals, and as such was 'the worthy successor of ancient kings'.

Although the Sieng Keu rebellion was put down without much difficulty, Sayakoummane's death was followed by minor revolts and disturbances. No new king was appointed and Champasak remained under the control of Bangkok whose new king, Rama I (1782–1809), was primarily concerned in maintaining the Siamese dominance over its peripheral territories. Rama I decided that Champasak would do better with a vassal king and to reward Fay Na, the son of Phra Ta, for his past help against Sieng Keu and other rebels by making him king. However, to ensure the loyalty of the people of Champasak he also made Chao Nou and Chao Set, the two grandsons of Sayakoummane who had murdered Chao O in Attopeu, senior ministers of Champasak.

King Fay Na opposes the Siamese

KING FAY NA (1791–1811) had no intention of being a mere figurehead for the Siamese. As Archaimbault says, he in many ways was more conscious of his royal responsibilities than many of the kings of the Champasak dynasty who followed him. Although a usurper placed on the throne by the Siamese, he was in many respects a true descendant of King Soysisamout. He was determined to rebuild Champasak and recreate its greatness.

He began by building a new capital at Kau Khan Kong, which today is the village of Ban Muong Kau opposite Paksé. By moving his capital further northwards, he hoped to be able to control the more distant principalities that may by then have stretched as far north as modern Nakhon Pathom and Thakhek.

In the new capital, he built a special vihara for the Crystal Buddha, the palladium of Champasak, which he had escorted there with great pomp. His reign lasted sixteen years and was mostly devoted to reorganising and rebuilding the country. His main achievement was his skill in opposing the ever continuing efforts of Bangkok to subsume the whole of the realm. Their chief method was to offer local Chaomuongs and rulers the apparently greater freedom of reporting directly to Bangkok, so severing their allegiance to Champasak. Fay Na countered this to a large extent by the creation of new muongs. Although many were small and insignificant, his strategy did successfully counter the Siamese and prevented the complete dismemberment of his kingdom.

On the debit side, by moving his capital so far north, he cut across the traditional trade routes as well as the political structure that had developed from the times of Phra Kru Nhot Keo. In doing so he opened the way for new claims and new territorial disputes that the Siamese would do all they could to exploit.

On Fay Na's death in 1811, Rama II sent a Commissioner to inquire into the question of the succession. By some accounts the Commissioner on the authority of the Siamese king appointed Chao Nomuong, a son of King Sayakoummane, as king. But, if this is true, Chao Nomuong seems to have reigned for only three days before dying.

The Crystal Buddha taken to Bangkok

ON LEARNING OF his death, Rama II sent a gold plaque investing Chao Nou, the son of the deceased king. There is, however, a disturbing similarity with the description of the previous reign. Is it probable that two kings should follow each other, each reigning only three days and then dying without explanation? One modern historian, Chao Sanhprasithna Champasak lists only Chao Nou and does not mention the father, Chao Nomuong, as being crowned, so there may be some confusion in the different Annals between the father and the son.

The Commissioner was left once again with a vacant throne. But he turned to what may have seemed to him, and for his career, to be a more important matter. He asked the Court whether Champasak had any valuable treasures from the past. He was told that they had only one, the Crystal Buddha. This because of its antiquity was of great value, but to the people of Champasak it was of inestimable value as it was the palladium of

ILLUSTRATION 17 Vihara at Wat Phu

© Peter & Sanda Simms

the kingdom and symbolised the essence of the nation. The Commissioner reported this to Rama II, who ordered him to return to Bangkok, bringing the Crystal Buddha with him!

A solemn procession of Champasak nobles and monks was organised and the Buddha set off for Bangkok. At Saraburi, it was transferred to a pirogue with, in the centre, a parasol ornamented with gold threads to protect the Buddha figure from the sun. Great respect was shown and the bow of the ceremonial pirogue was carved with the representation of a dragon. So, accorded the greatest honour, it was rowed down to Bangkok and to the Royal Palace on the banks of the Menam Chaophraya, where it still rests today.

In Champasak, the removal of the Buddha had a devastating effect. It seemed to everyone from noble to peasant as though the very heart of the country had been taken away. Rama II may have hoped that as a result, Champasak would disintegrate and that Siam would be able to take it over piecemeal. By failing to appoint a successor to king Fay Na, he may have thought to have hastened the disintegration of the country. If so, it was a vain hope as although there was an interregnum from 1807, (or 1811 depending on the date of the death of Fay Na) to 1813, Champasak continued to maintain its integrity as strongly as ever.

ILLUSTRATION 18 Lintel at Wat Phu, provenance Khmer

© Peter & Sanda Simms

Chao Phommanoy: a troubled Reign

WITH THE NEW king, the crown left Sayakoummane's family. It was given to Chao Phommanoy, (1813–1819) who was the son of a former Rajavong, Chao Soury Nho. Chao Soury Nho was one of Chao Soysisamout's sons and a brother of Chao Thammathevo. To divide the responsibility as much as possible and so weaken the authority of the king, Rama II appointed one of Chao Phommanoy's cousins, Chao Thammatika, the eldest son of Chao Thammathevo, as Maha Oupahat.

As Rama II had expected, it was not to be a happy combination. Within a few months the King and his Oupahat were in dispute and were forced to go to Bangkok for the Siamese to adjudicate. Rama II decided against the Oupahat who was told he would remain in Bangkok.

Chao Phommanoy had hardly returned to his kingdom before the Chaomuong of Ubon Ratchathani renounced his allegiance to Champasak and placed himself under Bangkok, who rewarded him with a new muong. In the same year, 1814, the Rajavong of Khong also renounced his allegiance and was made a Chaomuong of his birthplace, a village near Yasothon.

Saket Ngong and the Lao Theung Rebellion

BUT MORE SERIOUS trouble was brewing among the upland peoples, who were then known as the Kha. In 1817, a monk named Saket Ngong, or sometimes called merely, Sa, who had been living in Siam, claimed magical powers. Among other things he showed how he could tame the sun's rays

173

to make flames and boasted that if he wished, he could set fire to the town of Champasak.

He also claimed to be able to make himself invisible at will and by some clever artifice seems to have been able to create this effect. The people flocked to him, specially the montagnard from around Attopeu. They raised an army and capturing pirogues rowed down to the Island of Khong where King Phommanoy and his Court were residing.

Chao Phommanoy sent his new Oupahat, Chao Khamsouk, to reconnoitre. On his return, he reported that the river was covered with pirogues and the air was full of strident cries. The king promptly called all his nobles and told them to send their families away to safety. He then gathered his own family together and fled.

It was not the kind of behaviour that the warrior kings of Bangkok expected of their vassals. As soon as Bangkok learnt what had happened Phommanoy was called to Bangkok and the Siamese army was given the responsibility for restoring law and order. Chao Anou, the king of Vientiane, who as part of vassalage was responsible for the safety of the borders with Vietnam and Cambodia, immediately sent his son, Chao Nho, with an army to assist the Siamese commander.

Saket Ngong had become so overconfident that, by one account, he had used up his magical powers through overindulgence with young girls. He was no longer able to make himself invisible and his followers, thoroughly disillusioned, deserted him. He escaped to the eastern hills, but was tricked by Chao Nho's troops and was captured. He was then sent to Bangkok for execution.

Chao Phommanoy died soon after his arrival in Bangkok. His reign had seen the loss of nearly all that Fay Na and his predecessors had gained. By the time of his death, Champasak was little more than a colony of Bangkok. Its muongs stripped one by one from its control so that there was little north of the Nam Mun that owed it allegiance.

In 1818, Chao Anou, who had a very warm relationship with Rama II, pleaded for his son to be made the new king of Champasak and Chao Kham Phong, a Vientiane minister and relative, to be his Oupahat. Despite opposition within his Court, Rama II agreed and the Champasak crown passed once more back to the Vientiane nobility.

Chao Nho: a vassal of Bangkok

CHAO NHO (1819–1827) proved himself a willing servant of Bangkok and very soon was hated by the people of Champasak. His arrogance and petulance were not the sole grievance. He had a new census taken and new, heavier taxes applied. Among the many abuses of his power he ordered the hereditary clans that provided rowers for the royal pirogues, to undertake what was in everyone's eyes demeaning work as casual labourers building a new defensive wall around the capital

However, his final undoing came about not through his misrule of Champasak, but through the calamitous war his father, Chao Anou, King of Vientiane, mounted against King Rama III (1824–1851) of Siam. In 1827, at his father's request, Chao Nho marched the Champasak armies through the northern territories of his kingdom where a large number of Lao families had over the years migrated in order to escape persecution in Vientiane. He ordered their rounding up for deportation to Vientiane, one objective being, presumably, to provide more conscripts for the Vientiane army.

He then marched against Ubon Ratchathani. However, the Lao families who were being forced to follow his army, when they heard that a Siamese army was approaching rose up against Chao Nho, who then found himself attacked from the rear, while threatened by the Siamese from the front.

Taking refuge in flight, Chao Nho tried first to enter Champasak town, but his people, at last able to take their revenge against him, shut their gates and refused him entry. He and his retinue crossed the Mekong and took refuge in a montagnard village. The Siamese army having reestablished themselves in Champasak ordered Chao Houy, a son of the Chao O who had been murdered in Attopeu, to mount an expedition against Chao Nho. This he did willingly, having been the person who had encouraged the townspeople of Champasak to refuse sanctuary to Chao Nho.

Eventually, Chao Nho and his Court were tracked down and he, his relatives, his courtiers, jewellers, blacksmiths and mahouts were taken to Bangkok in 1827.

From 1829 to 1893, the Siamese took administrative control over the former kingdoms of Vientiane and Champasak, including the numerous principalities and semi-independent towns that had been vassals of the two former kingdoms. However, in Champasak where a social structure and the royal family had survived the defeat, they only did so with great difficulty and sometimes at the cost of having to give individual rulers, chaomuongs, or village chiefs, considerable autonomy.

The Champasak Dynasty returns to the Throne

Rama III appointed Chao Houy (1828–1841) as the seventh king, and his brother, Chao Nak, as the Maha Oupahat. Chao Houy fought hard to restrict the powers of Bangkok, but it was to be a losing battle. After Chao Houy had been made king, Rama III had an Act passed modifying all the titles held by the Champasak nobility that, in effect, reduced them by at least one rank.

A new census was called and heavier taxes were imposed. As well, to emphasise their new status, Chao Houy and Chao Nak had each to report to Bangkok every three years taking with them tribute in the form of a golden tree, as well as objects made from ivory, numbers of rhinoceros horns, and cloth made from ramie, a prized East Asian plant.

The Siamese policy of creating new muongs that reported directly to the Bangkok administration was increased. The whole of the Korat plateau was repopulated with whole villages who were forced to remove out of the Vientiane kingdom and resettle in the new territories. Rama III ordered the whole of central Laos to be systematically raided, the villages split up and scattered to create new centres that, without the social structure of being part of their muong could then be controlled by the Siamese. Vientiane as a kingdom ceased to exist, and Champasak was able to preserve only with the greatest difficulty is own existence.

In 1840, Chao Houy, who had been ill, fell from his elephant, striking one of its tusks as he fell. He was not to recover from the fall, and died within a few days aged 63.

Bangkok tightens its grip

HIS BROTHER, CHAO Nak (1841–1851), who had been the Maha Oupahat, was allowed to accede to the throne and ruled for ten years until, in 1851, he was called to Bangkok over a border dispute. It is not known exactly what happened while he was there, but he was said to have contracted cholera from which he died, aged 76. He too had tried to stop the encroachment of the Siamese, following once again the strategy of creating new muongs himself. But power now lay with the Siamese and there was little that he had been able to do except to slow down the inevitable devolution of power.

From 1851 to 1853 an interregnum followed Chao Nak's death. One reason may have been that in 1851 Rama III died and a new policy was being evolved by Rama IV, who is better known as King Mongkut (1851 – 1868). The succession in Champasak may not have appeared to be very pressing compared with the many other problems that the new king faced in his own Court at Bangkok.

It was not until 1853 when Chao Boua, who was acting as a regent, carried the annual taxes to Bangkok that Mongkut finally decided to appoint him king. However, before Chao Boua could receive the golden plaque, he, as so many other rulers before him, was stricken with a sudden illness and died.

Immediately, an open dispute broke out between Chao Sene, the son of the former king Chao Nak (1841–1851), and Chao Seng, the son of king Phommanoy (1813–1820). Their immediate claims to the throne seemed to have been so well prepared that they both fell under suspicion that they might have been involved in Chao Boua's unexplained death. Nothing, however, was proved. Once again an interregnum (1853–1856) followed,

Mongkut was determined to modernise Siam in every way possible, but he could not rely on the wholehearted support of his own Ministers. The following example from Champasak illustrates the kind of difficulty that he faced.

King Mongkut's Reforms and his new Colonial policy

IN 1853 KING Mongkut had a Commissioner, Anurak Phupet, sent to the Champasak capital to collect new taxes and to confirm Chao Seua, the Oupahat, in the position of Regent, or possibly King. However, when Anurak arrived, he found that Chao Seua had died and there were two claimants to the throne, Chao Sene and Chao Seng, who had been so suspiciously quick in putting forward their claims on the death of King Boua.

When the Siamese Commissioner, Anurak Phupet, returned to Bangkok with the taxes, he told King Mongkut of the rivalry between the two princes for the throne. Rama IV ordered Anurak Phupet and a second Commissioner, Luang Saksena, to return to Champasak to resolve the matter.

When the Commissioners arrived they took advantage of their position by taking bribes from the two candidates, as well as extorting money from the other nobles. This came to the knowledge of King Mongkut who recalled them. He put the two Commissioners on trial and, finding them guilty, confiscated all their possessions. As well, to show the people of Champasak that he believed in impartial justice, he arranged for the money and valuables that had been taken from the nobles of Champasak to be returned to their owners.

Mongkut hoped that by punishing the two Commissioners severely, he could make his courtiers realise that the old feudal days when an appointment was an opportunity to enrich oneself, were over. It is hardly surprising that King Mongkut was not immediately successful, but he did lay down the framework for a more modern and dedicated government service.

177

After this interregnum, Chao Kham Nhay (1856–1858), a son of Chao Houy was appointed king. He reigned for only two years, dying at the age of twenty-seven.

His reign was followed by another interregnum that lasted from 1858 to 1863. During part of this time Chao Chou, a son of Chao Phommanoy, acted as Regent, but he greatly misused his powers, at the Court he made free with the wives of his nobles and officials, and throughout the country he maltreated the ordinary people appropriating from them whatever he wanted. His misrule was reported to King Mongkut, who had him brought to Bangkok.

From then until the end of the Siamese period, Champasak was ruled over by Chao Khamsouk (1863–1899), a son of Chao Houy. Before the end of his reign the history of Champasak had become merged with the history of Laos as a whole. How the French gradually managed to take over Laos and Champasak from the Siamese will be told in Chapter Thirteen.

There were, however, two major developments during Chao Kham-souk's reign that should be mentioned here. The first was a Siamese measure whereby slavery was made illegal throughout Champasak. The second was the opening in 1887 of a telegraph line between Bangkok and Champasak. From that time on, it was possible for the central government to maintain immediate and total control over the outlying provinces. It came too late to be of use to the Siamese, but it became the basis of the new administration to be set up by the French.

Champasak becomes a French Protectorate

FROM 1893, THE French removed the provinces of Attopeu and Saravane from the realm of Champasak and Chao Khamsouk, freed from Siamese control, found himself administering Champasak under the French. He died in 1899 aged sixty-two, and was succeeded by Chao Nhouy, who has become better known to the western world as Chao Rasadanay. He was to rule until 1934, when the French ceased to recognize him as king, instead giving him the lower title of Governor of Champasak. Immediately after acceding to the throne Chao Rasadanay was faced with a major rebellion by the montagnards.

The Highlands of southern Laos

THE LEFT BANK of the Mekong from the southern borders of the Xieng Khouang Plateau to the southern frontiers of Champasak was a part of

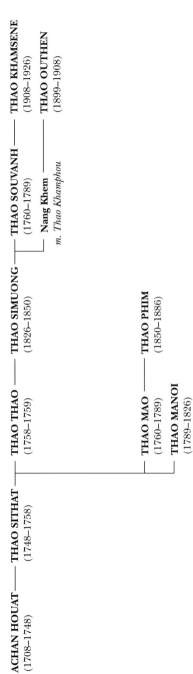

GENEALOGICAL TABLE 10 The Chaomuongs of Khong – Achan Houat to Thao Khamsene (18th, 19th and 20th centuries)

179

Laos that over the centuries had been least influenced by the events in the kingdoms of Luang Prabang, Vientiane and Xieng Khouang. In that region of high mountains and valleys, the Lao Loum, the Lao who were the inhabitants of the cities and valley agricultural land, probably constituted far less than 40 percent of the population.

The great majority of the people was the so-called *Kha*, more recently called the Lao Theung. They were the descendants of the indigenous peoples of early Indochinese and the Mon-Khmer. With the arrival of the Tai from the twelfth century onwards, the Lao Theung were driven up into the mountains where they had to develop a new, often impoverished, way of life making the best they could out of the barren soil of the uplands.

Their eastern frontier was the Annamite Chain, the great ridge of mountains that separated the Tai and Lao Theung from the Vietnamese. Although the frontier had never been demarcated, it had, from the times of Fa Ngum, been recognized as a physical entity. Fa Ngum and the King of Annam had agreed that where the rivers ran into the sea and the houses were built on the ground, the territory was Vietnamese. While, where the rivers flowed into the Mekong and the houses were built on stilts, the people owed allegiance to Lan Xang.

Although the western side of the Annamite Chain formed apart of Lan Xang, its administration whether by Vientiane, Champasak, or the local Lao Loum rulers was unorganised and haphazard. The degree of control changed year by year depending on the strength or weakness of the local rulers.

Even at the best of times, beyond trying to collect taxes from the more accessible Lao Theung villages and to exact the annual corvée from them, they left the Lao Theung very much on their own. There was little law and order and the Lao Theung had to be ready to defend themselves against slave traders, Lao Loum, Vietnamese, Chinese or even a different tribe of their own Lao Theung people.

In the south, the most important Lao Theung region was around the Bolovens Plateau. Except for the more important towns such as Attopeu, Saravane and some of the larger trading towns, there was little attempt to maintain a Vientiane or Champasak administration. The Lao Theung were left to manage their own affairs along tribal lines. There was already enough cause for discontent and any increase in the harshness by the new overlords, the French and Siamese, would be cause enough to take up arms.

The Kha Rebellions

WHEN LE BOULANGER wrote his History of Laos in the 1930s, he commented that there was no known cause for the rebellions that spread so rapidly across the Bolovens and were to continue spasmodically for thirty-five years from 1901 to 1935. With the perspective of the last sixty years of research, there is now no doubt that the division of the former kingdom of Champasak and of its neighbouring territories between the French and Siamese administrations was the reason that discontent escalated so rapidly into armed revolt.

By the 1893 Franco-Siamese treaty, France took possession of the whole of the Left bank of the Mekong, while the Siamese occupation of the former Lao territory of the Korat plateau was given the appearance of legality and permanence. To the people on both sides of the Mekong this division of territory brought great hardship. The great Mekong river that had for centuries united the families on its two banks, now suddenly became a dividing line that separated them. For once the Lao Loum and the Lao Theung were united in their frustration.

By 1893, the Siamese system of Commissioners administering a territory under the direct control of King Chulalongkorn had become finely honed. With the completion of the telegraph line from Bangkok to Champasak in 1887, Bangkok could keep itself informed of every event, literally within minutes of its happening. Decisions could be made rapidly and seemingly more efficiently. But these decisions had never been discussed with the local people and Bangkok did not take into account the strength of local feelings and the opposition that was developing against this new way of governing. Chulalongkorn began the implementation of laws against the slave trade, against opium trafficking and, worse still, the imposition of even larger taxes that included many people who had never been taxed before.

The French on their side of the river also began to take action against the slave trade, to introduce measures that would organise the sale of opium as a way of raising money for the Treasury and, like the Siamese, to extend and increase the collection of taxes.

By 1901 there had been some popular manifestations of discontentment and, in 1889, a revolt in the northeast of Siam had spread rapidly and had not gone unnoticed in the rest of the country. The chief rebel was a former Buddhist monk who claimed to be a *Phou Mi Boun*, a holy man possessed with special magical powers. He had been joined by other ascetics and soon the countryside was full of rumours of terrible disasters that were about to overwhelm the country.

As well, as a symbol of the upset in the social order that Chulalongkorn's reforms and the arrival of the French had made, there were prophecies that pebbles would become gold and silver and that gold and silver would become pebbles. While pumpkins and gourds would become elephants and horses. To the ordinary peasant, there was only one meaning. The social order was about to be reversed: the rich would see their wealth turn to stones, while the poor would see their stones and even the vegetables in their gardens turned into immense wealth.

In 1901, near Oudone, matters came to a head. A holy man and also a former Buddhist monk, named Bac My claimed magical powers. Among other things that any bullets fired at them would turn into frangipani flowers and are harmless. His followers claimed, and he never denied their claims, that he was the Maitreya, the next human being who would become a Buddha, the successor to Gautama. Tradition had it that the coming of the next Buddha would be a time of great change and for the supporters of Bac My it was one more confirmation that a gigantic revolution was about to take place.

Although the revolt took place within the demilitarised zone, the Siamese had no hesitation in sending in troops to put it down. This they managed to do by the next year, 1902. The French, however, did not protest this breach of the treaty as they had political problems in Paris and were themselves facing the same rebellion in the Bolovens region.

The Siamese dealt so firmly with the revolt that Bac My moved across to the Left Bank and turned the rebellion against the French. The new French colonisers showed both ineptitude and bad faith in their dealings and soon had the whole of the Bolovens in the possession of the rebels with an enormous loss of property and wealth.

By 1902, it is estimated that there were more than 100 *Phou Mi Boun*, white clothes ascetics, who had given up their life in the jungle searching for truth to lead a crusade against the French and the new form of government.

The rebellion was to continue until 1935. Suffice it to say that among the leaders of the *Phou Mi Boun's*, the most important after Bac My was Kommadam a Chieftain of the Nya Heun tribe.

In August 1902, one of the ring leaders Pho Kadouat was driven back to Tchepone and was killed the next year. Bac My, or Ong Keo, as he then called himself was driven back into the hills as was Kommadam. By the end of 1902, although it did not seem so at the time, the worst of the rebellion was over. There were further outbreaks until November 1907 when Bac My was taken from house arrest and then bayoneted to death 'while trying to escape'. Two days later Kommadam was treacherously attacked while under a truce to negotiate but managed to escape. He survived until 1935 when he was betrayed by one of his followers and killed and his son, Sithone was imprisoned until released by the Japanese during the war. Sithone later joined the Pathet Lao where he became the principal representative of the Lao Theung, was made a Vice-President of the Lao Communist government and on his death was given a state funeral on his death.

As can be seen these Kha rebellions spanned the whole period of French rule and as it was, to a large extent caused by the failures of the inexperienced French administration. As law and order were by then a French responsibility and the rebellion was connected with other events in Laos as a whole, it is better left to be treated fully in the second volume of this history on the French administration and postwar Laos.

Champasak ceases to be a kingdom

CHAMPASAK CONTINUED AS a French colony until 1941 when France was overrun by the German armies. Thailand took this opportunity to take possession of Champasak and other parts of the Right Bank of the Mekong. These it continued to administer until the end of World War II in 1945. In the same year, Chao Rasadanay had died and had been succeeded by his eldest son, Chao Boun Oum. Champasak was returned to France, but in 1946 Chao Boun Oum, the dynastic ruler, was persuaded into handing over the sovereign rights of Champasak to form a part of a new, independent Laos under the King in Luang Prabang.

By then modern Champasak, founded by Chao Soysisamout, had existed as an independent, or semi-independent, realm for more than 200 hundred years.

There had been both good as well as hard and bitter times, but the spirit that was first evoked by Phra Kru Nhot Keo in 1708 flourished throughout the years and was continued in the works of the poets and writers of the past. Of the most recent of these poets and artists was the great writer and intellectual Nhouy Abhay, who was himself a descendant of Achan Houat.

Most importantly, the passionate and individual spirit of Champasak can still be seen to have survived in its peoples' hearts, whether they are in Laos, or reluctantly living in exile abroad.

CHAPTER TWELVE

An Overview of Xieng Khouang History

FATE GAVE TO the kingdoms of Luang Prabang and Vientiane a geographical position that protected them from minor incursions. The price, however, was their constant involvement in the monumental battles between Burma and Siam. But, damaging as these wars were to their economies, both kingdoms possessed large areas of rich agricultural lands that helped speed their recovery when peace returned. As well, they held dominant positions on the great trade routes from mainland China southwards, and from the Indian Ocean to the South China Sea. The prosperity that came from the trade also helped them to quickly regain the wealth lost in fighting.

Muong Phoueune, or Xieng Khouang, or Tran Ninh, the many names are a testimony to the numerous changes the kingdom has experienced, did not have these advantages. It is a vast region of some 12,500 square miles largely comprising a semi-arid plateau that rises in parts to more than 4,000 feet.

This great plateau, the *Plaine des Jarres*, forms a bowl within the mountain ranges cutting it off from Vietnam, China, Luang Prabang and Vientiane. While these mountain ranges are an impediment to trade, they are worthless as a defensive wall. Once an army has passed through the numerous mountain passes, or along the rivers, and reached the plateau region, there are no natural obstacles to stop it attacking anywhere throughout the heartland of the kingdom.

It is on the southern hills of this plateau that the capital, Xieng Khouang, lies. It has been an inhabited area for many thousands of years. To the northwest of Xieng Khouang lie three major Bronze Age sites dating back 2,000 to 3,000 years surrounded by hundreds of stone jars. As mentioned in Chapter 2, no one knows who these people were but they were sophisticated enough to wear jewellery and must have had a highly organised society to be able to undertake, for whatever purpose, the task of

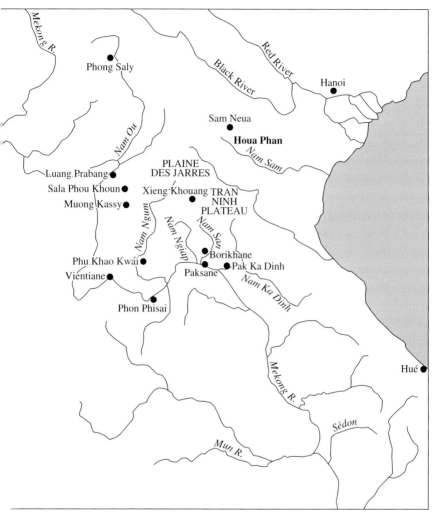

P 6 Xieng Khouang in the 18th and 19th Centuries

carving these hundred of jars: a task that must have been spread over several centuries.

The major site, with about 250 or more jars, lies between Xieng Khouang and the market town of Phongsavan. There are two other sites in the area one with about 90 jars and the other about 150. Perhaps one day, we shall discover new information that may tell us whether they were funerary jars and why so much effort was spent in their creation. The smallest jars in the three major sites weigh about 600 kilograms while the heaviest is well over a ton.

As with many of the bronze and iron age peoples of the world, they did not use local stone, but carved them from a sandstone that has been tentatively believed to come from a range of mountains more than 100 kilometres away towards Luang Prabang. Other sites on the Xieng Khouang plateau have been found, but none of them has more than about 40 jars each. As one turns away from one of these sites, it is with regret that one realises one is more conscious of wondering why they created the jars, than of feeling respect for the greatness of the people who expended so much time and energy in their creation.

The climate is no more hospitable than the land: it passes from the extremes of the heat of summer to the bitter freezing mists of winter. Despite all these disadvantages, it is a country that has produced a nation of people whose life and customs are individualistic and deeply ingrained. As with all Lao people, they carry within them a sense of their history. Even after deportation and having to live for a hundred or more years in a foreign country, they still remain and think of themselves as Phoueune, or P'uon.

The Descendants of Khun Boulom

THEY TRACE THEIR descent from the legendary Chet Chuong, the second son of Khun Boulom, who was given the whole of Muong Phoueune as his kingdom. To the northwest of his kingdom lay Xieng Thong, modern Luang Prabang, which had been given to his elder brother, Khun Lo.

History, as opposed to legend, begins with Fa Ngum's triumphant march northwards to regain what he considered his birthright, the kingdom of Xieng Thong. Repulsed by the rulers of the Vientiane valley, Fa Ngum's first significant capture was the town of Xieng Khouang. This he took with the help of the king's son, who, like Fa Ngum's own father, had been exiled for committing adultery. Marching northeast from Xieng Khouang after it had acknowledged Fa Ngum's suzerainty, he approached the borders of Annam. The king of Annam offered him a very favourable treaty and an alliance. Fa Ngum then marched north where he subdued the Sipsong Chau Tai whose territory lay along the Black and Red rivers, and finally descended on Xieng Thong. After three great battles, the king surrendered to him.

Muong Phoueune was only independent at times when it was strong and its neighbours were either divided, or busy about other matters, then it

ILLUSTRATION 19 *Plaine des Jarres*

© Peter & Sanda Simms

could live in peace and with freedom. But when either Vietnam, or Lan Xang, or later Vientiane, was strong and aggressive, it had usually to pay at least nominal tribute to one, sometimes all three, of its neighbours.

Muong Phoueune refuses Tribute to Lan Xang

FROM THE TIMES of Fa Ngum, the relations between Muong Phoueune and Lan Xang remained amicable. Then in the beginning of the sixteenth century, the king of Muong Phoueune felt strong enough to withhold his tribute. As a result in 1532, Chao Phothisarath (1520–1550), the king of Lan Xang, sent three envoys to claim the traditional payment. When they had not returned after two years, he sent another mission. By some accounts this mission learnt that the earlier envoys had been killed by the king of Muong Phoueune. Even in the days of very bad communications, it is difficult to believe that for more than two years the news of their deaths had not reached Xieng Thong. It is, of course, always possible that Phothisarath had learnt about it earlier, but had not responded as he could not decide on a course of action.

However, when it was certain that his envoys had been killed he chose to go war. It was a war that brought no immediate profit to either side. The army Chao Phothisarath sent against Xieng Khouang had little success and it was two years before Xieng Khouang admitted defeat and agreed to pay tribute.

More than a hundred years later, about 1650, the Lan Xang king, Chao Souligna Vongsa (1637–1694), was told of the beauty of Princess Ken Chan, the daughter of the newly crowned king of Muong Phoueune, Chao Kham Sanh (1651–1688). It is said that Souligna Vongsa became inflamed by the tales of the beauty of this *Pearl of Tran Ninh*, as popular memory calls her. Souligna Vongsa sent a mission asking for her hand, but Chao Kham Sanh refused the request, saying that she was not free and brusquely ordered the Vientiane mission to return taking with them the rich gifts they had brought.

Souligna Vongsa was so angry that he despatched an army to take the Princess by force if necessary and to bring her back. This time, the Lan Xang army quickly triumphed over Xieng Khouang and with Princess Ken Chan they rounded up and brought back some 500 families. As with all such deportations, there were two objectives: to weaken Muong Phoueune and to increase Vientiane's manpower. The deportees were settled near Vientiane and, even today, are known as the 'former P'uons'.

Souligna Vongsa obtained his bride, but the price was to be far higher than he imagined. Thirty eight years later when Chao Kam Lan (1688–

1700), the son of Chao Kam Sanh, came to the throne, the strongest feeling he possessed was a desire for revenge against Vientiane. It was also the main reason in 1707 when the former Lan Xang became two kingdoms, Luang Prabang and Vientiane, that Xieng Khouang, which was free to ally itself with either or both of the two kingdoms, chose Luang Prabang and did not hesitate to refuse to pay tribute to Vientiane. Xieng Khouang's feeling of outrage at Chao Souligna Vongsa's action had been so great that it had survived more than half a century.

Muong Phoueune is surrounded by Enemies

By 1723, Chao Kham Sattha (1723–1751), the grandson of Chao Kam Lan, was king. He too wished to remain independent, but the balance of power had changed. Vientiane had regained its strength and Xieng Khouang found it could only maintain its formal independence by paying tribute to three countries: to Vietnam, to Luang Prabang and to Vientiane.

When the Phoueune king, Chao Kham Sattha married Nang Wen Keu Sam Phiu, a daughter of King Inthasom (1729–1743) of Luang Prabang, he gave his full support to Luang Prabang in its wars against both the Burmese and the Siamese. He also raised an army to fight against the ruler of the Thakhek principality, which today is Khammouan. His close alliance with Luang Prabang brought him more enemies than friends.

Chao Kham Sattha is remembered for the many pagodas he built, his encouragement of Buddhism, and for the great number of Buddha statues he had distributed throughout the country.

Xieng Khouang was able to maintain a precarious independence by balancing Luang Prabang against Vietnam. In 1751 Chao Ong Lo (1751–1779) came to the throne with his younger brother, Chao Ong Bun, as his Oupahat. During 1771, he made the unwise decision to attack Vientiane. His army was totally defeated. He was fortunate enough to be able to escape and, outpacing the pursuit, made his way to Houa Phan, today's Sam Neua, where he began to raise a new army.

The Two Royal Brothers: Chao Ong Lo and Chao Ong Bun

In the meantime, Vientiane made his younger brother, Chao Ong Bun, the governor of Xieng Khouang. So as to gain time for his brother, Chao Ong Bun opened negotiations with Vientiane. He was clever enough to

189

maintain these negotiations until his brother was able to return at the head of a new army to Xieng Khouang.

Unfortunately, the two brothers then fell out, so that instead of creating a grand new army to fight against Vientiane, they turned on each other. Chao Ong Bun lost and offered his submission to his elder brother. They were reconciled, but any hope of breaking away, or of forcing Vientiane to acknowledge their independence, was lost. For the next 37 years, Xieng Khouang remained a vassal of Vientiane. To add to its difficulties, from 1771 a more dominant Vietnam began to emerge on its eastern borders.

The Attempted Renaissance of Muong Phoueune

As ARCHAIMBAULT HAS pointed out there are numerous discrepancies in the annals of Xieng Khouang over the exact course of the turbulent events that took place in the reign of Chao Somphou (1779–1803). Even the date when he ascended the throne is not known with any certainty. It was probably within a three-year period between 1779 and 1782. Uncertainty also clothes the date of his death in captivity in Vientiane. It was either in 1802 or 1803. In what follows, we have chosen what appear to be the more probable dates and course of events.

For some ten years, until about 1789, King Somphou, the son of Chao Ong Lo, devoted himself to rebuilding Xieng Khouang. According to some accounts he made his palace so large and magnificent that it rivalled the palace of the king of Vientiane. Like his grandfather he encouraged the spread of Buddhism. However worthy these activities were, it is also certain that as with so many of his predecessors, he harboured a bitter grudge against Vientiane and planned to break free from its hated suzerainty.

King Nanthasen (1782–1794) in Vientiane learnt of this hatred and decided to take precautions. By one account he sent his army against Xieng Khouang in either 1789 or 1790. By other accounts he tricked Chao Somphou into accepting an invitation to visit Vientiane and once he was there, imprisoned him.

An attack on Xieng Khouang appears to be the more probable as it would be at the same period, 1792, as the Vientiane army attacked and captured Luang Prabang. If there was a battle between Xieng Khouang and Vientiane, Chao Somphou's Xieng Khouang army met the Vientiane army at a place called Muong Hang and was defeated. Chao Somphou fled to Houa Phan and for the time being was left in peace while king Nanthasen's army completed its subjection of Luang Prabang.

The next year, the Vientiane commander, Chao Keu, managed to track down King Somphou and arrested him with two nobles. Chao Keu had orders that Chao Somphou should be killed on the way back when they reached Vientiane territory. Chao Keu and his party with its prisoners crossed the Nam Ngum and it was there, on Vientiane soil, that the executions were to take place. The two nobles were executed, but when it came to Chao Somphou's turn the sky suddenly clouded over, the rain began to pour down, and a bolt of lightning struck the executioner on the arm. This was taken to be an omen too powerful to ignore. The execution was suspended and Chao Somphou was taken alive to Vientiane and there Chao Nanthasen had him placed under guard in a comfortable house.

Chao Somphou's brother, Chao Xieng, however, decided to appeal to Vietnam as a suzerain power of Xieng Khouang. The Emperor of Vietnam collected an army of 3,000 Vietnamese and 3,000 Xieng Khouang soldiers and began to march on Vientiane. King Nanthasen foreseeing a long and expensive war that he might lose, offered a treaty with Vietnam whereby in future Xieng Khouang would pay equal tribute to both Vietnam and Vientiane. Soon after this Chao Somphou was allowed to return to his capital.

Chao Somphou is released

THERE HE FOUND that during the three years he had been in prison, two cousins, Chao Kang and Chao La, had taken power. With Chao Xieng, the brother who had called on the help of the Vietnamese, Chao Somphou attacked and beat them. Chao Kang and Chao La retreated to Muong Kassy and from there appealed to Luang Prabang for armed support. But Luang Prabang weakened by its war with Vientiane was in no position to help them and refused them any assistance.

Chao Somphou returned once more to his interests: embellishing his palace, the construction of the Boun Khong pagoda and the encouragement of Buddhism. In 1798, despite his personal feelings towards Vientiane, he sent the Xieng Khouang Sangharaja to Vientiane to ask for religious assistance and in the next year a senior Vientiane abbot was sent to Xieng Khouang to instruct its Sangha.

It was an important time in the history of Buddhism in Xieng Khouang as it was then decided to give up the Burmese form of Buddhism and to follow the Buddhist practices of the other Tai kingdoms. To mark the change, the Sangha gave up wearing the reddish-orange robes of the

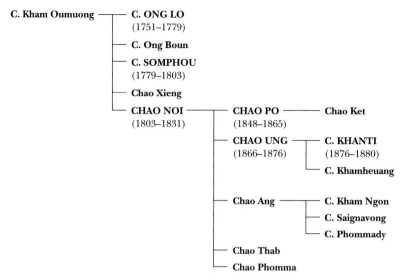

GENEALOGICAL TABLE 11 The Kings of Xieng Khouang – Chao Ong Lo to Chao Khanti, 1751 to 1880

Burmese monks, and reverted to the saffron-coloured robes that were worn throughout the Tai world.

The king of Vientiane, Chao Nanthasen, died in 1794 and was succeeded by Chao Inthavong (1795–1804). Chao Inthavong became jealous of Chao Somphou's achievements when he was told that Chao Somphou was building a city that would rival Vientiane in greatness. If this happened, he thought, Chao Somphou would be strong enough to take his revenge on Vientiane and try to conquer it. He therefore placed his brother, Chao Anou, at the head of a Vientiane army and ordered him to attack and capture Xieng Khouang. His soldiers succeeded in beating the Phoueune army. Once again Chao Somphou found himself arrested and taken back a prisoner to Vientiane for what proved to be the last time. There he remained until his death a year or two later in 1802 or 1803.

Chao Noi ascends the Throne

ON CHAO SOMPHOU'S death, his nephew, the son of his brother Chao Xieng, became king. He was to be known as Chao Noi and was only fourteen years old when he ascended the throne. Chao Noi (1802–1831), whose full name was Chao Southaka Souvanna Koumar, had started working in the administration from the time that Chao Somphou had been taken prisoner. He was then only twelve. As king, he proved to be very authoritarian and, among other measures, demanded that the tax collections be enlarged. With this revenue he continued the rebuilding of Xieng Khouang, especially his palace, and had a retinue of some 300 pages whom he ordered to be trained in fighting. He also built up a large reserve of arms, of elephants, and horses.

In 1814 he successfully put down a rebellion by the Kha people in the hills to the north. But in 1823 he faced a greater problem. His foster-brother who had been one of his closest friends, Phya Xiengdi, went secretly to Vientiane where he accused Chao Noi of wishing to become independent from Vientiane. He also claimed Chao Noi was oppressing his people with heavy taxes and had lost all popular support.

Chao Anou (1804–1828), who was by then the king of Vientiane, called Chao Noi to Vientiane where he kept him captive for three years. By one account, it was Chao Anou's brother, Chao Inthavong, who was responsible for Chao Noi's arrest and imprisonment. By this account Chao Anou was quite friendly with Chao Noi, arranged a marriage for him and saw that his stay in Vientiane was not too arduous. When, one day, Chao Noi successfully tamed a stallion that had refused to be broken by anyone else, Chao Anou was so pleased that he ordered his release and allowed him to return to Xieng Khouang.

If Phya Xiengdi had expected a reward for betraying his foster-brother, he was to be disappointed and decided to leave and to take refuge in Luang Prabang. From there he went to Bangkok where he continued to stir up trouble against Chao Noi. After Chao Noi's return to Xieng Khouang in 1826 or 1827, Phya Xiengdi was foolish enough to go back. Chao Noi wisely arrested him and had him executed.

The capture of King Anou

ONCE AGAIN THERE are different accounts of what happened. The one that has been most widely accepted is that Chao Noi had no reason to love Vientiane. When King Anou, whose rebellion against Rama III had ended so calamitously, fled for the second time from the Siamese, Chao Noi decided it presented an opportunity to negotiate Muong Phoueune's freedom from Vientiane.

Siam, as the conqueror, claimed sovereignty over all of Vientiane's former vassal states. Among these was, of course, Xieng Khouang. Chao Noi proposed to the Siamese commander that he, Chao Noi, should capture and deliver up Chao Anou, and, in exchange, Xieng Khouang would be given its independence. This was agreed to, although it seems a little naïve on the part of Chao Noi to have expected Siam, in its overwhelmingly dominant position, to ever honour such an undertaking.

Chao Noi sent out detachments of troops who soon found Chao Anou, with four of his wives, two sons, two daughters, a niece and his sisters, as well as other members of the family. All were trying to make their way to the safety of Vietnam and Emperor Minh Mang's court.

As a reward for the capture of Chao Anou the Siamese offered Chao Noi the throne of Vientiane. It was not so generous an offer as it might seem. The town of Vientiane and nearby villages had been razed to the ground and the people deported. As the king of Vientiane, Chao Noi would have gained the title of vassal king of an empty land, while his own kingdom, Xieng Khouang, by implication would have remained a vassal state. Not surprisingly he refused the Siamese offer. But he had not taken into account the violent anger felt by the Vietnamese Emperor at his surrender of Chao Anou who had become a Vietnamese vassal. Chao Noi remained in Xieng Khouang not suspecting any danger and within reach of Minh Mang's army,

The sons and grandsons of Chao Anou laid a complaint before Minh Mang who sent for Chao Noi to come to Hué and explain his actions. At first Chao Noi refused to leave Xieng Khouang, but he eventually set off for the Vietnamese Court. As soon as Minh Mang learnt he had started on his journey, troops were sent to meet him. His years as a king were over. The Vietnamese troops immediately arrested him and, as an indication of his future treatment, he completed the rest of the journey to Hué in a cage. He was brought before Minh Mang, who asked how he, a Vietnamese vassal king, had come to betray another king, who had also been granted Vietnamese protection?

The Arrest and Execution of Chao Noi

CHAO NOI, REALISING that he could not expect any mercy, replied that Chao Anou had earlier taken refuge from the Siamese in Vietnam, but Minh Mang had not been able to protect him then, or later. If the might of Vietnam was not powerful enough to protect Chao Anou, how could it expect his small kingdom to oppose the wishes of the Siamese?

Needless to say, Minh Mang refused to accept this explanation and Chao Noi was executed, while his wife and relatives were kept in Vietnam as prisoners for some sixteen years.

The descendants of Chao Noi do not accept this account, which they claim is based on Siamese and Vietnamese sources who wished to move the blame from their own countrymen to Chao Noi.

By their account, Chao Anou after his defeat by the Siamese sent his family to Xieng Khouang to be under the protection of Chao Noi. They deny that Chao Noi ever betrayed Chao Anou who, chased by Siamese and Luang Prabang troops, took refuge in the jungles around the village of Muong Kassy on the road to Luang Prabang. Eventually, driven by hunger and weariness he gave himself up to the surrounding troops.

They maintain that Minh Mang's arrest of Chao Noi was in consequence of his plotting with a Vietnamese faction at the court of Hué opposed to the Emperor.

Chao Sopsaisana Southakakoumar, one of Chao Noi's descendants, says that he worked with the late King of Laos, King Savang Vatthana, and other contemporary scholars, and they believed that Chao Noi did not betray the Vientiane king. However, with so much of Xieng Khouang's historical material lost, or destroyed, this will probably have to remain unresolved.

In 1832, the year following Chao Noi's execution, Minh Mang turned Xieng Khouang into a prefecture giving it the name *Tran Ninh, to guard peace.* The Vietnamese employed the most brutal methods in an unsuccessful attempt to force the people to take on Vietnamese ways, including Vietnamese dress. This, as might be expected, created a great sense of grievance and ever increasing discontent.

When Chao Noi had been forced to go to Vietnam to answer for the capture of Chao Anou, Chao San, the son of Chao Kang who had earlier rebelled against Chao Somphou, was appointed temporary Governor by the Vietnamese. He thought that in a little while he would be confirmed as *de facto* king. This, however, never happened, and he became increasingly disillusioned with Vietnamese rule. In the hope of breaking free from Vietnam, he secretly appealed for help from the Siamese king, Rama III (1824–1851).

Bangkok plans the Annexation of Xieng Khouang

KING RAMA WISHING to make the most out of this opportunity, but at the least possible risk to himself, sent only a small force of some 1,000 men to Xieng Khouang. They took over the town and assassinated the Vietnamese *Quan Phu*, the head of the Prefecture. The Siamese general then told Chao San that Vietnam would doubtless send an army to revenge the death of their official and with only 1,000 men he could not hope to resist them. The Siamese force would therefore have to leave immediately and he proposed that the people of Xieng Khouang should leave also to avoid the inevitable retaliation by Vietnam. He promised to settle the P'uon along the banks of the Mekong, where the Vietnamese would not be able to reach them.

Chao San accepted the idea and four thousand P'uon families decided to follow the Siamese troops to safety, taking with them all the archives and other written records in Xieng Khouang so that the Vietnamese would not be able to rewrite them, and, in this way, produce a false record for posterity. It seems likely that most of these records were lost.

However, as soon as the 4,000 families had crossed the Mekong, the Siamese announced that they were being taken to repopulate an area near Bangkok. When the people heard this, they begged to be allowed to return but Phra Varinthorn, the Siamese general refused. So Chao Sa and Chao Sali, brothers of Chao San, secretly organised a resistance and re-crossed the Mekong.

Disease combined with the hardships of the return journey took a heavy toll and few of them regained their former homes. When they did, they found a region without people under the control of Vietnamese troops who had been sent in to regain control. Chao Sa and Chao Sali managed to escape, but they were chased by the Vietnamese troops and in desperation killed themselves.

Chao San and some 1,000 families continued on to Phanom Sarakham near Bangkok where they were settled and their descendants are still to be found there. Chao San stayed with them until his death.

Vietnam tries to assimilate Xieng Khouang

In XIENG KHOUANG, conditions remained harsh and anarchic as the Vietnamese authorities tried to enforce the Emperor Minh Mang's policy of total assimilation. When the King of Luang Prabang, Chao Mantha Tourath (1817–1836), died, Xieng Khouang decided not to send its triennial tribute. Luang Prabang promptly called for help from Siam and they launched a joint attack on Xieng Khouang. It was from this campaign that Chao Rajaphai, the then Oupahat of Luang Prabang, was accused of having committed treason with the Vietnamese and was later called to Bangkok where Rama III found him guilty.

The attack against Muong Phoueune had been a punitive expedition and, when it was thought that the people of Xieng Khouang and the

Vietnamese had learnt their lesson, the armies of Luang Prabang and Siam returned to their capitals.

In 1841, Minh Mang died and was succeeded by the Emperor Thieu Tri (1841–1848). Thieu Tri and especially his successor Tu Duc (1848–1883) were to face increasing pressure from the French who wished to extend their small foothold in Cochin China. Gradually Hué had neither the means nor the interest to interfere to any great extent in P'uon affairs.

Despite the terrible years they had been through, the people of Xieng Khouang were determined to revive their independence and with it the system of rule under their own royal family. They had realised that they could not do anything while Minh Mang lived, but soon after his death a delegation of the senior nobles raised a large sum of money as a ransom and set off for the Court at Hué.

Xieng Khouang seeks the return of the Dynasty

WHEN THEY ARRIVED, they begged for the release of all the members of Chao Noi's family who had been held prisoner since his execution in 1832. Among them were all of Chao Noi's sons: Chao Po, Chao Ung, Chao Ang (Kam), Chao Thab, and Chao Phomma, as well as his numerous daughters.

The mandarin in charge of the prisoners wanted to know why they wished to rear 'these little ones of the tiger?' The Xieng Khouang delegation very wisely replied, using a slightly derogatory term, that they wanted 'those people' as by tradition their presence was essential in the performance of the buffalo sacrifice to the Guardian Spirit of Xieng Khouang. To allay any suspicions, the Xieng Khouang mission said they had no intention of restoring 'those people' to power. Emperor Thieu Tri evidently considered it was worth the risk, as he allowed them to go back to Muong Phoueune.

When the Emperor Thieu Tri died and Tu Duc ascended the throne, the Vietnamese Court decided to try to buy peace with the people of Xieng Khouang by giving the kingdom some independence. Some time before, the former Emperor, Thieu Tri, had released Chao Po, the eldest son of Chao Noi, with the rest of the royal family. The new Emperor Tu Duc decided the resistance would die down in Xieng Khouang if they were nominally under the rule of one of Chao Noi's sons. He therefore made Chao Po an Imperial Mandatory Prince in charge of the 'prefecture' as the kingdom had now become. However, as so often happens, the relaxation of authority only made people hungry for greater independence and the removal of all Vietnamese officials.

197

Revolt against the Vietnamese Rule

IN EITHER 1851 or 1855, an anti-Vietnamese revolt, stirred up by Siamese agitators, broke out. The Vietnamese were able to restore order, but, struggling to maintain their own territory against the French, they decided to give Xieng Khouang what they called independence. Chao Po (1848–65) was allowed to move to the capital, Xieng Khouang, where he was installed. His younger brother Chao Ung was made Oupahat, Chao Ang, the next of the brothers who had on his return taken the robe, was made Rajaput and Chao Ket, Chao Po's son, became President of the Tribunal.

Neither Chao Thab, nor Chao Phomma, the remaining sons of Chao Noi, was given any important post, and infuriated by their treatment, they left for Bangkok where they tried to stir up trouble. However, Rama IV (1851–1868), better known as king Mongkut, had just ascended the throne and had decided that it was essential Siam acquire a modern administrative and legal structure. The last thing he wanted was to invite a war with Xieng Khouang. He therefore had them exiled to Luang Prabang, where they lived out their lives without being able to do any harm to Chao Po or Xieng Khouang.

For the remaining decade of Chao Po's reign, the life of the principality was able to return to a certain tranquillity and order. However, events in southern China were to bring about a new era of anarchy and pillage that would last from the beginning of the 1870s to the turn of the century. A situation that was to be aggravated as a direct result of a new policy the Chinese government had decided to implement against their southern hill peoples, whose lands were close to the borders of Xieng Khouang and Tongking.

The Hill People flee from southern China

FROM THE 1840s the Chinese authorities had tried to extend their control and, especially, their system of taxation, over the hill peoples in their southern provinces. The revenue from the sale and transportation of opium was one of the greater attractions. The people who were most involved in its growth and sale were the Meo.

From 1856, the Chinese began a new series of massacres similar, but more widespread, than they had carried out in the 1840s. The immediate result was a mass migration over the mountain trails to the Red and Black river valleys. These sudden raids by the Chinese soldiery and the forced departure of entire villages were often the scenes of extraordinary bravery.

The older members of the clans sacrificed themselves as they fought rearguard actions to give the rest of the villagers the chance to put a few days' distance between themselves and the Chinese soldiers who were chasing them.

The Arrival of the Hmong

MEO IS A name that is no longer used as it is thought to be derived from the Chinese "Miao", *barbarian*. About 1972, Dr Yang Dao, the first Meo to gain a PhD from a French university returned to Laos and demanded the term be discarded. Instead, he asked that the word they used themselves, *Hmong*, which means a *free person*, should be recognised in place of Meo. This has now been accepted worldwide.

The two major Hmong clans to enter Laos were the Lo and Ly. They were at first bound together by marriage. But by a series of misadventures, and then by the dissolution of the marriage, this happy alliance was reduced to a series of killings, betrayals and the destruction of each other's villages. As we shall see, this bitter vendetta has continued to the present times. During the Second World War the Lo clan helped the Japanese, while the Ly formed a resistance to fight the Japanese. Later the Lo clan joined the Vietnamese communists, while the Ly remained loyal to the Royal Lao government.

Unlike some of the other hill tribes who entered Xieng Khouang, the Hmong invasion was a peaceful one. One reason for this was that they preferred the higher parts of the mountains that the Lao and the upland Tai did not farm. There the Hmong grew dry rice, wheat and barley, they hunted in the rich jungles and, as a cash crop, grew the opium poppy. Except for salt, they were practically self-sufficient. The only other necessary items they needed to purchase were metals: anything from pins to the toughened bars of iron they spent over a year, or more, boring out to make their single shot rifles.

Lastly, among the metals, they wanted silver, which their skilled jewellers turned into necklaces, arm bands and other solid silver jewellery. Some of this was worn by the men, but on the whole the women were ornamented with the wealth of the family, the only capital that they possessed.

They had little contact with the other peoples in Laos. Except when they came down to the markets, they were only to be seen very occasionally as a silent, almost ghostly, line with pack ponies moving through the jungle and across the plains to sell herbs from the forests, the skins of animals, their beautiful, woven blankets, and, of course, the most valuable of all, their opium. Although relatively newcomers to Laos, the Hmong played an increasingly important role in the events that followed the Second World War as will be seen in the history concerning the period.

While the Hmong brought peace and some commercial benefit to the region, very different kinds of people were also forced to flee from the Chinese army. They came to be known under the Siamese generic name of the *Ho*, meaning, '*Chinese*', although very few were ethnic Chinese. As we have described in the capture of Luang Prabang, they were a mixed collection of all races, whose only common denominators were the utter ruthlessness they displayed as they raided and burned their way across the northern regions of Laos, reaching as far south as Vientiane.

The Invasions by the Ho Pirates

BY 1864, THE trickle of displaced peoples from southern China had become a great flood, who were unable to find land on which to settle and, instead formed themselves into armed marauding bands of all nationalities, including renegade Europeans. They formed three large groups that took the names of the flags they displayed which were the Red, the Black and the Yellow Flags. The last also being known as the Striped Flags.

Within a decade they had terrorised the Black and Red River regions, ransacked the Sipsong Chau Tai, and then descended on Houa Phan, Sam Neua. They divided up the country between their three groups and began their raiding from the area around Luang Prabang to the eastern borders of Xieng Khouang.

In 1874 Chao Khamsouk, who was later to become King Sackarindr of Luang Prabang, attacked and scattered them, but they then reunited and directed their attacks against Xieng Khouang. Chao Ung (1866–1876) called on the Vietnamese to help and in the battle Chao Ung was killed and the Vietnamese troops fled leaving Xieng Khouang town defenceless. The Ho pillaged the town, which was largely deserted as the greater part of the inhabitants had earlier fled southwards to Vientiane, or along the banks of the Mekong. Others fled into the jungle where they lived for many years awaiting the defeat of the Ho. Later in the year, Chao Ket was also killed in the fighting. After the death of Chao Ung the leadership passed to Chao Khanti (1876–1880), who was a son of Chao Ung.

The French look to Xieng Khouang

AS THOUGH THE invasion of the Ho were not sufficient hardship, international politics had begun to intrude onto the scene. The Siamese were intensely conscious of the French determination not merely to govern Vietnam in its entirety but, as well, to 'protect' its frontiers by expanding into Laos. As the suzerains of Xieng Khouang and Luang Prabang, it was obvious to the Bangkok Court that unless it restored order and drove out the Ho, they would soon lose control of Luang Prabang and Xieng Khouang. If they lost the two former kingdoms, they would find it impossible to prevent the extension of French influence in Indochina and they would have to give up any ideas of a Tai nation united under their rule.

The new Siamese king, Chulalongkorn (1868–1910), therefore, decided to send expeditionary forces into the two vassal states to attack the Ho bases in the Sipsong Chau Tai. The French viewed the situation just as the Siamese did, but from an exactly opposite point of view. If the Siamese had been successful in controlling the Ho, they would have been able to confirm their position as the suzerain of Luang Prabang and Xieng Khouang and would have stopped any French extension of their territory to the West.

From the French viewpoint, the Siamese campaign had somehow to be brought to an end as soon as possible, and their troops removed from the Sipsong Chau Tai. While they were still there, the French would not be able to move in.

The Siamese Armies attack the Ho in the north

SOON AFTER CHAO Khanti took charge, he was given 600 Siamese troops to deploy as a guerrilla army around Xieng Khouang. The two groups of forces, the Siamese and the Ho were evenly balanced. There was also only 600 Ho but they had the advantage of operating from a secure base in the town of Xieng Khouang and the strength of desperation in knowing that they had nowhere else to go. It was not, therefore, surprising that Chao Khanti was unable to drive them out immediately.

As it turned out Chao Khanti's failure was not significant. Instead it was the ineptitude of the Siamese intervention in northern Laos that was to prove so disastrous. The Siamese failed to understand that they were no longer fighting the same war as they had fought for centuries against peasants, whose only wish was to get back to their land and live peacefully.

Instead they were facing landless, ruthless cutthroat bands, whose only possessions were their arms and their lives. Without land or villages of their own, when beaten in a battle, these mercenary bands merely scattered, before reuniting to attack the next weakest target they could find.

The situation had not improved by 1885, nine years after the Siamese had made Chao Khanti ruler and given him responsibility for getting the Ho out of Xieng Khouang. The Siamese were unwilling to accept that their own commanders were at fault and they decided to replace Chao Khanti by someone who would bring them victory. Only one thing held them back. They were afraid that if they arrested Chao Khanti in Xieng Khouang, many of his nobles would take refuge in Vietnam where the French would welcome and support them against the Siamese. To avoid this, they decided on a ruse. They told Chao Khanti and his family that they should come to Bangkok to be invested with new honours.

Chao Khanti is tricked into visiting Bangkok

NOT SUSPECTING ANYTHING, accompanied by the most important members of the Court, Chao Khanti and his family left for Bangkok. Once there, the Siamese showed the real reason for the invitation. They were imprisoned and none of them was to be allowed to leave Bangkok for the next eight years. During this time Chao Khanti died, as did a number of his nobles.

The Siamese failure to deal with the Ho was the prime cause for the Ho attack on, and capture of, Luang Prabang in 1887. Although King Chulalongkorn did not realise it at the time, this was the watershed between the Siamese and French influence. With the consequent decline in power of the Siamese in Luang Prabang and the Sipsong Chau Tai their influence in Xieng Khouang also waned. The end of Siamese sovereignty was only a few years away.

Xieng Khouang comes under French protection

BY 1899, FRANCE had forced the withdrawal of Siam, and Laos became an autonomous protectorate under the French Resident Superior. The French initially left the ruling families with their titles, but their power was more symbolic than real. 1899 marks the real end to the kingdom of Xieng Khouang. Chao Kham Ngon was followed by Chao Saignavong and Chao Phommady, but neither had any power as the ruler of Xieng Khouang.

The French officials had firmly reduced their position as rulers to that of officials, even so, they served Xieng Khouang as much respected members of the French Colonial Administration. It is in part thanks to their devotion to duty and care that Muong Phoueune still lives on in the hearts of its people.

CHAPTER THIRTEEN

Lan Xang Reunited as a French Protectorate

B Y THE MIDDLE of the nineteenth century Laos had ceased to exist as a single political entity. The destruction of the kingdom of Vientiane in 1828 had created a division between the southern principalities and the north. This the Siamese had exploited to the full, gradually extending their control over the whole of the country. From Champasak to the Sipsong Chau Tai, former Laotian kingdoms and principalities had become departments, or provinces, that were ruled directly from Bangkok.

As France's control over Tongking, Annam and Cochin China expanded so did her conflicts with the Siamese. In 1867, Cambodia became a French Protectorate increasing the number of border issues between the two countries. There was almost continuous friction as France extended her influence across the Annamite Chain to Xieng Khouang and from there southwards into the Khammouan. In 1888 the French hoped that a thorough survey carried out of the Khammouan region would produce evidence that might be used to undermine the Siamese claims to the region.

Britain's primary objective was to maintain the best possible relations with Siam. The reason was trade: Britain was involved in some 80 percent of the foreign trade that was developed out of the prosperous Menam Chaophraya Valley. She was not worried by France's expansion westwards from Vietnam so long as it did nothing to destabilise conditions in Siam, or disrupt the prosperous commercial traffic.

However, the Siamese found it difficult to accept the limitations that the British placed on her support. Britain was prepared to back Siam so long as in doing so it did not provoke France into starting a war in Europe. It was difficult, if not impossible, for Britain to be sure what France's reactions would be to any move she might make to help Siam. At times Britain appeared to the Siamese to be a weak and vacillating ally.

Pavie was asked to go to Hanoi in February 1889 and then on to Paris where he backed the idea of the projected topographical study of the

Khammouan. He suggested that the survey should include an investigation of the commercial and mining prospects. In November he returned, stopping in Bangkok to tell the Siamese government of the French intentions to carry out the survey. From there he went on to Hanoi. A *Syndicat Français* was created and it was put under Pavie's command. This time as head of the second French mission to Laos, he was no solitary explorer, but had a staff of very competent commercial and scientific personnel with 15 tons of supplies at his disposal. Having delegated responsibilities, Pavie returned to Luang Prabang, and the Syndicat split up into groups to cover Xieng Khouang, Khammouan, and Stung Treng.

In support of the Syndicat's exploration, the French produced the letters that King Mantha Tourath had sent to the Emperor Minh Mang reminding him of the Vietnamese suzerainty over Luang Prabang and Xieng Khouang. The French let the Siamese know that they, therefore, had claims not only to the former kingdom of Xieng Khouang, but possibly to the Khammouan as well as between the west bank of the Mekong and the Annamite Chain.

In April Pavie went back to the Sipsong Chau Tai and spent some time there winning the confidence of Deo Van Tri, who acknowledged the debt he owed to Pavie for having his brothers released by the Siamese. At the end of Pavie's visit he offered his formal submission to France.

To show his good faith Deo Van Tri gave Pavie a royal seal from China that had been taken when he and his Ho allies sacked Luang Prabang in 1887. It was an amalgam of gold and silver and weighed 5.9 kilograms. On the front was the picture of a camel kneeling before a pedestal waiting to be loaded and on the face of the pedestal in Manchu and Chinese characters was an inscription which Pavie translated as 'Seal of the King of Laos'. It had been given at the beginning of the Manchu Dynasty in exchange for a seal that had been granted by the Ming Dynasty. As the Manchu ruled from 1644 to 1911, it had most probably been presented to Chao Souligna Vongsa (1637–1694). Pavie later had it sent to the library of the Quai d'Orsay, in Paris.

The Vietnamese Migration

ONE RESULT OF the occupation of Annam and Cochin China by the French was a sudden exodus of people from Vietnam who belonged to a Vietnamese movement known as the *Can Vong, (Protect the King)*. Considered subversive by the French, they decided it was safer to leave Vietnam. Many of them settled as entire Vietnamese communities along the Mekong from

Savannakhet to Thakhek. They were to provide invaluable support for the communist Pathet Lao movement between 1945 and 1973 leading to the overthrow of the Royal Government in 1975.

They were following in the tracks of numerous Vietnamese mercantile families who, from the 1850s, had settled along the banks of the Mekong. During the last decade of the nineteenth century many thousands more Vietnamese, for one reason or another, migrated from Vietnam to Laos and Thailand, especially to Bangkok. They were to form the future basis for the Siamese communist movement in the 1930s and after.

The British in Burma

IN 1890, SIR George Scott, a brilliant, if rather maverick, colonial official arrived in Kengtung with a handful of soldiers to persuade the Saopha to accept British rule, as Britain had now replaced Burma as Kengtung's suzerain. The British claim to sovereignty over Kengtung meant that for the first time in Indochina, British and French frontiers would run together. However, neither the British officials in India, nor the Foreign Office in London, had any policy to meet such a potentially thorny situation. However, events were about to force them into creating a policy for Indochina that took account of the French presence.

France's next step towards winning control of Laos was the setting up of a number of French Bureaux in Siam and in the former Lan Xang. These were partly commercial, and partly official outposts, whose activities the French government could at any time deny. However, when it suited French policy, she could always claim that they possessed a semi-diplomatic status. It was a situation bound to cause friction with Bangkok, but both the French administration in Hanoi, and the government in Paris, believed that confrontation with the Siamese was the most likely strategy to forward their interests in Laos.

The French Consulate becomes a Legation

IN FEBRUARY 1892, the French Consulate in Bangkok was upgraded to a Legation and Pavie was made Resident Minister. His brief was, in his own words, to 'make Laos French'. He had every intention of fulfilling this task.

The policy of confrontation was exploited to the full by the French colonial lobby. Two incidents out of many were sensationally reported in the French press that whipped up popular feeling against the Siamese and against other governments, especially against the British, in the Indochinese region.

The first incident concerned a French Bureau in the small town of Tha Uthen, just north of Nakhon Phanom on the west bank of the Mekong river. There seems little doubt that, as the Siamese claimed, two of the French agents, Champenois and Esquilot, had been engaged in smuggling opium. Bangkok demanded their expulsion, despite strong protests from France.

This incident was followed soon after by the suicide of Monsieur Massie, the new French Consul in Luang Prabang, who was suffering from fever and had decided to take a boat down the Mekong to Saigon. He stopped at Khone and there, for no known reason, he committed suicide.

There was never any question of his having been murdered. But some of the more jingoistic of the French press claimed that he had been so insulted that he had taken his life. One example of the insults was that someone had attached a fishtail to the French tricolour!

Everything possible was done to exploit these two incidents as examples of the uncivilised behaviour of Siam. There were immediate demands in French newspapers that Siam pay reparations.

In December 1892, and again in April 1893, the British Government informed the French that by their annexation of the kingdom of Ava they had acquired sovereign rights in several districts on the east bank of the Mekong. These included the eastern part of Chiang Hung, in the Sipsong Panna. The British declared that they intended to transfer this territory to China, with the reservation that China might not transfer it to any other country without the agreement of Britain.

At the same time, the British government announced that they had also acquired the rights to Kengtung and the eastern part of this, Keng Cheng, they proposed offering on the same terms to Siam. The Keng Cheng capital was at Muong Sing, which the French considered a part of the kingdom of Lan Xang. However, this should not have caused any problems with France as at that time France had accepted the Siamese maps showing the kingdom of Luang Prabang, and therefore Muong Sing, as a part of Siam. There was no immediate French reaction to these British Notes, but there would be later.

Siamese fear of France's expansion

THE SIAMESE, WORRIED by France's continued efforts to extend its influence throughout the east bank territories of the Mekong, immediately strengthened the powers of the Royal Commissioners. Bangkok delegated to them absolute and all-embracing powers in their own region. One result of this was that King Oun Kham was deprived of any official means of questioning decisions implemented by the two Commissioners in Luang Prabang. Pavie took this issue up with the Siamese government, but to no effect. Instead the Siamese emphasised their determination to maintain this policy by strengthening their garrisons, especially opposite Vientiane, in Ubon Ratchathani and in Champasak.

In March 1893, the Anglo–Chinese agreement was signed transferring Chiang Hung to China. The transfer of Keng Cheng to Siam was to be the next. But by April tension between Siam and France had grown alarmingly and Britain was afraid that it might finally be reaching the point where it could spill over into Europe ... with the frightening possibility of Britain and France going to war. As a first measure, a British gunboat, the *Swift*, was sent to Bangkok to protect the lives of British subjects.

The next month, in April, the French sent three columns of troops into the east bank of the Mekong to occupy, by force if necessary, parts of Laos, despite the fact that Bangkok considered this Siamese territory. One column seized Stung Treng, another came from Vietnam down the road to Savannakhet, and a third followed a route that took them over the Annamite Chain to Khammouan, modern Thakhek.

In this third column was an Inspector Grosgurin whom the French claimed was leading a group of Vietnamese back from a post on the Mekong. They were apparently resting when some Siamese troops came up to arrest them. An argument broke out and one or two shots were fired. It was then discovered that Inspector Grosgurin had been killed. The French authorities blamed the Siamese, but one Cambodian eye witness was later to state that it was Inspector Grosgurin who had started the shooting. It is probably impossible to determine now exactly what happened. Whatever it was, this was the opportunity that the French had been looking for.

The Paknam Incident

As a result, France placed two gunboats, the *Inconstant* and the *Comète*, on alert and on 10 July Pavie informed the Siamese government that they were needed to protect the safety of the French community in Bangkok. He requested that Siamese pilots be sent to the mouth of the Menam Chaophraya at Paknam to bring the two gunboats up the river.

The Siamese replied the next day that no other country had two warships at Bangkok and they could not permit two French gunboats to enter the Menam. On 13 July the two French gunboats were sighted off Paknam and a British warship advised them to wait. Again, what happened next is not very clear. The commander of the Paknam fort had been ordered to refuse the French entry and it now appears that he fired some warning shots across the bows of the approaching gunboats. The Siamese later claimed that these were blanks. The French replied with live shells and forced their way through.

The two countries were on the brink of war and it was only the clear headedness of Prince Devawongse, who was in charge of foreign affairs, that saved the day. He went down to the quayside and congratulated the two gunboat captains on their bravery at forcing the entry. He also gave assurances that every consideration would be given to the French case.

This was not sufficient. Paris instructed Pavie to present an ultimatum to the government. This he did on 20 July. In it the French demanded that Siam immediately cede all territories on the east bank of the Mekong, including Luang Prabang. Secondly that they pay as reparations three million francs for the casualties suffered in the fight with the Paknam fort and, thirdly, that those responsible for firing on the French ships, as well as the murderers of Inspector Grosgurin be punished.

The Siamese agreed to the second and third demands, but refused to accept the cession of 90,000 sq. miles of previously undisputed territory. Pavie then informed them that unless the demands were met in full, he would leave Bangkok on 26 July. A declaration that was close to saying that a state of war would follow.

The French Blockade and the new Stipulations

ON 29 JULY, the French blockaded the Menam river mouth. Throughout this crisis, King Chulalongkorn had been so overcome by events that he had left everything in the hands of his Foreign Minister, Prince Devawongse. Two days later, he decided to capitulate. But it was too late and on 3 August when the French ended the blockade, they added new stipulations, which they claimed were to ensure that the agreement was kept.

The first was that until the evacuation of the east bank had been completed, they would station troops in Chantaburi, an important Siamese town close to the border with Cambodia. They also demanded that the Siamese should withdraw their troops from Battambang and Siemreap which the Siamese had had stationed there as the suzerain power of Cambodia. The last stipulation was that the Siamese army had to remain

25 kilometres away from the west bank of the Mekong, so preventing their giving support to the Siamese administrative centres on the Mekong, such as Mukdahan, Nakhon Phanom and Nong Khai. To compensate for this, the Siamese greatly increased the size of their police force.

The Franco–Siamese Treaty of 1893

THE FRANCO–SIAMESE TREATY was initialled on 3 October and the former kingdom of Lan Xang became a protectorate of France for the next 56 years until 19 July 1949. The Siamese, not to mention the modern Thai, have always held up this treaty as an example of the worst aspects of colonialism, but it should be borne in mind that the people who were to suffer most from it were not the Siamese, but the Lao. It was Siam that had been responsible for the total destruction of the kingdom of Lan Xang. They had then colonised a territory that had never been their's, but had been a part of Lan Xang or, previous to that, had been independent principalities.

By taking the Mekong as the frontier, the French secured their possessions in Vietnam and in the northwest extended them beyond their wildest claims. The Siamese, admittedly lost some Lao territory that they had expropriated over the previous few decades, but they gained a legal sovereignty over the whole of the Korat plateau, over the eastern part of the Muong Nan, that had been a Lao, not a Thai, muong, and is the present-day Sayaboury province. The Franco–Siamese agreement in fact legalised an enormous extension of Siamese territory that they had expropriated in the course of the wars against Vientiane and Luang Prabang.

The real losers were the Lao people who had lived on both sides of the Mekong and suddenly found themselves divided from their relatives and friends. As well, the new treaty allowed Siam and Cambodia to take possession of a large part of the kingdom of Champasak, both on the Korat plateau and on the lower Mekong.

The East Bank becomes French

THE END OF the Siamese colonisation of the east bank had come suddenly and the administration of the new French protectorate had initially to be a very *ad hoc* affair. The best that the French administration in Hanoi and Paris could do was to second officials from Vietnam to take control over their new possessions.

As usual they turned to Pavie and on 5 June 1894 they made him Commissioner General of Laos and sent him to Luang Prabang. It was a startling transformation. Only seven years earlier, on his first visit, he had been the sole and unsupported representative of France. Now he was the most powerful foreigner in Laos. It was an amazing achievement. He immediately set about forming a French organised administration.

In July, Pavie began to implement one of his major decisions that was to influence the future of the country, both during the French Protectorate and after. On 6 July he went down to Vientiane and took the first steps to having it rebuilt as an important town. Acutely aware of the political realities of the geography of Laos, Pavie realised that Vientiane was the centre of the country and, lying on the borders of the new Siam, should be the focal point for the country's administration.

He proved to be right. In 1898, Vientiane was made the administrative capital and became the only truly international city in the country. From Vientiane Pavie continued south to set up another administrative group in Champasak.

The French takeover of Laos did nothing to reduce tension in the region. Britain continued to be extremely worried by the possibility of disagreements with the French over events in Indochina. In London, the idea of forming a buffer state between the British and French possessions became increasingly popular. For once the British chose the right man to take charge of their negotiations. It was Sir George Scott, who was as individualistic and intellectually informed as Pavie. He was ordered from the Shan States to Bangkok, from where he was to head the Border Commission to decide on the territory to form the buffer state.

The Muong Sing Commission

SCOTT LEFT BANGKOK in October, and travelled first by river, then rode cross-country with twenty elephants the Siamese had given him. The whole journey of 884 miles from Bangkok to Keng Hung (Chiang Hung) took him 63 days. The other members of the Border Commission started from Rangoon and came up through the Shan States.

He met them in the middle of December and arrived in Muong Sing on Christmas day. They found the French flag flying over the *Haw* of the ruler, or *Myosa*, who, on hearing that it was the British who had arrived, took to his heels and hid. It was to be some days before he could be persuaded to return.

Muong Sing was the capital of Keng Cheng, a vassal state of Kengtung that now belonged to the British. Some idea of the difference in colonial strategy of the British and French may be seen in the vicissitudes that the poor Myosa of Muong Sing had suffered. Following the treaty with China whereby Britain gave to her Chiang Hung, the Myosa had been told that his territory was being transferred to Siam and he should transfer his allegiance there. He duly offered the traditional gold and silver flowers to the nearest Siamese official. With the setting up of the Border Commission it was decided that he should return to the British so that Muong Sing's allegiance could be decided formally.

He, therefore, sent a letter to the Siamese informing them of the new orders. His letter was intercepted by a French official and returned to him with the information that he was now French and should fly the French flag.

It was in this way that Scott found Muong Sing already French territory and he promptly had the French flag removed. Pavie arrived on 1 January 1895, and was furious at what he chose to take as an insult.

However, the French and British appeared to have worked harmoniously together, exchanging champagne and making the most of the simple amenities around them.

But if they could be in harmony socially, in their work it was different. Scott had come to the conclusion, and was later to change the official British view, that a buffer state would present Britain and France with endless problems. As he pointed out, it would be a safe haven for rebels from both sides and would be a haunt for criminals and every other unwanted member of society.

Pavie, however, probably with less freedom to alter the terms of his brief, remained committed to the idea of forming a buffer state. The Commission worked from 15 January to 8 April and produced a series of agreed maps of the territory, but could not reach any consensus on where the demarcation lines should be drawn.

It was decided that a new joint Commission would be opened in Europe and by 15 January the next year, 1896, it was agreed that British Burma would extend to the west bank of the Mekong and the French territory would run eastwards from the river. Chiang Hung remained Chinese and the western part of Keng Cheng remained a part of British Burma.

Pavie's last visit to Luang Prabang

From Muong Sing, Pavie returned for his last stay in Luang Prabang. In his memoirs he comments that the King and royal princes attached a great deal of importance to their being invested in their titles by him. Pavie had

had their titles printed on parchment in Hanoi and the king had the finest jewellers in Luang Prabang prepare ornamented silver cylinders to hold them.

On 16 April 1895 Pavie solemnly presented these titles first to the former king, Tiao Oun Kham, who had abdicated for reasons of health in 1889, then to King Sackarindr who had succeeded him, and finally to the Maha Oupahat, Tiao Boun Khong. Three days later Pavie returned to Bangkok.

In seven years, almost single-handed, he had reunited a large part of the three former kingdoms of Lan Xang.

In 1899, Upper and Lower Laos became an autonomous protectorate under a Resident Supérieur who reported to the Governor General in Hanoi. The Kingdom of Luang Prabang was given a special position within the Protectorate with the king acting on the advice of the French officials. The rest of Laos was administered as a French colony. It was not the best of all possible solutions, but it gave back to the Lao people a renewed sense of national unity that would probably have been lost had they remained a Siamese colony as already the influence of the Siamese was very strong and Siamese was used at the Court of Luang Prabang.

Treaties and Conventions

On 7 October 1902, a Franco–Siamese Treaty was signed. It was never ratified, as Paris had second thoughts about the possible implications: some officials were afraid that it could imply the recognition of Siamese sovereignty over areas that France might later wish to claim.

A further attempt by France and Siam to reach a satisfactory agreement was made on 13 February 1904. Siam then agreed that the west bank territories of modern Sayaboury, with its southern boundaries lying where the kingdoms of Luang Prabang and Vientiane had placed them in 1707, should be returned to Laos. They also agreed to the return of parts of Champasak to Laos. However, Stung Treng and a large section of the former Champasak kingdom remained a part of Cambodia.

Two months later, on 8 April 1904, a Franco–British Convention was signed defining the French and British zones of influence in Asia. The agreement was one of the consequences of a new policy put forward by King Edward VII who, in 1903 paid an official visit to Paris. Britain and France from being traditional enemies entered into a new alliance, known as the *Entente Cordiale*, that would bring them into the First World War in 1914 on the same side.

Champasak incorporated into Laos

THE 22 NOVEMBER 1904, saw the end of the kingdom of Champasak. It was formally made a part of Laos, and the administration was taken over by French officials who reported to Vientiane. This was a severe blow to Chao Rasadanay, a descendant of Princess Sumangala, who had been the king of Champasak under the suzerainty of Bangkok. When the French had assumed power in 1893, he had been downgraded to Governor of Champasak. The transfer of his regal powers to Vientiane was the final blow and, in 1934, when he died the French did not choose anyone from the family to replace him as Governor. Later, in the 1940's, after the fall of France, the French in Indochina came under pressure from the Japanese and, in an attempt to gain local support, Boun Oum, the eldest son of Chao Rasadanay, was recognised as having an official position in Champasak.

One last attempt to legalise the situation with Siam was made at a Franco–Siamese Convention on 23 March 1907. This treaty formally gave to Siam all territories on the Right Bank of the Mekong, with the exceptions of modern Sayaboury and a part of Champasak. It was, in historical terms, completely unfair and was as unpopular with the Lao as the earlier Franco–Siamese agreement of 1904.

On 4 March 1905 King Sisavang Vong was in Paris as a student when he learnt of the death of his father King Sackarindr. He was to reign as King of Luang Prabang until 19 July 1949 when Laos became an independent nation and the two parts were once again united. Sadly, though it was not the Laos that had once been Lan Xang. Much of the territory that had been lost through the different treaties and agreements during the nineteenth century was not, as we shall see, to be returned.

So Laos was ruled as two separate entities. The King of Luang Prabang had only the province of Luang Prabang and Sayaboury as his domain. The provinces, or former kingdoms, of Namtha, Muong Sing, Xieng Khouang and Phong Saly were excluded until 1916 when Phong Saly was made the Fifth Military Region and, with Sam Neua, was included as part of the realm of Luang Prabang.

On 14 April 1917, the French imposed a Charter for the kingdom that stated that the titles and positions of Rajavong, Rajaput and Maha Oupahat would become extinct on the death of the incumbents. However, 21 August 1941, to compensate the King of Luang Prabang for the valuable teak forests in Sayaboury Province that had been expropriated by the Siamese, the French decided to raise Luang Prabang to the status of a Protectorate.

ILLUSTRATION 20 King Sisavang Vong as a young man
(CMIDOM Droits Reservés)

As well, the provinces of Vientiane, Xieng Khouang and Namtha were included within its territory. It was also decided to re-establish the position of Maha Oupahat, which was given to Tiao Phetsarath, the eldest son of the previous Oupahat, Tiao Boun Khong. Phetsarath held this post until

ILLUSTRATION 21 Princess Khamfanh, who married King Sisavang Vong, and Princess Sammathi, Luang Prabang, c. 1900

© Archives Nationales, Aix-en-Provence

10 October 1945 when the King stripped him of all titles and honours for his support of the Lao Issara. In 1957, the king re-instated Tiao Phetsarath with the honorary title of Maha Oupahat, but without any official post to go with it.

Much as one deplores the terrible depletion of the Lao territories that took place in the nineteenth century, it at least entered the twentieth century with a king bound together with the rich memories of Lan Xang and the consciousness of the individuality of being Lao. The extinction of the royal titles of Champasak and Xieng Khouang is a fitting, but sad, end to the history of the great kingdoms of Lan Xang. The twentieth century was to see new greatness, first under King Sisavang Vong and then under his son, King Savang Vatthana. Laos of the twentieth century is a history that rightly deserves a book of its own.

The Kings of Lan Xang Variant Dates with Sources

Souvanna Khampong	before 1316–1343?	Le Boulanger, 31
Fa Ngiao	1343, approx.	Sila, 64
Fa Kham Hiao	1349 approx	Sila, 64
Fa Ngum	1353–1373	Le Boulanger, 31; Dommen, 64; Hall, 81;
	1353–1371	Sila, 64; Manich, 67
	1353–1368	Stuart-Fox, 93
Sam Sen Thai	1373–1416	Le Boulanger, 31; Sila, 64; Manich, 67; Hall, 81; Stuart-Fox, 93
Lan Kham Deng	1416–1428	Le Boulanger, 31; Hall, 81
	1417–1428	Sila, 64; Manich, 67; Stuart-Fox, 93
	1416–1427	Dommen, 64
Maha Devi dominance	1428–1438	Manich, 67; Stuart Fox, 93
	1427–1440	France-Asie Laos, 59
Phommathad (10 months)	1428–1429	Le Boulanger,31; Hall, 81
	1428	Manich, 71
Kham Teun (3 years)	1429–1430	Le Boulanger, 31
Yukorn (8 months)	1430	Sila, 64
Khon Kham (18 months)	1431–1432	Sila 64
	1431	Manich, 71
Kham Temsa (5 months)	1433	Sila, 64; Manich, 71
Lusai (6 months)	1434, c.	Sila, 64; Manich, 71
	1434–1435	Le Boulanger, 31
Khai Bua Ban	1435–1438	Sila, 64; Manich, 71
Kham Keut	1435–1438	Le Boulanger, 31; Hall, 81
	1438–1440	Sila, 64
	1436–1438	Manich, 71
Interregnum	1438–1431	Manich, 71
	1440–1443	Sila, 64
	1453–1456	France-Asie Laos, 59
Chakkaphat	1438–1479	Le Boulanger, 31; Dommen, 64
	1441–1478	Manich, 67

	1456–1479	Sila, 64
	1442, c.–1479	Wyatt, 84
	1438–??	Stuart-Fox, 93
Souvanna Banlong (Then	1478–1485	Sila, 64; Manich, 71
Kham)	1479–1486	Le Boulanger, 31; Hall, 81; Stuart-Fox, 93
La Sen Thai	1486–1496	Le Boulanger, 31; Hall, 81; Wyatt, 84
	1485–1495	Manich, 71
	1485–1497	Sila, 64
Som Phou	1496–1501	Le Boulanger, 31; Hall, 81; Wyatt, 84
	1497–1500	Manich, 71
	1497–1501	Sila, 64
Visoun	1500–1520	Sila, 64; Coedès, 66; Stuart-Fox, 93
	1501–1520	Domment, 64
Phothisarath	1520–1550	Le Boulanger, 31
Setthathirath (Chiang Mai)	1546–1551	Wyatt, 84
	1547–1550	Sila, 64
Setthathirath (Lan Xang)	1550–1571	Manich, 67; Saveng, 87
Sen Soulintha: Regent	1571–1572	Sila, 64; Saveng, 87
Sen Soulintha: King	1572–1575	Sila, 64
Tha Heua	1575–1579	Sila, 64; Manich, 67; Saveng, 87
Sen Soulintha reinstated	1579	Hall, 81; Saveng, 87
	1580–1582	Sila, 64
Nakhon Noi	1582–c. 1583	Le Boulanger, 31; Sila, 64; Hall, 81
Interregnum	1583–1591	Le Boulanger, 31
Nokeo Koumane	1591–1596	Le Boulanger, 31; Coedès, 66; Hall, 81; Saveng, 87
	1591–1598	Sila, 64
Vorapita becomes Regent	1598	Sila, 64; Manich, 67
Thammikarath (Voravongsa)	1596 or 1598	Sila, 64; Saveng, 87
	1603	Le Boulanger, 31; Coedès, 66
	1596–1622	Dommen, 64
end of reign	1621 or 1622	Sila, 64
Oupagnouvarath	1622–1623	Le Boulanger, 31; Sila, 64
Bandith Phothisarath II,	1623–1627	Le Boulanger, 31; Sila, 64
Mone Keo	1627–unknown date	Sila, 64
Tone Kham,	1627, between and 1633	Sila, 64
Vichai,	1627–1633	Sila, 64
Souligna Vongsa	1633–1690 or 95	Sila, 64
	1637	Coedès, 66
	1637–1694	Le Boulanger, 31; Dommen, 64; Saveng, 87; Stuart-Fox, 93

Tian Thala usurps throne	1690	Sila, 64
	1694 only	Le Boulanger, 31; Hall, 81
Ong Lo	1690–1695, c.	Sila, 64
	1694–1698	Manich, 67
Nantharat	1695, c.	Sila, 64
	1699	Saveng, 87
Sai Ong Hue	1693	Saveng, 87
	1696 or 1700	Coedès, 66
	1698–1709	Sila, 64
	1698	Manich, 67
	1700	Wyatt, 84
	1700–1707	Le Boulanger, 31; Dommen, 64; Hall, 81

Glossary

Glosary of words and phrases to illustrate the meaning, or the transliteration we have preferred

Agna	A title used on the Island of Khong equivalent in rank to, or in some instances greater than, the title *Chao*.
Ai-Lao	*alt. spelling:* Ailao, Chinese name for the Shans from the times when they were living in Yunnan province in the early centuries of the CE.
Ban	Village
Bassi	A ceremony for renewing the spiritual ties between family and friends, especially held at Phi Mai (qv).
Boun Mo	A person dedicated to serving and appeasing the spirits, the Phi. He still has an important role in Lao life and is believed to possess spiritual powers. He is usually skilled in medicine assisting at births and deaths. For most of the Laos in the countryside, he is the only doctor available.
Buddhism	The Tai in Yunnan came into contact with Buddhism in the beginning of the CE. In what was to be Laos, they were influenced by both the Theravada School of southern India and Ceylon as well as by the Mahayana School from Tibet. Theravada Buddhism from Angkor became the recognised religion of Lan Xang during the reign of Fa Ngum about 1359.
Castes	Varna. The Brahmins introduced the concept of castes, but the Tai never permitted the social segregation as practised in India. The four Varna are: the Brahman, the priestly caste; the Kshatriya, the ruling, knightly, caste; the Vaisya, the trading and agricultural caste; and finally the Sudra, the servile class whose social duty was

to serve the other three. King Sam Sen Thai did, however, divide his people into two classes: Nobles, which included all officials and merchants as one category, and peasants as the other. There appears to have been a third, unacknowledged, class who were the equivalent to the Sudra.

Champasak	The modern state of Champasak dates from about 1707 when Princess Sumangala's son, Chao Soysisam-out, was made king. (v. Chapter 11)
Chao	the spelling we have adopted for the noble title before the reign of King Mantha Tourath (1817-1836) and, at all periods, for the kings and nobles of Champasak and Xieng Khouang. (v. Tiao)
Chaoheuane	A married princess who is a Chao by birth: *heuane* = house. (Champasak)
Chaomuong	Chao = head, owner, or a noble + Muong = country, city, or town. In the former days, it was the prerogative of the King to promote a village or town to the status of a Muong. In many parts of the country, the chaomuong ruled like a king over his Court and people, with the power of life or death. He was directly responsible to whoever could enforce the right to be his suzerain.
Chaonang	An unmarried princess who is a Chao by birth. (Champasak)
Chiang Tung	v. Kengtung, Shan States
Chiang Hung	*alt. spelling*: Chiang Rung, Jenghung (Chinese)
Chiang Mai	*alt. spelling*: Chiangmai
Chiang Rai	the second most important city of Lan Na
Chiang Rung	*alt. spelling*: Chiang Hung
Chiang Saen	*alt. spelling*: Chiang Sen, lies to the south of Chiang Mai
Chiang Thene	19th century vassal state of Kengtung, given by Britain to China
Chiang Tung	*alt. spelling*: Kengtung
Haw	Palace of the Ruler. (Shan)
Hmong	Name now used for a highland people formerly known as Meo. Meo is traditionally believed to have been derived from the Chinese *Miao*, barbarian. About 1972, Dr Yang Dao, the first Hmong to gain a PhD from a French university, returned to Laos and demanded the term Meo no longer be used.
Hongsavadi	*alt. spelling*: Hamsavadi. Burma: fl. 16th century

Houei	Stream
Keng Cheng	*alt. spelling*: Chiang Khaeng
Kengtung	*alt. spelling*: Chiang Tung, we have used the Shan spelling
Khoueng	Province: the region administered by a Chaokhoueng.
Lan Na	*alt. spelling*: Lanna
Lao Loum	*alt. spelling*: Lum. Those Lao who are to be found in the towns and villages of Laos: the Lowland Lao. They constitute about 40% of the population. They are related to the Lao Tai(qv), who are a highland people.
Lao Soung	The Hmong (Meo) and Yao and other mountain clans, who are not ethnically related to the Lao Loum or Lao Tai.
Lao Tai	Upland Lao: they include the White, Black, and Red Tai
Lao Theung	Descendants of the proto-Indochinese peoples who spoke a Mon-Khmer language. Over the centuries they were referred to as the *Kha*, a Lao word for slave. The largest groups are the Khmu (alt. Kamu) in the north and the Kwi and the So in the south.
Mahadevi	*Great Goddess*, the title of the most senior Queen, also used in the Shan States.
Maha Thevi	v. Mahadevi
Meo	v. Hmong.
Mom	Title given to the wife of a noble, who was born a commoner.
Muong	In modern times an administrative area run by a Chaomuong, in the past a semi-autonomous area that was usually directly responsible to the king.
Muong Thaeng	Present name: Dien Bien Phu
Myosa	A Burmese word that literally means eater of towns and in Burma proper was applied to tax collectors who were given the right to collect taxes over a limited area in exchange for an agreed sum. In the Shan States it was used as the name for the person deputising for the Ruler and sometimes, in his own right, was the Ruler of a Mong (in Lao a Muong).
Nam	Water or River.
Nang	Nang, a girl, or woman without a title. (Champasak). Nang, or Nangsao, also means an unmarried girl in most of the Tai world.

Nya	Honorific title, especially applied to one of a princely family who has not inherited the title Chao. (Champasak)
Nyanang	Honorific title, especially applied to a woman of a princely family who has not inherited the title Chao.(Champasak)
Pha	Cliff or Limestone mountain
Phai Nam	twin capital with Vientiane in 14th century. Phai Nam = *sharpened bamboo*.
Pi Mai	lit. the New Spirits, the equivalent of the western New Year, when family ties are renewed, friends and acquaintances come together to obtain release from the sins or errors of the previous year and to start afresh.
Phou Keo	A term sometimes used to denote the people of Annam.
Phoueune	Name of the inhabitants of Xieng Khouang from *Phou* (people) + *Eune*.
Phoueune, Muong	name of the former kingdom of the Phuan, now Xieng Khouang.
Rajavong	The third most important position in the hierarchy of the royal family, directly below Oupahat
Ranks, Civil Service	Samien; Phouxouei; Oupahat; Chaokhoueng and Chaomuong.
Ratsabout	The fourth most important position in the royal hierarchy, follows after Rajavong.
Sangha	The Buddhist Order (Church), hence Sangharaja: the Chief monk or Head of the Order.
Saopha	Title of a Shan Ruler, literally *Lord of the Sky*, cf. Chao Fa
Sena (Fr. Séna)	The most senior royal council, whose members were chosen by the King and Royal Family. It usually included the most important of the nobles.
Siphandone	The region around the island of Khong, meaning *Four Thousand Islands*.
Sipsong Chau Tai	*The Twelve Hundred Tai Groups*
Sipsong Panna	*The Twelve Hundred Rice Fields.*
Sisattanakhanahud	One of the names for Lan Xang in the time of King Setthathirath
Song Koi	Indigenous name for the Red River.
Swa, Muong Swa	Earliest recorded name of Luang Prabang
Tasseng	Sub district comprising 5 to 10 villages, controlled by a Tasseng

Thene   modern Dien Bien Phu, *alt. spelling*: Thaeng, Thene
Tiao   The spelling of the title we have adopted for the nobility
               of the Royal House of Luang Prabang, starting from the
               reign of King Mantha Tourath (1817-1836). (v.Chao)
Tran Ninh   v. Xieng Khouang. Vietnamese name meaning *to guard*
               peace, a reference to its position as a frontier country on
               the borders of Luang Prabang, Vientiane and Siam.

APPENDIX THREE
Bibliography

Archaimbault, Charles, *L'Histoire de Campasak*, Journal Asiatique, Vol. 249, No. 4, 1961.

——, *Les annales de l'ancien royaume de S'ieng Khwang*, B.E.F.E.O. Vol. 53, No. 2 (1967), p. 557–673, maps biblio.

——, *Mémoires of T'au P'an, à Muang K'am le 20 September 1932, Histoire du Muang P'uon*, B.E.F.E.O. Vol. 53, No. 2 (1967), pp. 627–647.

Aung Thwin, Michael, *Pagan: The Origins of Modern Burma*, Hawaii University Press, Honolulu 1985.

Barney, G. Linwood, *The Meos of Xieng Khouang Province* in Southeast Asian Tribes, Minorities and Nations Vol. 1, Princetown University Press, 1967.

Berkeley, California, *Indochina Chronology*, IEAS, (quarterly), 1982.

Bernard-Thierry, Solange, *Le Roi dans la littérature cambodgienne*, France Asie, Vol. XII, Nov.–Dec., 1955.

Bernatzik, H.A., *Les Esprits des Feuilles Jaunes*, Plon, Paris, 1951.

Berval, René de, *Présence du Cambodge*, Vol. 12., France-Asie, Saigon. November–December, 1955.

——, *Présence Royaume Lao*, France-Asie, Saigon, 1956.

——, *Kingdom of Laos: The Land of the Million Elephants and the White Parasol*, France-Asie, 93 Nguyên-van-Thinh Street, Saigon. 1959.

Borgé, Jacques, & Viasnoff, Nicolas: photographs, Viollet, Roger, *Archives de l'Indochine*, Éditions Michèle Trinckvel, Paris, 1995.

Brown, Roxanna M., *Bronze Drums of Laos*, Arts of Asia, Vol. 5 No. 1, 1975.

Bunnag, T., *The Provincial Administration of Siam, 1892–1915*, Oxford University Press, Kuala Lumpur, 1977.

Burchett, Wilfred G., *Mekong Upstream*, Red River Publishing House, Hanoi, 1957.

Burnay, J and Coedès, G., *The Origins of the Sukhodaya Script*, Siam Society, 50th Anniversary, Vol. 1. p. 188, Bangkok, 1954.

Butcher, Tom and Ellis, Dawn, *Laos*, Awol Book, Pallas Athene, London, 1993, pp. 187.

Caply, Michel (Jean Deuve), *Le Japon et l'Independence du Laos*, Revue d'Histoire de la Deuxième Guerre Mondiale, No. 86, pp. 67–81, April, 1972.

Cocks, S.W., *A Short History of Burma*, Macmillan and Co, London, 1910.

Coedès, George, *L'Épigraphie cambodgienne*, France Asie, Vol. XII, Nov.–Dec., 1955.

——, *Fragments de la Grande Stèle du Prah Khan d'Angkor*, France Asie, Vol. XII, Nov.–Dec., 1955.

——, *La fondation de Phnom Penh au XVe Siècle, d'après la Chronique cambodgienne*, France Asie, Vol. XII, Nov.–Dec., 1955.

——, *Edit des Hôpitaux de Jayavarman VII*, France Asie, Vol. XII, Nov.–Dec., 1955.

——, *The Making of South East Asia (translation)*, Routledge & Kegan Paul, London, 1966.

Conze, Edward, *Buddhism Its Essence and Development*, Bruno Cassirer, Oxford, UK, 1951.

Cordell, Helen, *Laos, World Bibliographical Series: Volume 133*, Clio, Oxford, England & Santa Barbara, California. 1991.

Corthay, CH., *Le Laos, Découverte d'un Champ Missionaire*, Henri Cornaz, Yverdon, Switzerland, 1953.

Davis, Bonnie, *The Siam Society under Five Reigns*, Siam Society Bangkok, pp. 222, 1989.

de Marini, G.F., *Relation nouvelle et curieuse du Royaume de Lao*, 1660, reprinted Revue Indochinoise 8 (1910).

Decoux, Jean, Admiral, *A la Barre de l'Indochine*, Plon, Paris, 1949.

Decovert, Jeanne and Rochat, Georges, *L'Appel du Laos*, Henri Cornaz Yverdon, Switzerland, 1946.

Deuve, Jean, *Le Royaume du Laos 1949–1965*, Ecole Française d'Extrême Orient, 1984.

——, *Le Laos, 1945–1949*, Université Paul Valery, Montpellier, 1992.

Deydier, Henri, *Introduction a la Connaissance du Laos*, Saigon, 1952.

——, *Lokapâla: Génies, totems et sorciers du Nord Laos*, Plon, Paris, 1954.

Dommen, Arthur J., *Conflict in Laos, The Politics of Neutralization*,, Pall Mall Press, London. 1964.

——, *Laos, Keystone of Indochina*, Westview Press, Boulder and London, 1985.

——, *Documentary materials in the American archives for the history of the Kingdom of Laos, 1941–1962*, South East Asia Research Vol. 3 No. 2 Sept. 1995.

Doré, Amphay, *Aux Sources de la civilisation Lao: Contribution ethno-historique a la connaisance de la culture louang-prabangaise*, Mémoires Présenté pour le

Doctorat d'état et Lettres et Sciences Humaines. Paris: Cercle de la Culture et de Recherches Laotiennes. 1987.

Embree, Ainslie, T., *Encyclopaedia of Asian History (4 Vols.)*, Charles Scribner, New York, 1988.

Ennis, Thomas E. *French Policy and Developments in Indochina*, University of Chicago, 1936; reprinted Russell & Russell, New York, 1973.

Fauville, Henri, *La Présence Etrangère en Birmanie, A Travers les Siècles*, sudestasie, Thailand, 1996.

Fiasson, Jeannine, *Au Laos avec mes Hommes et mes Éléphants*, René Juilliard, Paris, 1961.

Finestone, Jeffrey, *Royal Family of Thailand: descendants of King Chulalongkorn*, ed. Narisa Chakrabongse, White Mouse Editions, 1989.

Fleeson, Katherine N., *Laos Folk-Lore of Farther India*, Fleming H. Revell Company, New York, 1899.

Gentil, Pierre, *Sursauts de l'Asie Remous du Mekong*, Charles-Lavauzelle & Co. Paris, 1950.

Golap Chandra Barua, Rai Sahib, *Ahom-Buranji (with parallel English translation), from the Earliest Time to the end of Ahom Rule*, Assam Administration, printed at the Baptist Mission Press, Calcutta, 1930.

Grison, Pierre, *Angkor, ou l'Univers Manifesté*, France Asie, Vol. XII, Nov.–Dec., 1955.

——, *Presence Historique du Cambodge*, in *Presence Cambodge*, France Asie, Vol. XII, Nov.–Dec., 1955.

Groslier, Bernard & Athaud, Jacques, *Angkor Art and Civilisation*, Thames and Hudson, London, 1957.

Gunn, Geoffrey C, *Political Struggles in Laos (1930–1954)*, Editions Duang Kamol, Siam Square, Bangkok, 1988.

Hagesteijn, Renee, *Circles of Kings: Political Dynamics in Early Continental Southeast Asia*, Foris Publications, Dordretch-Holland 1989.

Hall, D.G.E., *A History of South-East Asia (4th ed.)*, Macmillan, London, 4th Ed., 1981 reprinted 1994.

Halpern, Joel M., *The Lao Elite: a Study of tradition and innovation*, Rand Corporation, Santa Monica, 1960.

——, *Government, Politics, and Social Structure in Laos: A Study of Tradition and Innovation*, Southeast Asia Studies, Yale University, 1964.

Harvey, G.E., *History of Burma*, Longmans's Green and Co. London, 1925.

——, *Outline of Burmese History*, Orient Longmans Ltd. Bombay, reprinted 1954.

Hoshino, Tatsuo, *Pour une histoire Médiévale du moyen Mékong*, Duang Kamol, Bangkok. 1986.

Houmphanh Saignasith, *Quelques notions et renseignements utiles sur la Monarchie Lao et les Différentes Maisons Princières de Luang Prabang, MS.*

———, *Dates Importantes des Evenements Politiques et Autres au Laos*, Houmphanh Saignasith (Typescript), Paris, 16 April 1993.

———, *Brève Historique de Phrabang, Palladium du Royaume du Lane Xang*, Houmphanh Saignasith (Typescript), Paris, April 1994.

———, *Dualités entre le Vang Luang et le Vang Na, Parts I and II*, Typescript, original 1991, revised July, 1996.

Htin Aung, Maung, *A History of Burma*, Columbia University Press, New York and London, 1967.

Jaisvasd Visouthiphong, Prince, *Hommage a Sa Majesté Sri Savang Vatthana: Roi du Lane Xang*, Association Fa-Ngum, Paris, 1990.

Kachorn Sukhabanij, *The Thai Beach-Head States in the 11th–12th Centuries*, The Silapakorn Journal, Vol. 1, No. 3, September & No. 4, November, 1957.

Karnow, Stanley, *Vietnam: A History*, Random House (Pimlico), 1994.

Katay D. Sasorith, *Souvenirs d'un Ancien Écolier de Paksé*, Editions Lao Sédone, Laos, 1958.

Lafont, Pierre Bernard, *Aperçus sur le Laos*, Comité de l'Alliance Française au Laos, 1959.

———, *Bibliographie du Laos* (2 vols.), Ecole Française d'Extrême Orient, 1978.

———, *Les Recherches en Science Humaines sur le Laos*, CHCPI, 1994.

Lancaster, Donald, *The Emancipation of French Indochina*, OUP, 1961.

Le Boulanger, Paul, *Histoire du Laos Français: Essai d'une Étude chronologique des Principautés laotiennes.*, Plon, Paris. 1931.

LeBar, Frank M. and Suddard, Adrienne, *Laos: its people its society its culture*, HRAF Press, Newhaven, USA, 1960.

Levy, Banyen, *Legends and Fables in the Kingdom of Laos*, edited by Réné de Barval. France-Asie, Saigon. 1959.

Levy, Paul, *Histoire du Laos*, Presses Universitaires de France, 1974 (Que sais-je? No. 1549).

Lieberman, Victor B., *Burmese Administrative Cycles – Anarchy and Conquest c. 1580–1760*, Princeton University Press, Princeton, N.J.

Lintingre, Pierre, *Les rois de Champassak*, Paksé, Inspection Générale du Royaume, 1972.

Marr, David G. and Milner, A.C., *Southeast Asia in the 9th to 14th Centuries*, Institute of Southeast Asian Studies, Singapore, 1986.

McAleavy, Henry, *Black Flags in Vietnam. The Story of a Chinese intervention.*, George Allen & Unwin, London, 1968. Illus.

McCarthy, James, *Surveying and Exploring in Siam*, London, 1900.

McCloud, Donald G., *Southeast Asia Tradition and Modernity in the Contemporary World*, Westview Press, Boulder. San Francisco. Oxford.

Mangrai, Sao Sai Muong, *Paung Daw U Festival*, Journal of the Siam Society, Bangkok, July 1980.

Manich Jumsai, M.L., *History of Laos*, Chalermnit Press, Bangkok, 1967.

———, *History of Laos*, Chalermnit Press, Bangkok, 1971.

Mangkra Souvanna Phouma, Prince, *L'Agonie du Laos*, Plon, Paris, 1976.

Marchal, Henri, *Symbolisme des temples hindous et khmèrs*, France Asie, Vol. XII, Nov.–Dec., 1955.

Mathieu, A. R., *Chronological Table of the History of Laos*, France-Asie, Saigon, 1959.

Mitton, G.E. (Lady Scott), *Scott of the Shan Hills; Orders and Impressions*, John Murray, London, 1936.

Mordant, General, *Au Service de la France en Indochine*, Saigon, 1950.

Mouhot, Henri, *Travels in the Central Parts of Indochina (Siam), Cambodia, and Laos during 1858–60*, John Murray, London, 1864.

Nhouy Abhay, *Aspects du Pays Lao*, Comité Littéraire Lao, Vientiane, 1956.

Notton, Camille (translator), *Annales du Siam*, C. Lavauzelle, Paris, 1926, 3 Vols.

———, *Annals du Siam, Vol.III, Chronique de Xieng Mai*, Librairie Orientaliste Paul Geuthner, 13 rue Jacob, VIe. Paris, 1932.

Oger, Michel, *La Légende de Mahathevi*, Bulletin des Amis du Royaume Lao 7/8.

Oun Sananikone, *Khouam Louk, ou Le Passé*, Cornell University, (Data Paper Series, No. 100), 1975.

Parmentier, Henri, *L'Art du Laos* (Vol. I & II), EFEO, Hanoi, 1954.

Pavie, Auguste, *A la Conquête des Coeurs, Le Pays des Millions d'Éléphants et du Parasol Blanc, Les Pavillons Noirs, – Deo Van Tri*, Presses Universitaires de France, Paris, 1947.

———, *Au Pays des Millions d'Éléphants et du Parasol Blancs (a la Conquête des Coeurs), Préface de Loïc-René Vilbert*, Terre de Brume Éditions, Rennes, 1995.

———, *Etudes diverses II: recherches sur L'historie du Cambodge, du Laos et du Siam.*, Leroux, Paris. 1898.

Pedrazzanni, J, *La France en Indochine de Catroux à Sainteny*, Arthuad, Paris, 1972.

Penth, Hans, *A Brief History of Lan Na – Civilizations of North Thailand*, Silkworm Books, Chiang Mai, 1994.

Phayre, Sir Arthur P., *History of Burma, including Burma Proper, Pegu, Taungu, Tennasserim, and Arakan, from the Earliest Times to the end of the First War with British India.*, Trubner & Co. London, 1883.

Phetsarath, Tiao, *Notes sommaires sur l'historie du royaume de Luang Prabang*, Founds Dupont, EFEO.

Philips, C. H. (ed.), *Handbook of Oriental History*, Royal Historical Society, London, 1951.

Pluvier, Jan M., *A Handbook and Chart of South-East Asian History*, Oxford in Asia, Kuala Lumpur, 1967.

———, *Historical Atlas of South-East Asia: Handbook of Oriental Studies*, E.J. Brill, N.Y., 1995.

Quaritch Wales, H.G., *Siamese State Ceremonies – Their History and Function with Supplementary Notes*, reprinted by Curzon Press Ltd. Richmond, 1992.

———, *Ancient South-East Asian Warfare*, Bernard Quaritch, London, 1952.

Reinach, Lucien de, *Le Laos, Édition Posthume, Revue et Mise a Jour par P. Chemin Dupontès, Préface de M Paul Doumer, Ancien Gouverneur Générale l'Indo-Chine*, Librairie Orientale et Americaine, E. Guilmoto, Éditeur, 6, rue de Mézières, Paris, 1911.

Rispaud, Jean, *Introduction à l'historie des Tay du Yunnan et de Birmanie*, France-Asie, xxii, No. 166 (1961).

Sanhprasith na Champassak, *Aperçu General de la Famille de Champassak*, Privately published, France, 1995.

Savang Vatthana, King of Laos, *Annales du Laos, Luang-Prabang, Vientiane Tranninh et Bassac*, Publiées la Vingt-Deuxième Année du Règne de S.M. Sisavang-Vong Roi du Luang Prabang.

Saveng Phinith, *Contribution à l'Histoire du Royaume de Luang Prabang.*, École Françaises d'Extrême-Orient, Vol. CXLI, Paris, 1987.

Siam Society (ed), *Siam Society 50th Anniversary Commemorative Publication*, Siam Society, Bangkok, 1954, 2 Vols.

———, *Siam Society Selected Articles, relationship with Burma*, Siam Society, Bangkok, 1959, 2 Vols.

Sila Viravong, Maha, *History of Laos (trans)*, Paragon, New York. 1964, first published 1959.

Simon, Hélène, *Auguste Pavie, explorateur en Indochine*, Éditions Ouest-France, Rennes, 1997.

Sisouk na Champassak, *Storm over Laos: A Contemporary History*, Frederick A Praeger, New York, 1961.

Smithies, Michael (ed.), *Descriptions of Old Siam*, Oxford in Asia Paperbacks, Kuala Lumpur, 1995.

Stuart Fox, Martin, *Who was Maha Thevi?*, Siam Society Journal, Vol.81, Part 1, 1993 page 103.

———, *A History of Laos*, Cambridge University Press, 1997.

Stuart-Fox, Martin & Mary Koryman, *Historical Dictionary of Laos*, The Scarecrow Press, New Jersey & London, 1992.

Sunet Phothisane, *The Importance of the Pheune Khoun Bolom for Lao History*, translation of a paper presented at the National Conference on Lao History. Vientiane. 1990.

Tarling, Nicholas, *The Cambridge History of Southeast Asia, Vol. I: From Early Times to c. 1800, Vol.II, The Nineteenth and Twentieth Centuries*, Cambridge University Press, 1992.

Thongchai Winichakul, *Siam Mapped; A History of the Geo-Body of a Nation*, University of Hawaii Press, Honolulu, 1994.

Touby Lyfong, *The Meo of Laos*, Vientiane, 1956.

Toye, Hugh, *Laos: Buffer State or Battleground*, OUP, 1968.

Tuck, Patrick, *The French Wolf and the Siamese Lamb: The French Threat to Siamese Independence, 1858–1907*, White Lotus, Bangkok,1995.

Twitchett, Denis & Loewe, Michael (ed.), *The Cambridge History of China, Vol.I The Ch'in and Han Empires, 221 B.C.–AD 220*, Cambridge University Press, Cambridge, 1986.

——, *The Cambridge History of China, Vol.3. Sui and T'ang China, 589–906, Part I*, Cambridge University Press, Cambridge, 1979.

Vo Thu Tinh, *Les Origines du Laos.*, Sud-est Asie, Paris. 1983.

Vongsay Kithong, *La Formation de l'Etat Laotienne*, Unpublished, Thèse en vue du doctorat en science politique, Toulouse, 1967.

Wood, W.A.R, *A History of Siam*, reprinted Bangkok.

Wuysthoff, Gerrit van, *Le journal de voyage de Gerrit van Wuysthoff et de ses assistants au Laos (1641–1642)*, editor Jean Claude Lejose, 2nd ed. Centre de Documentation et d'Information sur le Laos., 1993.

Wyatt, David K, *Siam and Laos, 1767–1827*, Journal of Southeast Asian History, 4/2, 1963 (pp. 13–32).

——, *Thailand: A Short History*, Yale University Press, New Haven and London, 1984.

Wyatt, David K. & Aroonrut Wichienkeeo (Ed.), *The Chiang Mai Chronicle (trans)*, Silkworm, Chiang Mai, 1995.

Young, Gordon, *The Hill Tribes of Northern Thailand*, (5th. Edition), Siam Society, Bangkok, 1974.

Zasloff, Joseph J and Unger, Leonard (ed), *Laos: Beyond the Revolution*, Macmillan Academic and Professional Ltd. London, 1991.

Index

237